Motherhood Memoirs

Mothers Creating/Writing Lives

Published by:
Demeter Press
140 Holland Street West
P. O. Box 13022
Bradford, ON L3Z 2Y5
Tel: (905) 775-9089
Email: info@demeterpress.org
Website: www.demeterpress.org

Demeter Press logo based on sculpture "Demeter" by Maria-Luise Bodirsky
<www.keramik-atelier.bodirsky.de>

Cover Artwork: Lori Lyn Greenstone, "Ekphrastic Mama," 2007, collage and water media, 24 x 36 inches. Private collection.

Printed and Bound in Canada

Library and Archives Canada Cataloguing in Publication

        Motherhood memoirs: mothers creating/writing lives
/ Justine Dymond and Nicole Willey, editors.

Includes bibliographical references.
ISBN 978-1-927335-16-1

Cataloguing data available from Library and Archives Canada.

Motherhood Memoirs

Mothers Creating/Writing Lives

edited by

JUSTINE DYMOND AND NICOLE WILLEY

DEMETER PRESS, BRADFORD, ONTARIO

For Marjorie
—J.D.

For Jacob and Isaac, who made me a mother,
and to my parents, Cheryl and Walt, who gave me the model.
—N.W.

Table of Contents

Acknowledgements

I would like to thank my colleagues and friends Professors Rebecca Lartigue, Jody Santos, and Nicole Willey for reading my chapter in draft form and offering insightful suggestions; Lynn Martin, Technical Services Specialist at Babson Library, and Rachael Naismith, Assistant Director for Information and Research, at Babson Library for their help with ILL loans; my partner in life, Louis Faassen, for wisdom, guidance, delicious meals, and unflagging support; Nicole Willey for imagining this entire project in the first place; and our contributors for their work and patience. Of course, there are three people without whom none of this would be possible for me: my parents, Kenneth and Rosetta Dymond, and my daughter, Marjorie Faassen Dymond.

—Justine Dymond

I would like to thank Kent State University Tuscarawas for the Faculty Professional Improvement Leave that provided the time for me to do much of the research and drafting for this book, the course release that gave me time for revision, and for travel support; my colleagues and friends Andrea Adolph, Lisa Brindley, Tony Dallacheisa, Laurie Donley and Beth Osikiewicz for listening and helping me talk through both the finer and more pragmatic points of the process; Justine Dymond and Christopher Roman for reading early (and late) drafts of my chapter, and for helping it to become what it is; Beth Knapp and Jake Rader for key clerical support, and Cody Hutchison for teaching me some of the intricacies of word processing. To my sisters and brothers in the e-mail chain—Janelle and Todd Moffett, Cassie and JR Rummel, thank you for listening and for being eager to read this. To my parents

Walt and Cheryl Willey—not only did you provide me with support throughout this process, but you have also given me the tools for and have encouraged me to do work that is meaningful. Two people get thanked twice. Justine Dymond, my friend and complement, believed in this idea and enriched everything about this process and our final product. And, Christopher Roman, my first reader, final editor, sounding board, and also my partner in domesticity and parenting, makes my day-to-day not only possible, but pleasurable. And finally, my sons, Jacob and Isaac Roman-Willey, who have shown me, time and again, what matters, while helping me to laugh along the way.

—Nicole Willey

We would like to thank Katie Barsevich for her tireless copyediting, and Springfield College for helping to support her work financially; the University Research Council of Kent State University for financial support; Andrea O'Reilly and ARM, now MIRCI, for providing a forum for mothers' voices; and all of our contributors. You have tirelessly worked to help us achieve our collective vision for this book, and in so doing, have become the community we needed.

—J.D. and N.W.

Introduction

Creating the Collection

JUSTINE DYMOND AND NICOLE WILLEY

> *I told myself that I wanted to write a book on motherhood because it was a crucial, still relatively unexplored, area for feminist theory. But I did not choose this subject; it had long ago chosen me.*
> —Adrienne Rich, *Of Woman Born* (15)

> *…Memoir is the record of an experience in search of a community…*
> —Nancy K. Miller, "But Enough About Me, What Do You Think of My Memoir?" (432)

> *It's hard to write and to have kids. Don't let anyone tell you that it's not. You cannot get lost in the easy wind and downy flake of motherhood and then turn around, focus, and produce work. You have to be cunning, practical, and selfish. You have to steal time. Time is your enemy, your gift, your wanton desire, and you never have enough of it.*
> —Stephanie Brown, "Not a Perfect Mother" (31)

THIRTY-FIVE YEARS after the publication of Adrienne Rich's groundbreaking work *Of Woman Born* (1976), much more has been written about mothering and motherhood.[1] Motherhood memoirs have become a staple in book sales today. Amazon.com, the ubiquitous book source for almost everyone, has 461 (and counting) results under the search term "motherhood memoir." In the early days of what would become a publishing onslaught, Anne Lamott's *Operating Instructions: A Journal of My Son's First Year* (1993) and Anne Roiphe's *Fruitful: A Real Mother in a Modern World.* (1996) offered some of the first autobiographical accounts of motherhood that dared to speak the truth about the writers' experiences as mothers. Mary Kay Blakely's *American Mom: Motherhood, Politics, and Humble Pie* (1994) and Susan Johnson's *A Better Woman: A Memoir* (1999), among others, continued a healthy trend of mothers breaking a long-held silence in the genre of memoir. As Sidonie Smith and Julia Watson note in their discussion of life writing, "publishers seek the next hot topic and market particular kinds of memoirs to niche audiences" (*Reading Autobiography* 127). Motherhood memoir is the current "hot topic," and a proliferation of these works have extended from the 1990s into the present.

In this collection, we look directly at motherhood memoirs, mothers' own voices, in an effort to expand scholarly attention to this genre and to begin a discussion of its merits along with its shortcomings. In taking the motherhood memoir seriously, and in examining individual memoirs while (in many cases) sharing our own stories in a personal voice, this collection enacts a commitment to creating a community of mothers and others who are interested in transforming the institution of motherhood and mothering practices.

This book, like many, started at a conference. We were both at the beginning edge of our academic careers, and simultaneously, fairly new mothers, when we met on a panel Nicole had put together at NeMLA one spring on the topic of the rhetoric of motherhood. Nicole's first son Jacob had been born just about a year before, and sometime during that fall—the long fall semester that brought the return to teaching/relief from constant childcare/being walked in on by a custodian while strapped to a breast pump in her office/utter exhaustion—Nicole realized that reading *Brain, Child* and *LiteraryMama.com* obsessively, while finally throwing *Parents* magazine and *What to Expect, The First Year* across the room, was not enough. Why did writing about mothering draw her in so much more deeply than anything else? And why did some of the voices make her angry enough to, literally, throw books across the room, while others made her laugh and cry and helped her feel a sense of community? Instinctively in search of a community, Nicole pulled together her first panel on this topic, and met Justine, whose daughter was two years old. Her proposal to discuss Ayelet Waldman's "Mommy Track" detective hooked Nicole, and the first stirrings of this collection happened in the hallway after our panel.

Now Marjorie is attending third grade, and Jacob second. His little brother Isaac is in preschool, with kindergarten looming. We spent a few more years organizing panels, talking to participants, and generally getting the word out about our idea. Our picture of what kind of work we wanted to do and encourage changed as we became further enmeshed with the newly expanded canon of motherhood memoir. Though it didn't happen overnight, sometimes the discovery of these many books did feel revelatory, like voices springing out of the predawn, sleepless, breastfeeding darkness, just in time to help us along our path. Except, of course, these voices were not brand new. The works that are discussed herein are perhaps newly recognized as a highly marketable grouping, but mothering stories have been here all along. We felt it was time to give these stories the respect they deserved, by offering a space for serious and rigorous discussion about this genre. At the same time, one of the hallmarks of the motherhood memoirs we enjoy the most has to do with a singular voice, honesty, and the willingness to do what Anne Lamott did before many others, which was to show the hardness, ugliness, and tenderness, and therein reveal the deeply moving space that is a woman becoming a mother. Many of our contributors put their own life writing alongside the voices of the mothers in the texts they examine, giving the reader access to another corner of this mothering community—the community we have been so interested in finding and cultivating during the genesis of this collection.

Andrea O'Reilly has suggested in "The Motherhood Memoir and the 'New Momism': Biting the Hand That Feeds You" that if motherhood memoirs were required reading for all new mothers, they could create a revolution in mothering (209). Indeed, these works have felt revolutionary to us, and worth a collection of their own, one that will examine them in their fullness and variety. We aim in this collection to continue a conversation about mothering, life writing and autotheory, each a field with its own rich history, in the nexus of the motherhood memoir. The authors here examine and critique motherhood memoir, alongside the texts of their own lives, while seeking to transform mothering practice—highlighting revolutionary praxis within books, or, when none is available, creating the possibility of social change.

Because there are so many obstacles waiting for new mothers, and still present for those of us who aren't so new, the motherhood memoir does, as O'Reilly suggests, give mothers an insight into the realities that await us. For instance, Joan Richards writes about the struggles of achieving academic promotion while caring for two sons, one who has been diagnosed with a brain tumor, in *Angles of Reflection: Logic and a Mother's Love* (2000), shedding light on this complicated journey of academic life and illness. Ayun Halliday tracks the development of her 'zine, *The East Village Inky*, alongside the raising of her small children in *The Big Rumpus: A Mother's Tale from the Trenches* (2002). In *The Middle of Everything: Memoirs of Motherhood* (2005), Michelle Herman discusses her transformation from a writer, who needs "silence, uninterrupted hours, desk cleared of everything but the work at hand," to being a mother: "In those used-to-be days, I would have found it impossible to believe that I would ever be able to write under the conditions I do now, daily, without even thinking of them as 'conditions' or noticing what they are" (80). Adrienne Martini undertakes her own mothering story in *Hillbilly Gothic: A Memoir of Madness and Motherhood* (2006), in which she uncovers the struggle of mothering through postpartum depression. Rebecca Walker adds her voice to the discussion of mothering, choice, and ambivalence in *Baby Love: Choosing Motherhood after a Lifetime of Ambivalence* (2007). These are just a sampling of some of the motherhood memoirs we uncovered during the early stages of our preparation of this collection.

These full-length works are supplemented by a multitude of short motherhood memoirs, some that appeared originally in paper and online literary magazines such as *Brain, Child* and *Literary Mama.com*. Short-form memoir appeals to mothers who often, for the sake of limited time, can only dip in and out of another mother's life, in order to attend to her own. In *Mothers Who Think: Tales of Real-Life Parenthood* (1999), editors from *Salon.com*, Camille Peri and Kate Moses, collected short memoir by known writers, including Ariel Gore and Anne Lamott, and other less well known, but not less affecting, mothers in the trenches. Ariel Gore culled the best of the writing from her 'zine in *The Essential Hip Mama: Writing from the Cutting Edge of Parenting* (2004), and Andrea Buchanan and Amy Hudock's *Literary Mama: Reading for the Maternally Inclined* (2006) did the same for its online journal. A movement has clearly been born, and the time has come to give these works the analytical attention that both mothering studies and autobiographical studies suggest should happen, but have not yet completed.

We agree with Jocelyn Fenton Stitt and Pegeen Reichert Powell who note in their introduction to *Mothers Who Deliver*, "Mothering studies has come of age" (2), as mothers/scholars/writers put their lived experience next to their scholarly skills to define and interrogate motherhood as an institution and mothering as practice. In the decades following the Second Wave, mothering studies has built a firm foundation. Showing just how central, and how unexplored, mothering was as a topic in *Of Woman Born*, Adrienne Rich was a pioneer in opening up the discussion about mothering. Nancy J. Chodorow continued the discussion in *The Reproduction of Mothering: Psychoanalysis and the Sociology of Gender* (1978). These urtexts were soon followed by many books and collections on the topic of motherhood as an institution. Of course, mothering studies owes a great debt to Sara Ruddick's work, including her groundbreaking *Maternal Thinking: Toward a Politics of Peace* (1989). Jane Price Knowles and Ellen Cole edited *Motherhood: A Feminist Perspective* (1990), following a psychoanalytic approach to the field. The collection *Double Stitch: Black Women Write about Mothers and Daughters* (Bell-Scott et al. 1991) brought together the voices of influential women such as bell hooks, June Jordan, Sonia Sanchez and others. Donna Bassin, Margaret Honey, and Meryle Mehrer Kaplan edited *Representations of Motherhood* (1994), which featured some of the earlier and script-changing essays by Sara Ruddick, Patricia Hill Collins, and Jessica Benjamin. Andrea O'Reilly and the Association of Research on Mothering (ARM), now the Motherhood Initiative for Research and Community Involvement (MIRCI), continues to provide a forum for and publication venues for this important writing.[2] Sharon Abbey and O'Reilly make clear that writing about motherhood "tends to defy boundaries and category restrictions" (16) in their collection *Redefining Motherhood: Changing Identities and Patterns* (1998). The following year, Susan Maushart further uncovered the realities of mothering in her work *The Mask of Motherhood: How Becoming a Mother Changes Our Lives and Why We Never Talk about It* (1999). One critic gives a good sketch of the feminist theoretical discussions of motherhood up to the late 1990s:

> If there is consensus to be found in these debates, it is that conventional sentiments about motherhood inadequately describe and serve to mystify the actual circumstances of most women who mother, even as they may also sublimate the fear

and resentment of men who cannot be mothers, or of the always unsatisfied inner child. It is commonly recognized, in some circles at least, that the position of the mother in our culture and our language is riddled with its history of psychic and social contradictions. Motherhood offers women a site of both power and oppression, self-esteem and self-sacrifice, reverence and debasement. (Hansen 3)

In light of these contradictions, we focus on motherhood memoir in an effort to locate "the actual circumstances of most women who mother," focusing on the extent to which mothering is "a site of both power and oppression."

More evidence for the coming-of-age of mothering studies is found in O'Reilly's collection *Mother Outlaws: Theories and Practices of Empowered Mothering* (2004), which became one of the first textbooks explicitly meant for use in courses on mothering studies. Shari MacDonald Strong collects the work of mothers/writers/activists who discuss the importance of forging ties between mothering and social policy in *The Maternal Is Political: Women Writers at the Intersection of Motherhood and Social Change* (2008). And it is not surprising that academic mothers, in a variety of disciplines, decided to weigh in on the topic of mothering and the academic life in *Mama, PhD* (Evans and Grant 2008). Even more recently, we have seen the release of *Mothers Who Deliver: Feminist Interventions in Public and Interpersonal Discourse* (2010), edited by Jocelyn Fenton Stitt and Pegeen Reichert Powell. Their collection clearly embodies the fact that mothering studies as a distinct field is here to stay; further, this book points us to look beyond simply describing what we see in the effort to push us all toward change (5-6).

Mothering studies helps us to bridge the divide between sociology, psychology, feminist studies and the literary field of maternal narratives, as in Elaine Tuttle Hansen's *Mother Without Child: Contemporary Fiction and the Crisis of Motherhood* (1997). The study of motherhood memoirs grows out of a tradition of acknowledging and examining the maternal narrative in literature. Alice Walker's *In Search of Our Mothers' Gardens* (1983) took up the issue of motherhood in life and letters through her personal essays. Marianne Hirsch systemically traced the maternal narrative, and noted the absence of the mother's voice, in *The Mother/Daughter Plot* (1989). Brenda O. Daly and Maureen T. Reddy's collection *Narrating Mothers: Theorizing Maternal Subjectivities* followed in 1991. *Motherhood and Representation: The Mother in Popular Culture and Melodrama* by E. Ann Kaplan appeared in 1992, with the project of tracing fictional representations of motherhood in the 19th and 20th centuries. Jo Malin's *The Voice of the Mother: Embedded Maternal Narratives in Twentieth-Century Women's Autobiographies* (2000) bridges the search for maternal narratives and autobiography studies, as she finds that some women's autobiography is only able to be written with the mother's story (embedded) within the daughter's. *The Grand Permission: New Writings on Poetics and Motherhood* (Dienstfrey and Hillman 2003) analyzes the poetry of mothering, while offering snapshots of poet-mothers' lives. The connection between mothering studies and literary mothers/mothering becomes explicit in Elizabeth Podnieks and Andrea O'Reilly's *Textual Mothers/Maternal Texts* (2010). Their collection redresses the absence of mothers in literature that Alice Walker and Marianne Hirsch noted decades ago with an undertaking to seek out and explore maternal narrative in the areas of fiction, poetry, and life-writing genres. They convincingly argue that "if feminist theory is not the means to a resolution, matrifocal narratives may well be" (5). Though some of these texts offer a combination of analysis and memoir about mothering, the intersection of life writing and mothering does not become a singular focus until *From the Personal to the Political: Toward a New Theory of Maternal Narrative* (2009). Andrea O'Reilly and Silvia Caporale Bizzini offer in their collection a two part discussion of mothering—the first section includes motherhood memoir, and the second section is a collection of essays that analyze maternal narrative in the genres of fiction and memoir. These chapters on memoirs by Rachel Cusk, Jane Lazarre, Anne Enright and others begin the discussion that we wish to continue in this collection. With one exception (Harriet Jacobs' *Incidents in the Life of a Slave Girl*), the texts under examination in our two efforts do not overlap. Further, and as we will discuss below, the essays in our collection purposely set out to *merge* the memoir and analysis through autotheory.

As a distinct subgenre, motherhood memoirs also remain relatively unexplored in the field of life writing. Even Sidonie Smith and Julia Watson's excellent compendium *Reading Autobiography: A Guide for Interpreting Life Narratives*, now in its second edition, only gives one sentence to the subgenre of motherhood memoir: "A new genre to emerge in the past decade has been labeled the Motherhood Memoir, as in Anne Roiphe's *Fruitful: A Real Mother in a Modern World*, in which women write about how becoming mothers affects their working lives, sexuality, and writing lives" (270). Margo Culley notes in her introduction to *American Women's Autobiography: Fea(s)ts of Memory* that "autobiography studies ... has in fact dealt with only a tiny, tiny fraction of what has been published as autobiography ... most critics have focused on a narrow group of highly 'literary' texts and/or texts of writers known for their public achievement" (5). Though Culley levels this criticism in 1992, and though it is clear that women's autobiography and mothering studies more broadly have been taken up with gusto since her book was published, motherhood memoir as a genre is still underrepresented in scholarly studies. Indeed, in Helen M. Buss's 2012 study *Repossessing the World: Reading Memoirs by Contemporary Women*, she notes that "Despite the welcome existence of anthologies ... and the veritable boom in the publication of memoirs by women, the genre has received little academic attention. The study of memoirs from a theoretical and critical perspective informed by scholarly research is now overdue" (7-8).

While it is not our purpose here to exhaustively review all of the literature on autobiographical theories,[3] we do want to highlight some of the works that have influenced our thinking about motherhood memoir. G. Thomas Couser, in *American Autobiography: The Prophetic Mode* (1979), lent credibility and academic rigor to the genre by examining, in individual biographies, how autobiographical writing traces not only an individual's history, but the history of entire communities. He writes, "If literary genres can become institutions, then autobiography has become an important American institution, one with a rich tradition. Like our best institutions, it is flexible and democratic: it welcomes participation" (201). Providing a basis for the importance of autobiographical writing in the literary history of the United States, exploring its popularity, and beginning to theorize the form, he helped to open up autobiography as a legitimate genre for consideration.

The following decade brought an explosion of work on women's autobiographical writing in particular. Domna C. Stanton's collection *The Female Autograph* (1984) coined the term "autogynography" and brought attention to previously ignored works. It was followed by Estelle Jelinek's *The Tradition of Women's Autobiography: From Antiquity to the Present* (1986), Sidonie Smith's *A Poetics of Women's Autobiography: Marginality and the Fictions of Self-Representation* (1987), and Shari Benstock's collection *The Private Self: Women's Autobiographical Writings* (1988), all of which added immeasurably to this field of study and its intersections with literary and feminist theory. In 1988, Bella Brodzki and Celeste Schenck provided *Life/Lines: Theorizing Women's Autobiography*, and they remind us that the "death of the author" heralded by Roland Barthes and the further destabilizaton of the self by Michel Foucault present particular difficulties for the woman subject as writer of auto-biography. Nancy K. Miller joins this conversation by showing that if the author is dead, then the death "prematurely forecloses the question of agency for [women]" (106) in *Subject to Change: Reading Feminist Writing* (1988). At once utilizing and resisting the conventions of the decade in literary theory, critics focusing on women's autobiography remind us again and again that they have concerns peculiar to women and selfhood to address.

The definition of the self and the destabilization of the author are taken up by many other writers. Couser is "considerably more skeptical than [he] used to be of the authority of the genre" (vii) in *Altered Egos: Authority in American Autobiography* (1989), though he remains convinced that "autobiography may seek to order, even to alter, a world beyond the textual" (vii). Margo Culley in her collection *American Women's Autobiography: Fea(s)ts of Memory* (1992) maintains that women writ-ers of autobiography are aware of and play with fixed notions of "self" and "truth" as "[t]hey dismiss static and unitary notions of the self and remain skeptical of any totalizing 'self knowledge.' They know that the autobiographical process *creates* truth even as it attempts to recover and record it" (18). If destabilization is the norm for conceptions of the self, it also is true for the genre of autobiography itself. As Julia Watson and Sidonie Smith argue in their introduction to *De/Colonizing the Subject: The Politics of Gender in Women's Autobiography* (1992), "Autobiographical writing surrounds us, but the more it surrounds us, the more it defies generic stabilization, the more its laws are broken, the more it drifts toward other practices, the more former 'out-law' practices drift into its domain" (xviii).

Defining the genre of motherhood memoir is itself one of the difficul-ties in creating a study around motherhood memoir. We are following Smith and Watson in *Reading Autobiography* in their shift from "genre to discourse," as a way to open up the exclusionary genre of autobiography, once the "highest achievement of individuality in Western civilization" into modes of life writing that encompass a broader historical and literary sample (3). We *do* assume that memoir will be about a particular time and particular events in the author's life. We also assume that, like autobiography, motherhood memoir is "not a single unitary genre or form" (Smith and Watson *Reading Autobiography* 18), with "memoir" being a term that "seems more malleable" even than "autobiography," and a term that highlights the relationship between the public and private (Smith and Watson *Reading Autobiography* 4). We agree with Podnieks and O'Reilly when they argue in their introduction to *Textual Mothers/Maternal Texts* that "Autobiography (including the diary and memoir) is an especially valuable arena in which we can register and understand the ways that women inscribe an 'I' or series of 'I's' in the authoring of their own maternal selves, accounting for and expressing awareness of factors such as the body, sexuality, gender, race, class, and nationhood" (7). Motherhood memoir, as we understand the term, is a site for self-representation of the mother as she negotiates her multiple roles and how her roles are interpolated by the other aspects of her subjectivity.

Further, because genre categories are often about the "establishment of limits, the drawing of exclusionary lines, the fierce protection of idealized generic (and implicitly sexual and racial) purity" (Schenck 285), we follow Celeste Schenck's lead in "All of a Piece: Women's Poetry and Autobiography" in recognizing that motherhood memoir can appear in genres that are not *strictly* or *only* memoir. Marlene Kadar, Linda Warley, Jeanne Perreault, and Susanna Egan also note in *Tracing the Autobiographical* (2005), "We have ... as a group found 'auto/biography' to be a flexible term, one that implicates self and other(s) in a context in which a dialectic of relationality is both acknowledged and problematized" (3). And as Smith and Watson remind us, "what is called 'autobiography' is not at this historical moment (and, we would argue, never has been) a unified form" (*Reading Autobiography* 127). And so we attempt to grapple with a relatively unexplored subgenre within an exciting if contradictory field. This collection thus examines many "traditional" motherhood memoirs, but it will also examine diaries, blogs, a variety of visual arts, and slave narrative as well. The authors make a compelling case for looking at mothers' stories where they are found, and giving them the critical attention they deserve.

We are studying motherhood memoirs, because they, like the writing on mothering collected in *Mothers Who Deliver*, give voice to the problems experienced while mothering: "Motherhood's dilemmas and ideological contradictions are spelled out, often chillingly, in these texts" (Stitt and Powell 2). In this collection, we as editors along with our contributors are interested in exposing the obstacles and problems facing mothers (postpartum depression, grief, poverty, racism, and homophobia, to name a few). We are also interested in exposing the problems that occur during the process of mothers writing about mothering. Bringing these essays together allows us to move in the direction of understanding these obstacles in a collective and historicized context.

Additionally, though we wish to examine motherhood memoir for its possibilities in critiquing the status quo, like Stitt and Powell, we also aim to go beyond critique toward transformation (5-6). As Helen M. Buss notes, memoir "is becoming a discursive practice in which material realities and imaginary possibilities coexist" (2). In this collection, we wanted a conversation that would build upon the work of Joanna Frye, Ivana Brown, and others who look at memoirs by mothers that "initiate alternative understandings that resist the hazardous cultural constructions with which we continue to wrestle" (Frye 188). If the memoirs themselves are not able or willing to go to the next step and actually point the way toward changing mothering practice for the better, then we as mothers/writers/scholars are going to help open up new models for mothering. Some of the memoirs we discuss are clearly pointing to new and revised ways to mother—Lisa Federer's chapter on the nonbiological lesbian mom blog, for instance, begins to show the way to truly revolutionary redefinitions and paradigms for lesbian co-mothers, through the autobiographical texts themselves. Others, such as Rachel Robertson's discussion of parenting children with autism in her own life and in memoir, shows some of the limitations found within current memoirs, while nonetheless pointing a way forward in her analysis and lived experience.

And, as the example of Robertson's essay shows, we want to do this analytical work within a community that is willing and able to put its own lived experience into the scholarship. Indeed in examining our own lived experience—our subjective selves, our multiple positionalities—we allow for change through our scholarship and autotheroetical writings. In privileging motherhood memoir as a site for change, we are privileging the mother's representation of herself. We assume that "mothers are the agents of discourse, responsible for its delivery, rather than the passive recipients of received wisdom" (Stitt and Powell 7). Motherhood memoir has given women the opportunity to "'unmask' motherhood: to speak honestly, authentically of what it means to be a mother" (O'Reilly "New Momism" 209). And we, as the critics, are putting our self-representations alongside the memoirists'. Our collective self-representation thus aims for a double-pronged transformation, of mothering *and* scholarly practice. Just as memoir—and all life-writing—is "a historically situated practice of self-representation" (Smith and Watson *Reading Autobiography* 14), so is scholarship. Many essays here interrogate the tensions of maternal narrative—the negotiation of the historical location of writer and readers, narrative and linguistic constraints, and the slippery ground of memory—alongside the tensions of the "objective" scholar and the reader who engages with and identifies with texts through her intellect *and* her emotional being.

As mothers/scholars/writers we cannot separate these seemingly varied roles, nor do we want to. Instead, since "our mothering did not exist in a sphere that was distinct from our scholarship" (Stitt and Powell 9), we have aimed to nurture the cross-pollination of our multiple "selves." All of the writers in this collection write within a continuum that privileges their lived experiences in their scholarly work, though their voices are uniquely their own, and often, but not always, clearly autobiographical. As Deborah Holdstein and David Bleich note in their introduction to *Personal Effects: The Social Character of Scholarly Writing*, "We of course do not think that such [personal] reference is a requirement or that it should appear in every study; rather, that regardless of the announced level of subjective involvement of the scholarly author, both authors and readers need to have on their hermeneutic agenda, as readers and as writers, the task of locating scholarly authors through personal and social criteria" (1-2).

Of course, we would be remiss not to acknowledge a fairly long and extremely strong tradition of women of color writing criticism through the lens of their own experience. Cherríe Moraga and Gloria Anzaldúa edited the important collection *This Bridge Called My Back: Writings by Radical Women of Color* the same year that bell hooks published *Ain't I a*

Woman: Black Women and Feminism (1981). These works were followed by Audre Lorde's *Sister Outsider* (1984), hooks' *Feminist Theory: From Margin to Center* (1984), and Anzaldúa's *Borderlands/La Frontera* (1987). All of these works privilege the narrative "I" of the author/critic in their explorations of political landscapes and the lived realities of women of color. Moraga explains part of the reason for utilizing first person in her current website: "I was never talented enough to get away with any easy fictions not wrought out of the viscera of my own life" (par. 1). While we should not take her lack-of-talent claim at face value, she nonetheless exposes the importance of dealing with the realities, and difficulties, of her lived experience within her art and critical work.

Further, Trinh T. Min-ha's *Woman, Native, Other: Writing Postcoloniality and Feminism* (1989) reminds us that this type of academic yet personal writing leads to a different kind of relationship between writer and reader: "Touch me and let me touch you, for the private is political. Language wavers with desire" (37). In engaging with autotheory, or autocritical writing, we and our contributors are engaging in this intimate relationship with our readers, and with the authors we have analyzed. Like Audre Lorde, we encourage this type of personal mediation with the texts we are treating because our lived experience as mothers/writers/scholars helps us to understand these works and share them with others. Mothering is *not* analogous to a diagnosis of cancer, but Lorde's words here remind us of why we are examining motherhood memoir through our own subjective experience: "And yes I am completely self-referenced right now because it is the only translation I can trust, and I do believe not until every woman traces her weave back strand by bloody self-referenced strand, will we begin to alter the whole pattern" ("The Cancer Journals" 276).

Of course autotheory has appeared in somewhat more traditional scholarship as well.[4] Joanne Braxton begins her book *Black Women Writing Autobiography: A Tradition Within a Tradition* (1989) with this statement, "I believe, with the critic James Olney, that students of autobiography are themselves vicarious autobiographers, and I know that I read every text through my own experience, as well as the experiences of my mother and grandmothers" (1). In this collection we read through our experience as well, and share that experience when it is helpful to the critical narrative. In fact, this type of autotheoretical writing may be one of the great pleasures for critics of autobiography:

> The practice of autocritique has thus become more central to theorizing life writing, and for aficionados may be one of the pleasures of work in the field ... the interweaving of personal and public stories continues to be a hallmark of theorizing life writing, which both the consciousness-raising practices of 1970s feminism and the workers' and everyday life stories of the earlier twentieth century used as forms of prosopography with political goals. (Smith and Watson *Reading Autobiography* 231)

If the contributors in this collection are not uniform in the degree to which they utilize an autobiographical voice, what they *do* have in common is the desire to place the subjective experience of their lives in relationship to the works they are studying, so that they can use the fullness of their experience to inform their scholarship: "Our reading and a variety of other experiences in our lives do connect to make us very capable, dynamic respondents to the worlds around us and within us—and effective, learned readers of the texts we study" (Zauhar 105). We are scholars who need to rely on our holistic lived experience, and we are also mothers. As Bizzini writes: "Autobiographical writings make the mother the subject of her own discourse. It is through these texts that subjugated identities (that also exist within feminism) are revealed and discordant voices are heard" (45). And so through our variety of voices and our collective experiences, we have formed a community, one interested in the study of motherhood and memoir.

This longing for a community is a large part of what has given rise to the motherhood memoir, both its creation and its popularity,[5] because the writer writes in an attempt to represent her own personal relationships, while creating at the same time a relationship with her reader through the text (Felski 108).[6] Scholars like Jane Tompkins have noted the importance, and joy, of this author/reader relationship, one that only becomes possible when writing leaves the (perhaps false) notion of the objective third person narrator behind:[7] "I love writers who write about their own experience. I feel I'm being nourished by them, that I'm being allowed to enter into a personal relationship with them. That I can match my own experience up with theirs, feel cousin to them, and say, yes, that's how it is" (25). Those of us who have chosen the disciplines of literature and writing, and who have pursued academic appointments or who are committed independent scholars, in other words, those of us collaborating on this book, share the common history of a love of reading, or a relationship with texts and authors.

Despite the fact that we are insistently, if quietly, discouraged from using emotive words when discussing texts (Behar 16; Tompkins 39) or of forming close personal attachments with books and authors,[8] many of us still crave full engagement with a text, engagement that facilitates the building of a community through connected experiences. At least part of the reason we read memoirs is because "however solitary, memoir reading, like memoir writing, participates in an important form of collective memorialization, providing building blocks to a more fully shared national narrative" (Miller "But Enough About Me" 424). We are actively participating in the creation of a cultural storytelling, a cultural memory, which both gives meaning to our lived experiences and helps us find new models for our lives. We read memoirs, and share some of our own stories, to be a part of this shared narrative about mothering practice.

Focusing on our individual subject positions leads to the question of our differing relationships to privilege and marginality. As Stitt and Powell note:

> ...the intersections of maternal experience with class, race, and sexuality have created a divide between some White middle-class feminists who have historically seen the family as the locus of female oppression and some working-class women and/or women of color who have found refuge and resistance in their maternal praxis. (3)

We come to the field (both scholarly and lived) of mothering from a variety of perspectives, and we note with Blakely that all of us are considered "bad" mothers, at least some of the time: "Nobody's perfect, we knew, but mothers are somehow expected to exceed all human limits. This ideal is especially preposterous since mothers are likely to have more bad days on the job than most other professionals, considering the hours: round-the-clock, seven days a week, fifty-two weeks a year" (11).

While no one can be a "good" mother all the time, perhaps even more problematic is the way in which certain categories of women are removed from the possibility of being a "good" mother even before they begin. As Njoki Wane notes, some women are "judged 'unfit' on the bases of their social location ... disabled women, Black women, First Nations women, immigrant women, Jewish women, lesbian women, women who are the sole-support of parents, poor women, unmarried women, young women, and others" (235). Many of us writing in this collection have access to the institution of motherhood as "good" mothers more readily, while others are suspect before they begin by the arbitrary societal standards Wane notes. But motherhood memoir can allow us to question and "resist the simplistic notions of 'good' mother as selfless, 'bad' mother as selfish, and develop instead a fuller understanding of human mother as an active and thinking self" (Frye 191). To be recognized as mothers/scholars/writers and to enact change within each of those areas, we feel that to varying degrees all of the women in this collection—contributors and primary text authors alike—are writing from the margins.[9] We recognize the conundrum that mothers are at once everywhere and invisible, and that the invisibility of mothers happens most often at sites of struggle, and particularly when mothers are talking back to the status quo. Ideologies of motherhood are in constant circulation, but the work and experiences of mothering are often invisible, while the existence of family-friendly policies are sparse when they exist at all. Writing back to the status quo from the margins gives us the opportunity to critique the institution of motherhood. As Patrice DiQuinzio notes in *The Impossibility of Motherhood*, "[B]eing a mother and being mothered are both imbued with tremendous social, cultural, political, economic, psychological, and personal significance. Everyone has a stake in the social organization of mothering, but these stakes can vary greatly" (DiQuinzio viii).

But we are also aware that while we are speaking from the margins, there are wide ranges of privilege throughout the collection. We do not wish to erase the very real differences experienced by women that are created through race, class, country, sexual orientation, disability, and illness, to name a few factors. Every contributor in this collection is sharing part of her own story through a combination of subjective writing, autotheory, and choices made about topic and texts,[10] and the particularities of each story speak to varying levels of writing back from the margins. There are absences in this collection, absences that we hope the next volume on this topic will undertake. Motherhood is both an entry point to our interest in memoirs by mothers, and it is an evolving, always-shifting location from which we read, write, and reflect back on our mothering experiences.

While we hope that this book will build and add to the community of mother-writers, it is also a call for respect for our foremothers and our contemporaries, for the mother-authors who have put their words and lives out there for public consumption. Not all life writing is created equally, of course, but as a body it is worthy of study, and that is what this collection provides. It is not comprehensive—there are many more motherhood memoirs that are worthy of serious scholarly attention. But it is a start. This collection says, in response to the naysayers who have made it difficult for female authors of life writing to get serious attention in the academy,[11] that motherhood memoirs belong in the canon. This book, and the excellent essays herein, show that motherhood memoirs' time has come—they are worthy of our serious study, attention, and in many cases, approbation.

THE ART OF MOTHERHOOD

Engaged in an artistic endeavor, memoir authors craft and shape their stories; experience and observation become narratives. But this process is a recursive one. Motherhood transforms the artistic process, whether written or visual, and mothering is transformed by the creation of art. In creating memoir, we create new ways of understanding our lives. Motherhood can pose particular challenges and obstacles to artistic endeavor, but memoir can also be enriched by the experience of mothering or of being a mother, especially when that experience is explicitly interrogating the institution of motherhood. In writing about the minutiae and so-called mundane details of women's experiences as mothers, we start to see the patterns across varied experiences and how powerful mothering work can be. Not only is mothering worthy of expression and representation in art, but multitudinous acts of mothering *are* art.

This section begins with a discussion of the visual art of motherhood in Rachel Epp Buller's analysis of "memory work" in visual memoirs. Her essay explores the relationship between mothering and the act of remembering occasioned by creating artistic memoir. From Ayun Halliday's *East Village Inky* to Buller's own print-quilts, this chapter shows how individual memory production intersects with cultural representations of mothering. This essay begins our long conversation about how mothering can complicate and transform artistic practice for women. Another mother artist, Yelizaveta Renfro, writes about her own struggles as a mother-writer while analyzing how-to manuals for writing mothers. Her analysis discusses the obstacles mothers face in writing memoirs, or writing at all, while suggesting strategies for being a productive artist and mother. She reminds us that mothers will need tools that are different from other writers, and that we will have to work smarter (since we cannot work longer) than other writers, but that our writing—and our mothering—will be richer for the process.

Melissa Shields Jenkins shows through Elizabeth Gaskell's diary that mothers faced similar obstacles to their writing in the nineteenth century as they do today. Concerns about time, audience, and mothering practice, as well as conflict with her husband, inform her diary writing. Jenkins argues that Gaskell uses the struggles shown in her diary to create maternal fathers and transformative expressions of mothering in her fiction, giving us an early example of how women's writing about motherhood can turn into social commentary and even create the impetus for social change. This section ends with a return to the connection between written and visual art through Lori Lyn Greenstone's own "ekphrastic" portrait of herself as a mother. In this essay she explores the relationship between mothering and creating art in her own work as well as the works of Bernadette Mayer, Fanny Howe, and Anne Roiphe, showing that art in its variety is one way that mothers can express the anger, contradictions, and joys of their experiences.

The authors in this section, through their chapters here and their art elsewhere, identify and help us explore the patterns in the creation of art and in mothering itself (the impulse to create vs. the availability of time and space to do the creating; the memory-work of preserving familial history vs. the need to tell harsh truths), which allow us to move toward the possibility of naming the obstacles in mother/artists/writers' way, in a move to recognize problems and then move beyond them, allowing for transformation within mothering practice.

WHAT THE OTHER BOOKS DON'T TELL US

The chapters in section two explore areas that are not often honestly discussed, or discussed at all, in conversations about motherhood on the page and in public discourse, or even between mothers privately. The authors in this section discuss the hard facts. Pregnancy, childbirth, and mothering infants and young children can be complicated and exhausting. Coping with postpartum depression, a diagnosis of autism, or the death of a child may be, literally, unspeakable, as these topics often lead to self- and culturally-imposed silencing. These chapters give voice to these difficult topics and remind us that the expression of difficult truths can open conversations between readers and writers looking for meaning and community. One commonality in these essays is an explicit or implicit questioning of a society that allows women in these situations to suffer in silence. Acknowledging the degree to which medical paradigms of mental illness, terminal illness in children, diagnoses of autism, and even the pathologizing of childbirth and the "milkmother" stage create further alienation for mothers in these situations is the beginning step to questioning and changing the societal patterns that lead to the alienation in the first place.

Pamela Douglas invents and introduces us to the term "milkmother" as a way to describe mothers of infants to children who are under four, small children who have immediate needs that are often overwhelming to mothers. Douglas suggests in "Milkmother Memoir" that the medicalization of childbearing and rearing, as well as the relative dearth of memoirs from milkmothers, leave women underprepared for the reality of mothering. In recognizing this near absence, as doctor and writer, she breaks open an oppressive silence; her analysis also acknowledges the literary representations that offer portrayals of this period of a mother's experience, analyzing her own and other women's rare memoirs in this area. Another silence surrounds the issue of postpartum depression, despite its prevalence, and the truths women are allowed to acknowledge regarding their experiences. Against a backdrop of medicalized discourse about motherhood and media sensationalization of postpartum psychosis, Justine Dymond examines the spoken and unspoken in recent memoirs of postpartum depression, paying close attention to the fear of stigma that haunts both mental illness and the semblance of "bad" mothering. In comparing postpartum depression memoirs, Dymond shows how memoirists have paved the way for a fuller understanding of not only postpartum depression but mothering, too, privileging texts that question the larger culture's role in the silencing of this common occurrence.

Rachel Robertson explores the complexities of intimacy and representation in motherhood memoirs about raising children with autism, sharing her own experiences with this diagnosis in her son, while exploring the ways in which the representations themselves can hinder or assist the achievement of intimacy in the writers' actual lived experience. Understanding the various ways autism is represented enables everyone to notice how social constructions of "normal" create barriers in all of our intimate relationships. Finally, Kathleen Fowler examines memoirs of grief and loss as mothers express the experience of losing their children. Not only is it difficult for mothers to tell these stories, but people often do not want to hear their stories, since advances in medicine among the affluent have made the death of a child seem "unnatural" in the late twentieth century and beyond. In the space of motherhood memoirs though, a place for compassionate listening and dialogue is created, one that allows a conversation that exists and resonates throughout this collection. Sadly, Kathleen passed away before the publication of this book, and our sorrow in losing a member of our community resonates even more deeply now in the grief work she describes.

In giving voice to the unspeakable, these authors help us explore the fullness and complexity of the mothering experience, reminding us of the need to share and analyze our stories as a first step in changing societal mores for the better.

MOTHERS WITHOUT BORDERS

In the last section, our intention is not to close the conversation about motherhood memoirs, but to open a path to continued discussion. In that spirit, the chapters here explore how to collapse borders, the literal and figurative obstacles that have always been a reality for mothers. This section interrogates some common borders, and in the process, works to diminish their power and remove them. All mothers struggle with societal cues that can redirect our own impulses, but life-threatening pregnancy complications, homophobia, racism and poverty exacerbate the power of these messages.

When we internalize others' expectations for our mothering, the obstacles can seem nearly insurmountable. Tara McDonald Johnson's chapter begins with our own interiors as bounded by a concept of a border between the physical self and intellectual self. She asks how our experiences as mothers and intellectuals are informed by a culturally imposed duality of mind vs. body, and suggests a potential change of frame to allow mothers to be whole people, a process she experienced herself. In the next chapter, Lisa Federer examines the borders within and between virtual communities in the world of lesbian moms who blog, arguing that blogging provides community "that transcends geographical boundaries." At the same time, these writers blog in order to redefine their mothering/co-mothering role and status.

Just as all mothers need support networks, so too do women writers, particularly minority women writers who often face more obstacles than their white counterparts. Rather than focusing analytically on individual memoirs, Deesha Philyaw discusses the very contemporary issues facing African American mothers as they endeavor to write their motherhood memoirs, gathering advice and insight from editors, writers, agents and publishers who act as a supportive community of mentors to any aspiring memoirist. In her chapter's multi-vocal conversation, Philyaw sees a parallel between the historical invisibility of African American women's labor and the relative paucity of published memoirs by African American mothers. In the final essay, Nicole Willey bridges historical differences between Harriet Jacobs' rendition of her mothering in a slave narrative, and Richelene Mitchell's diaristic motherhood memoir from the 1970s. The context and history of these works help shed light on the relative dearth of motherhood memoirs by African American women, while showing us that these memoirs have been here all along, but were perhaps unrecognizable by conventional (and often oppressive) definitions of motherhood and memoir. Ultimately, the African feminist principles on display in these works provide transformative possibilities for all mothers in the form of redefinitions of mothering and the utilization of collective mothering practice.

Despite the wide reach of experience and texts here, all of the chapters grapple with common questions: how does motherhood shape our lives, and how does writing—searingly honest writing—about those lives transform the individual experience and institution of motherhood? While voices and format necessarily vary in these essays, their critical acumen is enhanced by the lived experience of the authors. The voices that surface in motherhood memoir reveal a community that gives shape to the struggles, pitfalls, revelations, and joys of motherhood. It is imperative that we listen.

ENDNOTES

[1]In this collection, we agree with Rich that there are "two strands: motherhood as *experience*, one possible and profound experience for women, and motherhood as enforced identity and as political *institution*" ("Motherhood in Bondage" 196-197). Andrea O'Reilly clarifies this distinction as follows: "while motherhood, as an institution, is a male-defined site of oppression, women's own experiences of mothering can nonetheless be a source of power" ("Introduction" 2). Most of what this collection critiques is not individual mothering experiences and practices, but rather the institution of motherhood.

[2]For an excellent summation of ARM's role in the development of mothering studies, see O'Reilly's "'Stories to Live By': Maternal Literatures and Motherhood Studies" in *Textual Mothers/Maternal Texts*.

[3]Smith and Watson's *Reading Autobiography* gives a thorough literature review on studies about and surrounding autobiographical studies issues; see particularly Chapter 7, "A History of Autobiography Criticism, Part I: Theorizing Autobiography" and Chapter 8, "A History of Autobiography Criticism, Part II: Expanding Autobiography Studies."

[4]The type of scholarship being enacted in this book is scholarly without being, strictly speaking, traditional. We have allowed our contributors to find the voice that works best for the type of scholarship and story they want to tell. Doing this kind of work values subjectivity, though it takes many forms:

> Many scholars, especially feminist scholars, have acknowledged the need to reflect on and theorize the ways in which personal history and experience shape the "subject" and the form of professional work, and especially of scholarly writing. One sign of the seriousness—and perhaps again the anxiety—with which scholars have approached this self-reflective project has been the proliferation of terms to describe such critical work: literary theorists Nancy K. Miller and Susan Suleiman have written (about) the uses of "personal criticism" and "mediated autobiography" respectively; anthropologist Behar's "vulnerable writing" has a reflexive quality in common with Linda Brodkey's—and Mary Louise Pratt's—"authoethnography." Feminist, social theorist Nancy Fraser describes the essays

included in her text, *Unruly Practices: Power, Discourse, and Gender in Contemporary Social Theory* as "exercises in situated theorizing." (Willard-Traub 46-47)

Although these terms and writing tasks are various and differently inflected, we would suggest they all signify an alternative intellectual practice which attempts to make sense of the personally situated nature of scholarly work, and to theorize what Gesa Kirsch and Joy Ritchie have termed, after Adrienne Rich, a "politics of location" (7) for that work. [5]Many reasons have been given for the rise in popularity of the memoir, and Nancy K. Miller comments on them here:

> There have been a variety of unsatisfactory, if not entirely false, answers—it is the well-worn culture of "me," given an expansive new currency by the infamous baby boomers who can think of nothing else; it's the desire for story killed by postmodern fiction; it's the only literary form that appears to give access to the truth; it's a democratic form, giving voice to minority experience in an anti-elite decade; it's a desire to assert agency and subjectivity after several decades of insisting loudly on the fragmentation of identity and the death of the author. It's voyeurism for a declining imperial narcissism. It's the market. ("But Enough About Me" 430-431)

[6]Rita Felski is here discussing memoir in a confessional form, as written by women, much more broadly. But the desire to demonstrate intimacies on the page, to share that story, and as a reader, to bond with the writer as a mother, is clearly applicable to motherhood memoir.
[7]Of course true objectivity in any type of writing, even traditional academic writing, is probably never possible: "To one degree or another, scholarly authors' lived experiences are already part of the different subject matters in the humanities. However, the conventions of writing urge writers away from the citation or use of these experiences" (Holdstein and Bleich 2). Laurel Richardson also comments on the subjectivity of the narrator: "The implied narrator is godlike, an all-knowing voice from afar and above, stripped of all human subjectivity and fallibility. But, in fact, science does have a human narrator, the camouflaged first person, hiding in the bramble of the passive voice. The scientist is not

all-knowing. Omniscience is imaginary, possible only in fiction" (18).
[8]Subjectivity, emotion, and relationship are supposed to be taken out
of our scholarly pursuits once we become professionals, so the received
wisdom goes:

> Many of us—when we learned to leave the world of the
> leisurely reader to become English majors and then English
> professors—learned that the way we responded to literature as
> professionals ought to be authoritative, objective, and engaging,
> but that we should not focus on ourselves as readers or on the
> way that a particular book may have affected us personally.
> The language of enthusiasm, of heightened sensitivity, had no
> place in our professional writing and was not involved in an
> articulate, perceptive analysis of/response to literature. . . .if we
> are personal, intimate, or if we try to create for our readers, or
> between our readers and ourselves, the affiliation we feel with
> the texts most important to us—we will be emoting, we will
> not be working, we will not be writing criticism. (Zauhar 105)

[9]Watson and Smith are talking about the autobiographical female subject
more generally here, but their words are instructive to this project as well:

> The subject in question is called variously *the colonial subject,*
> *the dominated object*, and *the marginalized subject* ... the writing/
> language that emanates from the position of the colonial subject
> is variously called the *discourse of the margins, minority discourse,*
> and *postcolonial discourse*. Whatever the label, that subject and
> that writing emanate from ... a position of damage. ("Intro-
> duction: De/Colonization and the Politics of Discourse" xvi)

[10]Another collection that allows for a continuum and exploration of
a variety of subjective critical voices is *The Intimate Critique: Autobiographical Literary Criticism* edited by Diane P. Freedman, Olivia Frey
and Frances Murphy Zauhar.
[11]Many of us wonder the extent to which the role women play in
memoir keep its reputation lower: "I'm not alone in thinking that the
predominance of women in the memoir bizz may also have something
to do with the genre's disrepute" (Miller "But Enough About Me" 431).

WORKS CITED

Abbey, Sharon and Andrea O'Reilly. "Introduction." *Redefining Motherhood: Changing Identities and Patterns.* Eds. Sharon Abbey and Andrea O'Reilly. Toronto: Second Story Press, 1998. 13-26. Print.

Anzaldúa, Gloria. *Borderlands/La Frontera: The New Mestiza.* 1987. 2nd ed. San Francisco: Aunt Lute Books, 1999. Print.

Bassin, Donna, Margaret Honey, and Meryle Mahrer Kaplan, Eds. *Representations of Motherhood.* Binghamton, NY: Yale University Press/ Vail-Ballou Press, 1994. Print.

Bell-Scott, Patricia et al., eds. *Double Stitch: Black Women Write about Mothers and Daughters.* Boston: Beacon Press, 1991. Print.

Benstock, Shari, ed. *The Private Self: Women's Autobiographical Writings.* Chapel Hill: University of North Carolina Press, 1988. Print.

Behar, Ruth. *The Vulnerable Observer: Anthropology That Breaks Your Heart.* Boston: Beacon Press, 1996. Print.

Bizzini, Silvia Caporale. "Writing as a Practice of Resistance: Motherhood, Identity, and Representation." *From the Personal to the Political: Toward a New Theory of Maternal Narrative.* Eds. Andrea O'Reilly and Silvia Caporale Bizzini. Selinsgrove, PA: Susquehanna University Press, 2009. 37-49. Print.

Blakely, Mary Kay. *American Mom: Motherhood, Politics, and Humble Pie.* Chapel Hill, NC: Algonquin Books, 1994. Print.

Braxton, Joanne. *Black Women Writing Autobiography: A Tradition Within a Tradition.* Philadelphia: Temple University Press, 1989. Print.

Brodzki, Bella and Celeste Schenck. "Introduction." *Life/Lines: Theorizing Women's Autobiography.* Eds. Bella Brodzki and Celeste Schenck. Ithaca: Cornell University Press, 1988. 1-15. Print.

Brown, Ivana. "Mommy Memoirs: Feminism, Gender, and Motherhood in Popular Literature." *Journal of the Association of Research on Mothering* 8.1-2 (Winter-Summer 2006): 200-212. Print.

Brown, Stephanie. "Not a Perfect Mother." *The Grand Permission: New Writings on Poetics and Motherhood.* Eds. Patricia Dienstfrey and Brenda Hillman. Middletown, CT: Wesleyan University Press, 2003. 25-32. Print.

Buchanan, Andrea J. and Amy Hudock, eds. *Literary Mama: Reading for the Maternally Inclined.* Emeryville, CA: Seal Press, 2006. Print.

Buss, Helen M. *Repossessing the World: Reading Memoirs by Contemporary*

Women. Waterloo, ON: Wilfrid Laurier University Press, 2012. Print.

Chodorow, Nancy J. *The Reproduction of Mothering: Psychoanalysis and the Sociology of Gender.* 1978. Berkeley: University of California Press, 1999. Print.

Couser, G. Thomas. *Altered Egos: Authority in American Autobiography.* New York: Oxford University Press, 1989. Print.

Couser, G. Thomas. *American Autobiography: The Prophetic Mode.* Amherst: University of Massachusetts Press, 1979. Print.

Culley, Margo. "What a Piece of Work is 'Woman'! An Introduction." *American Women's Autobiography: Fea(s)ts of Memory.* Ed. Margo Culley. Madison: University of Wisconsin Press, 1992. 3-31. Print.

Dienstfrey, Patricia and Brenda Hillman, Eds. *The Grand Permission: New Writings on Poetics and Motherhood.* Middletown, CT: Wesleyan University Press, 2003. Print.

DiQuinzio, Patrice. *The Impossibility of Motherhood: Feminism, Individualism, and the Problem of Mothering.* New York: Routledge, 1999. Print.

Evans, Elrena and Caroline Grant, Eds. *Mama PhD: Women Write about Motherhood and Academic Life.* New Brunswick, NJ: Rutgers University Press, 2008. Print.

Felski, Rita. *Beyond Feminist Aesthetics: Feminist Literature and Social Change.* Cambridge: Harvard University Press, 1989. Print.

Freedman, Diane P., Olivia Frey and Frances Murphy Zauhar, eds. *The Intimate Critique: Autobiographical Literary Criticism.* Durham: Duke University Press, 1993. Print.

Frye, Joanne S. "Narrating Maternal Subjectivity: Memoirs from Motherhood." *Textual Mothers/Maternal Texts: Motherhood in Contemporary Women's Literatures.* Eds. Elizabeth Podnieks and Andrea O'Reilly. Waterloo, Ontario: Wilfrid Laurier University Press, 2010. 187-201. Print.

Gore, Ariel, Ed. *The Essential Hip Mama: Writing from the Cutting Edge of Parenting.* Emeryville, CA: Seal Press, 2004. Print.

Halliday, Ayun. *The Big Rumpus: A Mother's Tale from the Trenches.* Emeryville, CA: Seal Press, 2002. Print.

Herman, Michelle. *The Middle of Everything: Memoirs of Motherhood.* Lincoln: University of Nebraska Press, 2005. Print.

Hirsch, Marianne. *The Mother/Daughter Plot: Narrative, Psychoanalysis, Feminism.* Bloomington: Indiana University Press, 1989. Print.

Holdstein, Deborah H. and David Bleich. "Introduction: Recognizing the Human in the Humanities." *Personal Effects: The Social Character of Scholarly Writing*. Eds. Deborah H. Holdstein and David Bleich. Logan, UT: Utah State University Press, 2001. 1-12. Print.

hooks, bell. *Ain't I a Woman?: Black Women and Feminism*. Boston: South End Press, 1981. Print.

hooks, bell. *Feminist Theory: From Margin to Center*. Boston: South End Press, 1984. Print.

Jelinek, Estelle C. *The Tradition of Women's Autobiography: From Antiquity to the Present*. Boston: Twayne, 1986. Print.

Johnson, Susan. *A Better Woman: A Memoir*. New York: Washington Square Press, 1999. Print.

Kadar, Marlene, Linda Warley, Jeanne Perreault, and Susanna Egan, Eds. *Tracing the Autobiographical*. Waterloo, ON: Wilfrid Laurier University Press, 2005. Print.

Kaplan, E. Ann. *Motherhood and Representation: The Mother in Popular Culture and Melodrama*. London: Routledge, 1992. Print.

Kirsch, Gesa E. and Joy S. Ritchie. "Beyond the Personal: Theorizing a Politics of Location in Composition Research." *CCC* 46: 1 (1995): 7-29. Print.

Knowles, Jane Price and Ellen Cole, eds. *Motherhood: A Feminist Perspective*. Binghamton, NY: Haworth Press, 1990. Print.

Lamott, Anne. *Operating Instructions: A Journal of My Son's First Year*. New York: Pantheon, 1993. Print.

Lorde, Audre. "The Cancer Journals." *Life Notes: Personal Writings by Contemporary Black Women*. Ed. Patricia Bell-Scott. New York: W.W. Norton, 1994. 275-280. Print.

Lorde, Audre. *Sister Outsider: Essays and Speeches*. Trumansburg, NY: Crossing Press, 1984. Print.

Malin, Jo. *The Voice of the Mother: Embedded Maternal Narratives in Twentieth-Century Women's Autobiographies*. Carbondale: Southern Illinois University Press, 2000. Print.

Martini, Adrienne. *Hillbilly Gothic: A Memoir of Madness and Motherhood*. New York: Free Press, 2006. Print.

Maushart, Susan. *The Mask of Motherhood: How Becoming a Mother Changes Our Lives and Why We Never Talk about It*. New York: Penguin Books, 1999. Print.

Miller, Nancy K. "But Enough About Me, What Do You Think of My Memoir?" *Yale Journal of Criticism* 13.2 (2000): 421-436. Print.

Miller, Nancy K. *Subject to Change: Reading Feminist Writing*. New York: Columbia University Press, 1988. Print.

Minh-ha, Trinh T. *Woman, Native, Other: Writing Postcoloniality and Feminism*. Bloomington: Indiana University Press, 1989. Print.

Moraga, Cherríe. "A Work-in-Progress: Send Them Flying Home, A Geography of Remembrance." *Welcome to CherrieMoraga.com*. Web. 3 May 2013.

Moraga, Cherríe and Gloria Anzaldúa, Eds. *This Bridge Called My Back: Writings by Radical Women of Color*. Watertown, MA: Persephone Press, 1981. Print.

Peri, Camille and Kate Moses, eds. *Mothers Who Think: Tales of Real-Life Parenthood*. New York: Washington Square Press, 1999. Print.

O'Daly, Brenda O. and Maureen T. Reddy, eds. *Narrating Mothers: Theorizing Maternal Subjectivities*. Knoxville: The University of Tennessee Press, 1991. Print.

O'Reilly, Andrea. "Introduction." *Mother Outlaws: Theories and Practices of Empowered Mothering*. Ed. Andrea O'Reilly. Toronto: Women's Press, 2004. 1-28. Print.

O'Reilly, Andrea. "The Motherhood Memoir and the 'New Momism': Biting the Hand That Feeds You." *Textual Mothers/Maternal Texts: Motherhood in Contemporary Women's Literatures*. Eds. Elizabeth Podnieks and Andrea O'Reilly. Waterloo, Ontario: Wilfrid Laurier University Press, 2010. 203-213. Print.

O'Reilly, Andrea. "'Stories to Live By': Maternal Literatures and Motherhood Studies." *Textual Mothers/Maternal Texts: Motherhood in Contemporary Women's Literatures*. Eds. Elizabeth Podnieks and Andrea O'Reilly. Waterloo, ON: Wilfrid Laurier University Press, 2010. 367-373. Print.

O'Reilly, Andrea and Silvia Caporale Bizzini. "Introduction." *From the Personal to the Political: Toward a New Theory of Maternal Narrative*. Eds. Andrea O'Reilly and Silvia Caporale Bizzini. Selinsgrove, PA: Susquehanna University Press, 2009. 9-31. Print.

Podnieks, Elizabeth and Andrea O'Reilly. "Introduction: Maternal Literatures in Text and Tradition: Daughter-Centric, Matrilineal, and Matrifocal Perspectives." *Textual Mothers/Maternal Texts: Motherhood in Contemporary Women's Literatures*. Eds. Elizabeth Podnieks and Andrea O'Reilly. Waterloo, Ontario: Wilfrid Laurier University Press, 2010. 1-27. Print.

Rich, Adrienne. *Of Woman Born: Motherhood as Experience and Institution*. New York: W.W. Norton, 1976. Print.

Rich, Adrienne. "Motherhood in Bondage" 1976. *On Lies, Secrets, and Silence: Selected Prose*. 1979. New York: W.W. Norton, 1995. Print.

Richards, Joan L. *Angles of Reflection: Logic and a Mother's Love*. New York: W. H. Freeman, 2000. Print.

Richardson, Laurel. *Fields of Play: Constructing an Academic Life*. New Brunswick, NJ: Rutgers University Press, 1997. Print.

Ruddick, Sara. *Maternal Thinking: Toward a Politics of Peace*. 1989. Boston: Beacon Press, 2002. Print.

Roiphe, Anne Richardson. *Fruitful: A Real Mother in a Modern World*. Boston: Houghton Mifflin, 1996. Print.

Schenck, Celeste. "All of a Piece: Women's Poetry and Autobiography." *Life/Lines: Theorizing Women's Autobiography*. Eds. Bella Brodzki and Celeste Schenck. Ithaca: Cornell University Press, 1988. 281-305. Print.

Smith, Sidonie. *A Poetics of Women's Autobiography: Marginality and the Fictions of Self-Representation*. Bloomington: Indiana University Press, 1987. Print.

Smith, Sidonie. "Resisting the Gaze of Embodiment: Women's Autobiography in the Nineteenth Century." *American Women's Autobiography: Fea(s)ts of Memory*. Ed. Margo Culley. Madison: University of Wisconsin Press, 1992. 75-110. Print.

Smith, Sidonie and Julia Watson. *Reading Autobiography: A Guide for Interpreting Life Narratives. 2nd ed.* Minneapolis: University of Minnesota Press, 2010. Print.

Stanton, Domna C. *The Female Autograph*. Chicago: University of Chicago Press, 1984. Print.

Stitt, Jocelyn Fenton and Pegeen Reichert Powell. "Introduction: Delivering Mothering Studies." *Mothers Who Deliver: Feminist Interventions in Public and Interpersonal Discourse*. Eds. Jocelyn Fenton Stitt and Pegeen Reichert Powell. Albany: SUNY Press, 2010. 1-18. Print.

Strong, Shari MacDonald, ed. *The Maternal Is Political: Women Writers at the Intersection of Motherhood and Social Change*. Berkeley: Seal Press, 2008. Print.

Tompkins, Jane. "Me and My Shadow." *The Intimate Critique: Autobiographical Literary Criticism*. Eds. Diane P. Freedman, Olivia Frey and Frances Murphy Zauhar. Durham: Duke University Press, 1993. 23-40. Print.

Tuttle Hansen, Elaine. *Mother Without Child: Contemporary Fiction and the Crisis of Motherhood.* Berkeley: University of California Press, 1997. Print.

Walker, Alice. *In Search of Our Mothers' Gardens: Womanist Prose.* San Diego: Harcourt Brace, 1983. Print.

Walker, Rebecca. *Baby Love: Choosing Motherhood after a Lifetime of Ambivalence.* New York: Riverhead Books/Penguin Group, 2007. Print.

Wane, Njoki Nathani. "Reflections on the Mutuality of Mothering: Women, Children, and Othermothering." *Mother Outlaws: Theories and Practices of Empowered Mothering.* Ed. Andrea O'Reilly. Toronto: Women's Press, 2004. 229-239.

Watson, Julia and Sidonie Smith. "Introduction: De/Colonization and the Politics of Discourse in Women's Autobiographical Practices." *De/Colonizing the Subject: The Politics of Gender in Women's Autobiography.* Eds. Sidonie Smith and Julia Watson. Minneapolis: University of Minnesota Press, 1992. xiii-xxxi. Print.

Willard-Traub, Margaret. "Scholarly Memoir: An Un-'Professional' Practice." *Personal Effects: The Social Character of Scholarly Writing.* Eds. Deborah H. Holdstein and David Bleich. Logan, UT: Utah State University Press, 2001. 27-50. Print.

Zauhar, Frances Murphy. "Creative Voices: Women Reading and Women's Writing." *The Intimate Critique: Autobiographical Literary Criticism.* Eds. Diane P. Freedman, Olivia Frey and Frances Murphy Zauhar. Durham: Duke University Press, 1993. 103-116. Print.

SECTION ONE
THE ART OF MOTHERHOOD

1.
Visualizing Motherhood

The "Memory Work" of Mother-Artists

RACHEL EPP BULLER

A S I BEGIN the process of visualizing motherhood through printed works on paper, the physicality of the art-making evokes a visceral satisfaction that startles me. My aching arm muscles, strained from the repetitive carving, are strangely pleasing. As I pull the prints, the smell of the ink takes me back in time. My body remembers the crackling sound of the ink rolled out with the brayer and the familiar cranking of the press wheel. Then I begin a new process, cutting and piecing, destroying and reassembling into a new whole. As I draw on ancestral traditions to sew these paper quilts, I am surprised by how good it feels to stitch the paper together.

In 2007, I returned to making art after a ten-year hiatus. Having put printmaking on hold first for graduate school and then for babies, it was the birth of my third and last child that spurred me back to finding my creative self, emerging from a postpartum haze. Becoming a mother was such an enormous shift in identity for me that I sought ways to express this, journaling extensively, and compiling many scrapbooks filled with hundreds of photographs, to record the milestones and the mundane. Much of this, however, centered more on the children and their development than on my own experiences. I returned to printmaking in part as a way to express what I recognized as a marked shift in my own identity as a person, a physical and emotional transformation. The series of work that emerged from that time functions for me as a visual memoir of early motherhood, a conscious staging of a time that I knew would be gone all too soon.

This concept of a visual memoir is not without precedent. Historically, the genre of memoir has entailed a first-person narrative, written

Figure 1: Rachel Epp Buller, "Middle Friendship Star," 2008, linocut print-quilt with hand stitching, 24 x 24 inches. Private collection.

perhaps as a short story, or series of stories, or as a longer, autobiographical volume. In recent years, however, a number of artists and artist-writers have expanded the genre by exploring the possibility of a family-based memoir in visual form. This is a somewhat surprising turn in the visual arts, where parenthood, or specifically motherhood, has only recently gained legitimacy as a serious source of artistic production (Buller; Liss; Chernick and Klein). Despite the advances of the Feminist Art Movement in the 1970s, motherhood was, with only a few notable exceptions, seen by many feminists as a traditional burden to be cast off or a role to be satirized for its stereotypes and limitations. Artist-mothers not infrequently hid the existence of their children from professional colleagues (Chernick and Klein 8). Within the last two decades, however, successful artists such as Renée Cox have brought heightened visibility and legitimacy to the theme of motherhood as a topic for art-making. This art world breakthrough, combined with the success of trade publishers in marketing motherhood narratives in recent years, has precipitated a new form: the visual memoir of motherhood.

I find that it is a process to get to this place, of the *visual* memoir. It is not easy to let go of the written word, to give up the control of explaining a personal experience to the viewer/reader. Perhaps for this reason, a number of maternal memoirists combine image and text, seeking a middle ground where both visual and verbal can play a role. The work to be discussed in this essay will thus follow two paths: graphic memoirists who combine text and image, and artists who transition to entirely image-based memoirs.

MEMORY WORK

The concept of visual memoirs may be understood in part through the recent surge of scholarly and artistic interest in memory. Memory research currently is being pursued in such diverse fields as philosophy, history, cultural studies, literature, film, media studies, psychology, archaeology, and architecture (Radstone 1). In addition, memory is a prominent topic of exploration in contemporary art: Christian Boltanski, Rachel Whiteread, Krzysztof Wodiczko, and Kara Walker are just a few of the many international artists who address issues of memory. By and large, their focus is cultural memory, a designation signifying that "memory can be understood as a cultural phenomenon as well as an individual or social one" (Bal vii). The artists and writers who work in the realm of memoir may begin their explorations of memory from a personal vantage point, but they often attempt to offer up in their work collectively shared points of reference as well, moving between individual and cultural memory.

Further, visual memoirs frequently engage with Annette Kuhn's theorized concept of "memory work." Kuhn argues that memory work is an *active and inquiring practice of remembering that connects individual and cultural memory*. She writes, "Memory work makes it possible to explore connections between 'public' historical events, structures of feeling, family dramas, relations of class, national identity and gender, and 'personal' memory.... [P]ersonal and collective remembering emerge again and again as continuous with one another" (Kuhn, *Family Secrets*

4-5). While Kuhn's understanding of memory work most often focuses on "working backwards" to, for example, mine old photographs for the memories they may hold, memory work can also be reconciled with a generative process, such as the creation of memoirs. Rather than analyzing a forgotten photograph in a scholarly manner, the artists discussed below perform memory work by actively remembering and recreating, in and through their memoir productions.

A key component of Kuhn's theories, and one exhibited to varying degrees in each of the visual memoirs, has to do with the relative veracity of memory. Memoirs are not documentary transcripts of events past but are instead subjective interpretations full of emotion and personal opinion. As Kuhn explains, "Memory work undercuts assumptions about the transparency or the authenticity of what is remembered, treating it not as 'truth' but as evidence of a particular sort: material for interpretation, to be interrogated, mined for its meanings and its possibilities. Memory work is a conscious and powerful staging of memory" (Kuhn, "A Journey Through Memory" 186). Each of the visual memoirists to be discussed performs memory in an active, often very public, manner, variously interpreting their own experiences to ends of humor, activism, nostalgia, or simply day-to-day survival.

FROM COMIC BOOKS TO GRAPHIC MATERNAL MEMOIRS

Recent decades have witnessed the rise of the graphic comic memoir. While the comic book of old might have had childhood and escapist, fantasy associations, Joan Gibbons argues that comic artists like Art Spiegelman, whose Pulitzer Prize-winning *Maus* comics told the story of his parents' Holocaust survival, have changed the literary landscape: "[T]he comic book is not necessarily a 'lowbrow' or a reductive medium but one that is also capable of psychological complexity and introspection" (Gibbons 88). In the years since Spiegelman brought attention to the comic as a vehicle for memoir, other graphic novelists have followed suit. Marjane Satrapi's *Persepolis* (2003) comics chronicle her childhood and early adult years living in Iran, during and after the Islamic Revolution, while Alison Bechdel's graphic novel *Fun Home: A Family Tragicomic* (2006) recounts her childhood and complex family dynamics, with issues of sexual orientation and suicide mixed in. Given the personal-historical direction of many contemporary comics, it is perhaps unsurprising that motherhood now finds shelter under the comic-memoir umbrella as well. However, the form of memory work practiced by these comic memoirists aligns closely with Kuhn's discussion of "memory texts." Kuhn defines this sub-genre of memory work by its "fragmentary, non-linear quality of moments recalled out of time. Visual flashes, vignettes, a certain anecdotal quality, mark memory texts..." (Kuhn, *Family Secrets* 5). Surely the vast majority of written memoirs include vignettes and anecdotes; so, too, do these visual memoirs draw frequently upon such fragmentary flashes of temporally dislocated narrative.

Ayun Halliday began writing the now-popular 'zine, *The East Village Inky*, in 1998. Halliday infuses her writings with near-constant self-deprecation and an exaggeration of the mundane, making evident her background in theater as she transforms the smallest parenting mishap into a laugh-out-loud anecdote. While Halliday privileges the text in her 'zines, her accompanying cartoon illustrations work with the narrative to enhance the hilarity, visually emphasizing the ridiculous despair of certain situations in mothering.

Begun when Halliday's first child was a year old, *The East Village Inky* was born as a mode of survival. Staying at home full-time, Halliday discovered that, "like many first time mothers, [I] slowly began losing my marbles" (Martini). What saved her sanity was the decision to chronicle her (mis)adventures in parenting in a tiny apartment in New York City. Her quarterly, handwritten, photocopied, and stapled-by-hand 'zine may include, in a single issue, pages on "Do it Yourself Recycling when the city of NY leaves you no option; Children's Music that won't make your gums bleed; Misadventures Behind the Wheel; PooPoo Bed; [and] Angry Fish" (Halliday issue 17, 2002). Interspersed within the narrative and squeezed into the margins, Halliday's line drawings of her husband, children, cat, and other assorted characters enhance the text by functioning as comic illustrations of the anecdotes or by imparting unrelated yet equally hilarious interactions between Halliday and her family.

Halliday's *EVI* is a continual staging of memory, a self-conscious and exaggerated reminiscence of quotidian existence. As part of her memory work, Halliday exaggerates the mundane in ways that make connections between her daughter's life and her own, longer-ago childhood. In issue 6 (1999), Halliday describes the hoopla surrounding her daughter's first case of head lice, then retells the story in issue 22 (2004) while embedding related stories from her own childhood within the narrative. In one embedded text, Halliday recalls her grandmother's vague warning about the dangers of sharing hats, a danger whose consequences Halliday's daughter later experiences for herself. Inge Stockburger argues that the inclusion of these stories from Halliday's own childhood is in part a discursive move meant to share the burden of the stigma regarding the lice infestation. In addition, Stockburger asserts, Halliday reaches back to childhood experiences "not only as a foreshadowing of a later event in her life, but also as a resource for making sense of this later event" (Stockburger 336). Part of this "making sense" includes a self-critique of her mothering skills: Halliday uses the embedded story humorously to implicate herself as an apparently careless parent for letting her child play with dress-up clothes.

An underlying component illustrated by Halliday's visual memoirs, and by motherhood memoirs in general, is the often gendered nature of memory work regarding the family. Stephan Feuchtwang argues that the transmission of memories between generations is "likely to be gendered, a different transmission by women and men, by mothers and fathers to daughters and to sons. Female transmission is likely to be less accommodated to or acknowledged by public commemoration except in the treasuring of the family and its female progenitor, themselves" (Feuchtwang 65). Halliday's valuation of the mundane serves as an implicit valuation of women, giving worth to the unpaid, unseen work of domesticity. In her acknowledgement of the *EVI* as a tool to survive the insanity of mothering young children, Halliday further participates in one of Kuhn's proposed purposes of memory work: "Bringing the secrets and the shadows into the open, allows the deeper meanings of the family drama's mythic aspects to be reflected upon, confronted, understood. This in turn helps in coming to terms with the feelings of the present, and so in living more fully in the present" (Kuhn, *Family Secrets* 6).

Packaged as a subscription 'zine, Halliday's memoir-in-progress is clearly targeted at a public audience, one who she hopes will identify with, or at least find amusement in, her verbal and visual exaltation of the nitty-gritty. In an interview, Halliday said, "I suspect that the depictions of Inky and Milo are as big of a draw as my own first-person narrative. They're the stars, the Gatsbys, and I'm just Nick living next door, reporting on the wonderful parties going on in the big house with all the lights on. What mother can't relate to that?" (Savage np). At the same time, Halliday aspires to more than just entertainment but to activism couched in/as humor: "I hope that [my work] will fall into the hands of women who are raising their children according to a very mainstream model and that it will turn them into bootie shaking, breastfeeding, co-sleeping, Barney bashing, zine reading, Bad House-keeping she wolves…" (Savage).

Fellow 'zine writer and comic artist Heather Cushman-Dowdee directs her work at a similarly public audience, but with a more obvious activist bent. Begun as a quarterly 'zine, then published as books and on her website as well, Cushman-Dowdee's *Hathor the Cowgoddess* is a memoir-in-progress of political motherhood. Unlike Halliday's work, *Hathor* fully integrates image and text in traditional comic-book style: the graphic imagery is primary but is only fully explicated by the bubbles of text conveying the spoken and thought words of her familial cast of characters.

Cushman-Dowdee experienced motherhood as a time of political awakening, as she searched for parenting advice and simultaneously encountered many questions about and hostile reactions to her decision to breastfeed. As she struggled to respond to these dilemmas of mothering through her art, Cushman-Dowdee developed a comic avatar in the form of Hathor the Cowgoddess. Hathor, the ancient Egyptian goddess of motherhood, childbirth, and midwives, among other things, was often portrayed as the cow that suckled the pharaohs. As a nursing mother herself, Cushman-Dowdee could find no more apt persona and so developed the Hathor persona as an activist-superhero-mother: "I began to use my artwork as a soapbox and invoked, assimilated or became Hathor the Cowgoddess as the best possible guide for my projects" (Cushman-Dowdee, *The Birth of Hathor* 16). Hathor's attachment parenting philosophy[1] includes six commandments: Homebirth, Breast-feed on demand, Wear your child in a sling, Practice the family bed, Unschool, and Save the World. In Cushman-Dowdee's hands, Hathor becomes a powerful superhero, waging battle on behalf of lactivists and attachment parents everywhere. Cushman-Dowdee carefully crafted Hathor's appearance to reflect her powers. As the artist describes her:

Hathor is the epitome of hipness. She wears jeans and small tees with revolutionary sayings. She dies [sic] her hair with abandon. She wears a sling and a baby as if it were the easiest accessory in the world. Her breast is almost always suckled and casually (politically) exposed. She is invariably barefoot, and her feet are giant to juxtapose her grounding to the weightlessness of her child. She goes barefoot even into battle. Her face is partially covered (except for the eyes) by the snout of a cow, which ties behind her head. She wears a headdress with a large golden breast in the middle, a pair of truncated (domesticated) horns and two large, soft velveteen cow ears. (Cushman-Dowdee, *The Birth of Hathor* 17)

In part by her use of an avatar, Cushman-Dowdee makes explicit her conscious performance of memory work. In her staging of memory and activism, Cushman-Dowdee so fully assimilates the character of Hathor that there is often little separation between them: "I am she and she is I" (*The Birth of Hathor* 16). Cushman-Dowdee blurs the boundaries between her art and her life as she integrates both with her activist zeal, producing a series that might be understood as visualizations of life-as-performance-art. She features herself, her husband, and her children in nearly all of her comics and bases them on factual events, creating on one level a serial graphic memoir of mothering. It is safe to assume, however, because of both its comic and political intents, that Hathor is a manipulation of those events, a Kuhnian memory text of non-linear vignettes and anecdotes that have been adapted or exaggerated to a specific end. This manipulation is made evident in part through differing types of text. Hathor's visually commanding presence is echoed by her short-and-sweet commands. As a goddess, Hathor does not hesitate to proclaim the superiority of her views. Hathor's children, on the other hand, are more likely to display word or thought bubbles articulating longer and more nuanced opinions to contribute to the dialogue at hand. These thoughtful expressions are sometimes at odds with the sharp political slogans ("Cage Free Kid," "Seen <u>And</u> Heard") emblazoned across their tiny t-shirts, further underscoring that Cushman-Dowdee's memoir of motherhood is just as much about activism as family.

In a multi-panel series from 2004, Cushman-Dowdee features both herself and her transformation into Hathor, as they battle together the culturally ubiquitous presence of formula feeding. Venturing out into public as Heather, with toddler and young child in tow, her character decides to attempt a "normal" life of "not talking about social ills, or politics or being outraged" (Cushman-Dowdee, *The Milk of Hathor* 24-26). Her plans go awry as she is confronted with parental discussions of infant formula brands, criticism of her use of a sling, a baby left to cry in a car seat, and magazine imagery of bottle-fed infants in the checkout line. Arriving home to find a large package of free formula delivered to her doorstep proves the final straw, precipitating Heather's transformation back into Hathor (Cushman-Dowdee, *The Milk of Hathor* 24-26). By compressing her experiences into a single series and by making visible her transformation into a lactivist superhero, Cushman-Dowdee carries out memory work by treating her memories as material for interpretation and by obviously staging the personal memories as performance for a wider audience.

MOVING TOWARD THE IMAGE

Kuhn's theory of memory work continues to resonate as artist-mothers turn to image-based memoirs. While Hal Foster notes a general "archival impulse" in much contemporary art when he writes of the artist as archivist, many visual memoirs of motherhood move beyond the documentary or the archival impulse. Not simply a process of remembering, the memory work conducted by visual memoirists follows Kuhn's construct by expanding upon individual memory to connect with a larger, shared cultural memory. Using individual experiences as the starting point, visual memoirists may position their work as broadly accessible—to all mothers, and maybe all parents—and this universality is perhaps eased by the absence of specific textual references. Removing the individualistic focus of names and verbal narratives from the presentation may make it easier to connect with viewers and with cultural memory.

Many artists who have embraced motherhood as a topic for art-making create their work in series, many of which might arguably function as memoirs, particularly of transitional periods. Susan Hiller's conceptual *Ten Months* project, for example, marked the gradual changes of the pregnant body. Closely cropped, landscape-like daily photographs of her pregnant form transformed her changing physicality into a calendrical presentation. Similarly, in *280 Days*, photographer Gail Rebhan chronicled the subtle bodily changes of pregnancy and imposed a kind of order on the "unruly situation" of impending maternity (Matthews and Wexler 66). In both cases, while the artists may have sought to archive their own individual experiences of a fleeting period, the somewhat abstracted nature of their public presentations allowed them to connect as well with the shared cultural memory of those who have experienced similar physical transformations.

Decades after her visual memoir of pregnancy, Rebhan presented a photographic memoir of the letting go that occurs in the mothering of twentysomethings. Rebhan's *Room* series (2007), a grouping of gridded photographs showing the borderline disaster area of her son's bedroom, offers both a narrative of a young man's detritus and a memoir of the changing nature of mothering as children grow. Rebhan states, "In the twentysomething work, I have become more of an observer rather than an active participant. My influence on my sons is not as great as when they were younger. I can no longer persuade them to assimilate my values uncritically" (174). Rebhan consciously stages the *Room* photographs, mining personal experiences but eliminating personal identification so that the works might also resonate with others at similar life stages.

In 2007, I embarked upon a series of prints that became my own visual memoir of transitional early motherhood. The *Identity Series* marks the changes, overlaps, and transformations of identity that occur in the life of the family with the addition of children. Initially conceived as a grouping of representational portraits, the series soon morphed into an abstracted idea of portraiture, taking as its formal basis one fingerprint of each member of our family. Printed individually, the fingerprints highlight unique genetic qualities; when layered, they can speak to the temporary masking of identity that occurs in the position of motherhood. In hand-stitched print blankets, issues of genetic difference overlap, literally and metaphorically, with larger implications of family position—individuality alongside and within familial identity. The most recent print-quilts combine sections of the fingerprints and fragments of the representational portraits, further playing on issues of identity and likeness. Many of these visual memoirs of motherhood use traditional patchwork quilting patterns and draw on a lengthy history of women's artistic creativity.

"Family Quilt" (2008) was my first visual exposition on the life of our family as it intersected with my fears of a lost identity. After earning a Ph.D. in Art History, I made the decision to stay at home for several

*Figure 2: Rachel Epp Buller, "Family Quilt," 2008, linocut print-quilt
with hand-stitching, 3' x 4'. Collection of the artist.*

years with our young children. The abrupt change from promising graduate student/scholar to stay-at-home mom was challenging, to say the
least. My personal and professional identities felt submerged beneath
the high needs of nursing infants and toddlers. In "Introduction from
The Myths of Motherhood," psychologist Shari Thurer dramatically
describes this phenomenon, how in some ways the new mother ceases

to exist: "She exists bodily, of course, but her needs as a person become null and void. On delivering a child … her personal desires either evaporate or metamorphose so that they are identical with those of her infant. Once she attains motherhood, a woman must hand in her point of view" (Thurer 335). Just as Ayun Halliday turned to *The East Village Inky* in part to save her sanity, so, too, did I return to printmaking after an extended absence to chronicle my situation and regain some semblance of my own separate being. In "Family Quilt," by assigning a color to each family member, I was able to showcase the individual identities of each family member with single fingerprints, as well as many permutations of color/identity layering. The varied layerings of enlarged fingerprints became a metaphorical layering of identities in which the color-identities masked each other in obvious ways, yet still allowed spaces for color-identities to shine through.

As I continued to work with the fingerprint prints and the intersections of familial identity, the combination prints developed more fully into an abstract memoir of motherhood. Physically fragmenting both the fingerprints and a series of earlier representational family portraits into squares and triangles, I set about the piece work of memory. No longer simply about my own frustrations of lost identity, I explored the genetic overlaps and distinctive characteristics of my three children, as seen in their visages as well as their thumbprints. Pieced, adhered, and hand-stitched into such traditional quilting patterns as Ohio Star, Four Patch, Nine Patch, Sawtooth, Jacob's Ladder, Friendship Star, and Pinwheel, these paper quilts in part allow me to draw on the staple feminine craft of our family's shared religious-cultural Mennonite heritage whose intricacies I never learned for myself. While the paper-quilts do not address specific events in the life of our family, they function more generally as a memoir of those early years of motherhood, the transitional time when my young children's identities seemed so fully merged with my own and then gradually began to separate. By basing them in part on idealized portraits from their early childhood, the print-quilts are a self-conscious nostalgic production; and yet, by fragmenting the images and combining them with the layered fingerprints, they draw attention to this problematic idealization and highlight the complexities of familial identities and relationships.

But while the print-quilts are very personal to me, pieced from intimate and, sometimes, difficult experiences, they are not documentary nor are they necessarily specific to our family. They are staged and abstracted productions, self-conscious memoirs that, in retrospect, I believe I created partly in the hopes of connecting with other mothers experiencing similar transformative experiences. Joan Gibbons argues, "The artist's ability to set the past within a social or collective framework is …vital to the success of memory…" (147). For me, the fragmenting, piecing, and reassembling of parts becomes a process of collective re-collection, not only a gathering together and mining of individual experiences and subjective emotions, but also a means for maternal connectivity.

In her extended analyses of memory work and memory texts, Annette Kuhn repeatedly emphasizes the continuity between personal and collective remembering. Whether discussing family albums or oral histories, Kuhn argues that such productions of memory can express "both personal truths and a collective imagination" (Kuhn, *Family Secrets* 165). Employing varied combinations of image and text, the visual memoirists discussed here address both the individual and collective maternal, "living" their memories by manipulating their experiences and performing Kuhn's concept of memory work. Bringing a visual component to the work of motherhood allows for lived experiences to be interrogated in a new way, mined for their meanings and presented not simply as commemorations but often as investigative critiques as well. Whether produced as comedic relief, tools of an activist agenda, a means of survival, or mementos of a quickly changing landscape, these varied visual memoirs of motherhood embrace the details of daily life so often overlooked in our histories (though not in our 'herstories'), uniting fragmentary images, anecdotes, thoughts, and feelings to evoke a collective response and stage a conscious performance of maternal memory.

ENDNOTES

[1]Dr. William Sears, a pediatrician, coined the phrase "attachment parenting" and promotes it in his many books, most notably in *The Baby Book* (1993) and more recently in *The Attachment Parenting Book* (2001).

WORKS CITED

Bal, Mieke. "Introduction." *Acts of Memory: Cultural Recall in the Present.* Eds. Bal, Jonathan Crewe, and Leo Spitzer. Lebanon, NH: University

Press of New England, 1999. Print.

Bechdel, Alison. *Fun Home: A Family Tragicomic*. New York: Houghton Mifflin, 2006. Print.

Buller, Rachel Epp, ed. *Reconciling Art and Mothering*. Surrey, UK: Ashgate Publishing, 2012. Print.

Chernick, Myrel and Jennie Klein, eds. *The M Word: Real Mothers in Contemporary Art*. Toronto: Demeter Press, 2011. Print.

Cushman-Dowdee, Heather. *The Birth of Hathor*. Self-published, 2005. Print.

Cushman-Dowdee, Heather *The Milk of Hathor: The Breastfeeding Comics*. Self-published, 2006. Print.

Feuchtwang, Stephan. "Reinscriptions: Commemoration, Restoration and the Interpersonal Transmission of Histories and Memories under Modern States in Asia and Europe." *Memory and Methodology*. Ed. Susannah Radstone. Oxford: Berg, 2000. 59-75. Print.

Foster, Hal. "An Archival Impulse." *October* 110 (Fall 2004): 3-22. Print.

Gibbons, Joan. *Contemporary Art and Memory: Images of Recollection and Remembrance*. London: I. B. Tauris, 2007. Print.

Halliday, Ayun. *The East Village Inky*. Self-published 'zine: 1998-present, in particular, issues 6, 17, and 22. Print.

Kuhn, Annette. *Family Secrets: Acts of Memory and Imagination*. London: Verso, 1995. Print.

Kuhn, Annette. "A Journey Through Memory." *Memory and Methodology*. Ed. Susannah Radstone. Oxford: Berg, 2000. 179-96. Print.

Liss, Andrea. *Feminist Art and the Maternal*. Minneapolis, MN: University of Minnesota Press, 2009. Print.

Martini, Adrienne. "An Interview with Ayun Halliday." *Bookslut* March 2005. Web. 15 October 2011.

Matthews, Sandra and Laura Wexler. *Pregnant Pictures*. New York: Routledge, 2000. Print.

Radstone, Susannah, ed. *Memory and Methodology*. Oxford: Berg, 2000. Print.

Rebhan, Gail. "Mothering Twentysomethings." *Reconciling Art and Mothering*. Ed. Rachel Epp Buller. Surrey, UK: Ashgate Publishing, 2012. 169-75. Print.

Satrapi, Marjane. *Persepolis*. Trans. Blake Ferris and Mattias Ripa. New York: Pantheon Books, 2003. Print.

Savage, Jennifer. "An Interview with Ayun Halliday." *Hip Mama*. 24

Sept. 2003. Web. 15 Oct. 2011.

Sears, William. *The Baby Book.* New York: Little, Brown and Company, 1993. Print.

Sears, William. *The Attachment Parenting Book.* New York: Little, Brown and Company, 2001. Print.

Spiegelman, Art. *The Complete Maus.* New York: Penguin Books, 1993. Print.

Stockburger, Inge. "Embedded Stories and the Life Story: Retellings in a Memoir and Perzine." *Narrative Inquiry* 18.2. (2008): 326-48. Print.

Thurer, Shari L. "Introduction from The Myths of Motherhood." 1994. *Maternal Theory: Essential Readings.* Ed. Andrea O'Reilly. Toronto: Demeter Press, 2007: 331-44. Print.

2.
How to Write Motherhood

Writing Guides for Mothers

YELIZAVETA P. RENFRO

O F ALL THE ADVICE I received in my MFA program about how to succeed as a writer, one kernel stands out in my memory. "Don't have children," said one of my male professors in one of my first classes. This was in 2001, before I had children of my own. I was recently reminded of his comment in a *Guardian* article that was a compendium of writing tips from several dozen writers ("Ten Rules"). One of Richard Ford's jumped out. "Don't have children," he admonishes. My MFA professor assigned John Gardner's *On Becoming a Novelist*, which offers advice that also excludes mothers—and, indeed, women. "If he has a wife and children," Gardner writes, "the writer cannot pay as much attention to them as his neighbors do to theirs" (47). Later, he writes, "I cannot work on a novel if I do not have long time blocks for writing—fifteen hours straight is for me ideal" (114). In his world view, not only is the writer male, but women—who tend to be wives—are the ones caring for the kids while the male writers do the real work, writing for fifteen hours at a stretch, producing masterpieces that only such prolonged concentration will allow them to pull off.

In *The Spooky Art*, Norman Mailer offers up a cornucopia of the writing lore that he has picked up in his five-plus decades as a successful writer of fiction and nonfiction. He fixates on protagonists who are brave and heroic, on war and boxing as subjects. He encourages writers to ask the question: "Do you have the inner sanction to create a man who's braver and tougher than yourself? The answer is yes." In the next paragraph, he admits, "I don't know how to pose the question for an author who's female. Can she, for example, write about a woman who is more sensitive than herself? Probably not" (85). Not only does he circumscribe women to the vague idea of "sensitivity" as being perhaps their greatest virtue, but he doubts their ability to pull off the feat of writing about it. In over three hundred pages, Mailer never mentions childbirth or motherhood. They are simply not on his writerly radar. Neither are children or fatherhood. These subjects seemingly have nothing to do with his life as a writer, though he was married a half dozen times and his children number just short of double digits. (And my MFA professor, I could add, had children from previous marriages.) So perhaps the "don't have children" rule carries the following postscript: But if you do, make sure your wife takes care of them so they don't interfere with your writing life.

And so, in hearing the advice of many experienced writers, I have often been left with a feeling that I was being excluded somehow: that either my experiences as a woman were not suitable subjects for literature, or that I was incapable of writing about the great and manly themes that mattered, or that what I wanted—to be a mother and writer—were mutually exclusive, and that by becoming a mother I would be giving up the intellectual life, that my mind would be deadened by a world of Barney and Elmo and the pre-articulate jabbering of toddlers, of stupidity brought on by lack of sleep and keeping company with howling babies. Some eight decades after the publication of Virginia Woolf's *A Room of One's Own* (which in itself is a type of writer's manual), its central concerns are still relevant. Though not a mother herself, Woolf recognized both that the work of motherhood and wifehood has prevented women from becoming writers and that the woman's experience—including the experience of taking care of children—needs to be written about. To this day, the validity of women's experiences and their abilities to write about them are still, in some circles, in question, are still pushed to the peripheries by writers who believe that motherhood as a subject is not as worthy as, say, war or politics or sports. The domestic life still stays in the home.

As I studied writing and as I pondered having children, these were my issues. Choosing to have children, what would I be giving up? Or choosing not to have children, what would I be giving up? What is it that is antithetical about having children and being a writer? And perhaps more importantly, how does motherhood transform our writing? How are the practical aspects of writing (such as time management) as well as questions of subject matter (writing about motherhood, for example) and even a writer's identity affected by becoming a mother? These questions seemed, in many ways, central to the ways in which writers viewed themselves and their peers and defined success. All through my MFA program, the comment my professor made early on stuck because motherhood was possibly on the horizon for me, though I had not yet committed to it. As it turned out, I would become pregnant the month I finished my MFA, would start a Ph.D. program three months later, would give birth in the middle of my second semester, have my second child after becoming ABD, and complete my Ph.D. as the mother of a five-year-old and two-year-old, while simultaneously having a book of short stories published.

In those years of my graduate education, I discovered another side to all this. The memoir genre has in recent years virtually exploded as writers of all backgrounds and experiences—including women and mothers—tell their stories. It isn't only the men with understanding wives and fifteen hours at a stretch who are writing. The "revolution in personal narrative," writes Natalie Goldberg, "is the expression of a uniquely American energy: a desire to understand in the heat of living, while life is fresh, and not wait till old age—it may be too late. We are hungry—and impatient now" (xx). She continues, "We are a dynamic country, fast-paced, ever onward.... In the core of our forward movement, we are often confused and lonely. That's why we have turned so full-heartedly to the memoir form. We have an intuition that it can save us" (xxi). Nowhere is this truer than in the country of motherhood. As mothers, we need that moment of pause, of respite, to look at the turmoil of a single day, the teething and weaning or dance classes and phonics homework, to locate and save ourselves. And writing mothers are doing it.

"Motherhood, while hardly new, is newly in vogue," writes Lisa Garrigues. "Bookstores have created whole sections for mothers, displaying not only manuals and magazines on the how-tos of parenting, but also fiction and memoir that celebrate motherhood, for the first time in history, as a worthy literary subject in its own right" (63-64). With the proliferation of motherhood memoirs, collections of essays on motherhood, websites devoted to writing by and about mothers, and workshops and classes designed to help mothers write about their mothering experiences, more and more mothers are taking up the pen—or sitting down at the computer—to write creative works of literary nonfiction, fiction, and poetry that are rooted in their identities as mothers.

This rise in the popularity of the "motherhood genre"—and especially the motherhood memoir—has led to the creation of a new sub-genre: the writing guide for mothers. Penned by mothers, these books by their very existence are proclaiming: Yes, you can be a mother and a writer. Yes, it is all possible in one coherent life. And it is possible not just for the elite, but for any mother who picks up the guide and a pen. Instead of proclaiming "don't have children," these guides say, in effect, "only mothers need apply." I want to look in some detail at three of these recent writing guides for mothers: Garrigues' *Writing Motherhood* (2008), Christina Katz's *Writer Mama: How to Raise a Writing Career Alongside Your Kids* (2007), and Barbara DeMarco-Barrett's *Pen on Fire: A Busy Woman's Guide to Igniting the Writer Within* (2004). These three writers—who are all mothers—bring their own experiences and approaches to the subject of the writing mother. By exploring these authors' varying perspectives on writing, I will define some of the special challenges that mother writers face, and I will also examine the deep connections between writing, motherhood, and identity.

In "Writing in Public: Popular Pedagogies of Creative Writing," Michelle Cross creates a typology for popular creative writing pedagogy, suggesting that most writing guides fall within one (or more) of four categories: literary pedagogy, commercial pedagogy, holistic pedagogy, and iconic pedagogy. Examining the writing guides in light of these categories will reveal that though the books target similar demographics, their guiding typologies vary. Two of the four typologies—commercial pedagogy and holistic pedagogy—are most relevant to this discussion. Cross defines commercial pedagogy as focusing "on literary texts in the context of a market-driven public culture. It implicitly conceives of creative writing as a vocation, and of the writer as professional labourer engaging in economic activity in an industry, more so than pursuing a path of artistic or spiritual self-discovery"; these types of guides have "an explicit recognition of the market as having a palpable presence in and influence on the writer's life and work" (69). Holistic pedagogy, on the other hand, "focuses on engendering a writing experience that contributes to the discovery, development, and healing of the writer's spiritual and emotional *self*, first and foremost. As it values process over product, writing over literature, and individual concerns over social concerns, holistic pedagogy tends to play up the personal and downplay discussions of craft, publication, famous authors, or literary themes" (70).

Garrigues' *Writing Motherhood* wholeheartedly embraces holistic pedagogy. "Write to discover, not to be discovered," she writes. "You will be more inclined to continue writing if your goal is to understand yourself, not to impress others" (36). Throughout her book, she stresses discovery and process over product. Motherhood is at the center of Garrigues' writing universe; for her, the exploration of one's life as a mother is paramount. She even describes a "holistic" writing schedule "that allows for children and parents, sickness and setbacks, fitness and friendship, breakups, breakdowns, and just plain breaks" (39). In other words, there is no separate writing life and mothering life. The writing occurs within the whole life; it is integrated into daily activities. "Just as mothering gives us material for writing," Garrigues writes, "so writing gives us tools for mothering" (22). Indeed, motherhood is so much a part of writing for Garrigues that she even borrows the language of motherhood to talk about writing, offering the "ABCs" of writing motherhood, as well as the writerly "Time Out" and "Playdate." Her writing exercises incorporate themes such as pregnancy, birth stories, baby names, and bedtime stories. For Garrigues, motherhood and writing are inextricably bound, each taking inspiration from the other. Writing, for Garrigues, is a process of knowing. She is not interested in the end result so much as in the writing itself. She has very little to say on the subject of publication. That, for her, is not ultimately the point.

In stark contrast, Katz's *Writer Mama* falls under the commercial pedagogy typology in its main goal of guiding the aspiring writer into launching a lucrative freelance writing career by developing a savvy knowledge of the commercial publishing industry. "This book will help you get published sooner," Katz promises in the introduction (2). The book is structured around "the progression of a typical career" in its various phases (7). Where, exactly, do children and motherhood fit in? The subtitle of the book is revealing: *How to Raise a Writing Career Alongside Your Kids*. The kids are clearly *alongside*, and not at the center of writing for Katz. One value of motherhood, she points out, is that it can be an avenue to publication. "Motherhood is in," she writes, and the writing mother can, for example, submit tips based on her personal experiences to parenting magazines in order to build a dossier of clips (3). The practical topics covered by Katz include targeting certain markets, writing cover letters, doing research, getting interviews, and pitching books. Motherhood itself as a concern is pushed to the side; most of her advice regarding children has to do with how to get them out of the way or get work done while they're underfoot. She discusses childcare options, for example, and also suggests, "Use televisions, VCRs, and DVDs in moderation, and as part of a regular routine you can use for writing time" (46).

It might seem easy to dismiss Katz's book for treating motherhood too flippantly, as an annoying distraction rather than a central concern vis-à-vis writing, and to criticize her for being overly interested in commercial success; in her world, you create work for a specific market in order to make money, rather than writing something from the heart and then hoping that it's good enough for publication. Her model is more akin to running a home business than discovering yourself. But Katz's focus on the economics of writing is in fact a central concern for many writers—and has been for decades. Economics, after all, lies at the heart of Virginia Woolf's book and is evident even in its title. The "room of one's own" that Woolf describes stands for a world in which women writers have the financial independence that enables them to have the physical space and the uninterrupted time to write. For all of its highbrow ideals and feminist concerns, Woolf's book also gets down to the economic nitty-gritty: a woman needs five hundred pounds a year to write. The economics of writing can no more be dismissed today than in Woolf's day. And for the mother who wants to write and needs to make money at it, Katz's guide may prove valuable.

In discussing her typologies, Cross writes, "While I do believe that many books about creative writing can be linked to these pedagogical types, I'm under no illusions that the types are comprehensive or mutually exclusive, and I recognize that rarely, if ever, would a particular text fit into a single category" (67). This is true of the third book under examination, DeMarco-Barrett's *Pen on Fire*, which, I should point out, is marketed at the "busy woman," not mothers exclusively, though many busy women are mothers, as is the author of the book, and her motherhood certainly informs the text. DeMarco-Barrett's book is a hybrid of the holistic and commercial pedagogy typologies. Like Katz, she covers many practical aspects of the writing life, including literary agents, rejection slips, and publication. She explains how a busy woman can make time for writing in her life. When her son was four, she held a writer's group in her kitchen: "jazz played over the speakers to drown out the sound of my son's videotape in the living room" (20). Presumably, like Katz, she used videos in moderation to make time for writing. Still, through much of the book, DeMarco-Barrett presents motherhood as just one of many obstacles that need to be overcome by the writing woman. Her son appears in several laundry lists of the daily demands on her life; for example, "I have a nine-year-old son, article deadlines, an hour-long weekly radio show interviewing writers" (xii).

And yet, at times, De-Marco-Barrett does focus on her motherhood. It does become her central theme, as in the following passage: "My son is a living art form, endlessly fascinating, even his little sounds when he drinks from a cup, takes a bite of a cracker, as he holds a book and tells the story as he remembers it, or bats the ball into the night sky . . . each moment feeds your art and is art, if you let it be" (22). This writing is more deeply focused on motherhood than anything in Katz's book. For Demarco-Barrett, writing is an introspective act, a way of reflecting on her identity as a woman and mother—in addition to being an economic activity. Not all writing, she realizes, leads to publication or commercial success, but nonetheless, the personal writing that remains private has value in itself.

These three writing guides suggest that mothers who take up the pen do so for myriad reasons, from the simple need for self-expression to the desire to forge a lucrative freelance career. The ways in which these guides straddle both the commercial pedagogy typology as well as the holistic pedagogy typology suggest the tension that many women feel between writing as an act of self-discovery and fulfillment and writing as an economic act to meet the demands of providing for a family. What, at their essence, do these guides share in common? What generalities about the writing mother's life can be gleaned from these books? And how do these guides differ from the writing guides of Gardner and Mailer? Gardner, we recall, advocated for long stretches—up to fifteen hours!—of writing time. Similarly, Mailer writes of putting in "eight or ten hours, of which only three or four will consist of words getting down on the page" (128). My MFA professor once stressed the importance of working on one piece at a time, perfecting a story before moving on to another. Amanda, a student in her early forties, a mother of three, took issue and spoke up. She was working on many pieces, she said. She would write some here, some there. It was like making dinner, she explained. It was like having many pots simmering on the stove at once, and you adjust the heat here, throw in a pinch of salt there. She might have also said: it's like being a mother and a writer at the same time. But she was in the minority. In fact, in retrospect, I think she was likely the only parent taking that class, and probably the only one over thirty. Our professor disagreed with her cooking metaphor. Perfect one thing before moving on, he said. He warned us of the dangers of never finishing anything if we work on too many things at once. He warned us of the hazards of dividing our attention. And that, precisely, is what motherhood requires of us, every day. Work for fifteen hours at a stretch?! The idea is beyond ludicrous to a mother of young children.

One key difference between the writing philosophies represented by the mothers' writing guides and those penned by Mailer and Gardner is how the writers experience—and work—in time. Garrigues, Katz, and DeMarco-Barrett all stress, again and again, that writing mothers are required to work in short bursts. For example, De-Marco-Barrett writes, "The real creativity-killer—the obstacle so severe that I've seen it stop promising writers before they even have a chance to begin—is time. With jobs, children, partners, and running their households to juggle, women in particular are busier than ever, with no space to nurture our creative selves. . . .The truth is, you can get a lot done in just fifteen minutes a day. We all have at least fifteen minutes somewhere—while the pasta boils, while a child bathes, while we're on hold with the phone company or on a coffee break or at lunch" (xii-xiii). In a similar vein, Garrigues describes how mothers get their writing done: "They write before their children wake up in the morning or after they have gone to bed at night. They write when their kids are at school or next door on a playdate. They write before the orthodontist or after the pediatrician. They write when the babysitter arrives or when their husband comes home. They write in notebooks, on napkins, on laptops—in coffee shops, at the public library, in a car or closet. In short, mothers write whenever, wherever, however, they can" (39). The ever-practical Katz has three sections on time, titled "Scrounge for an Hour in the a.m.," "Gather Every Afternoon Moment," and "Wring Every Second from the Evenings." In fact, she even advocates further fragmenting time in order to get more done: "Respond to e-mails—twenty minutes, go! Draft an article—twenty minutes, go! Proofread yesterday's draft— twenty minutes, go! Plan for next week—twenty minutes, go! You can get a lot done in short bursts if you practice working that way" (67). In

Katz's way of thinking, if a writer has an hour and a half, she might be even *more* productive if she gets four pots going on the stove at once.

In addition to working in brief bursts, the guides also recognize the mother's constant need to do more than one thing at a time, or, in popular jargon, to multi-task. All the mother writing guides share this special understanding of the nature of time (as do motherhood memoirs themselves, which are often about the fragmentation of—and chronic lack of—time in a mother's life). DeMarco-Barrett, for example, writes, "Women are used to switching tasks a million times a day, so for us natural multitaskers, writing in the midst of an experience shouldn't be a stretch and can be a fun, uninhibited way to get words down. Writing fast, writing in the midst of things, using whatever blips of time you have gives immediacy to your work and helps to break down barriers to writing" (39). And Katz suggests, "Can you get a few notes written in the waiting room at a doctor appointment, or during children's classes or activities?" (46). And because time is full to capacity and fragmented into fifteen-minute shards, mothers also often have the sense that we are constantly in danger of losing time, of frittering it away, of misplacing entire days in a fog of diaper changes, baths, snacks, tummy time, tantrums, potty time, naptime—and writing helps us to capture, to crystallize those moments as mothers, to step outside of mother time and gaze upon ourselves as mothers, upon these identities that we have taken on and now can hardly spare a moment to wrap our minds around. Who are we as mothers? Our writing tells us. Who are we *besides* mothers? Our writing tells us that too.

Along with the need for multi-tasking and the fragmentation of time, there is an accompanying sense that mothers do not own their time. Garrigues writes, "Time is a finite commodity for every woman (and man), but especially for mothers, who typically feel that our time is no longer our own. Every minute is accounted for, every second stolen by someone or something, a steady outpouring, so that some days we feel as though it is not just time that is slipping away but ourselves, wearing thin and wearing out" (53). Certainly many people work full-time jobs and must fit their writing in around their work schedules, and many aspiring writers consider writing their "real" work while their full-time job simply pays the bills. These paid jobs typically have clearly demarcated (albeit long) hours. Motherhood does not. And motherhood, for most mothers, is just as important—and arguably more important—than writing. You have to devote yourself to it completely, and you don't get to go home at five o'clock. Do I write a story or take care of my child? Presented with such choices, the answer is clear. We writing mothers must make real efforts to carve out writing time. Case in point: I sit in my basement office writing this while my children are upstairs with a babysitter. Later, I will write while my children are sleeping.

Many successful women writers who are mothers have recounted similar experiences. Jane Smiley, in a recent interview,[1] recounts her writing schedule when her children were small: "I've always written every day, for a few hours a day–maybe 1½ to 3. This fits in pretty well with the kids, because you aren't busy all day. It didn't change when my first one was born—I hired a babysitter who came two hours per day (in those days and in Iowa, she charged $10.00 a week)" (Luna). Not only does she work for relatively short periods at a time, but she also recognizes that writing is an act that takes time away from other pursuits. There could be "no procrastinating," she recalls, "since I was paying for the time" (Luna). And while "being a parent offers lots of times to just let your work problems go, and then have an idea come to you—while you're nursing, for example, or walking down the street to the store," Smiley also recognizes that there needs to be a clear demarcation between writing time and family time: "I think it's really important to define your work time and keep it separate. You go into your workspace and close the door, and think about your work, then you finish for the day and walk away from it" (Luna).

As Smiley suggests, writing by its nature is a solitary pursuit. Writing is unlike cooking or cleaning, growing a garden, even reading, because children can be included in those pursuits, but not in writing. Because at its essence writing is a single mind facing a single page. The children can't throw in a word now and then, like adding a dash of vanilla to the muffins. I must be away from my children to write—to really write, rather than just jotting things down or mulling over ideas or stuffing manuscripts into envelopes. And I do try to involve my children in my writing, in every way I can. My eight-year-old is the "author" of several of her own illustrated books; she has gone to my readings, and I tell her about each of my acceptances or successes. My five-year-old carries my manuscripts to the post office and places them on the counter to be weighed. But there is a real limit to their involvement. And so, every moment that I am writing—really writing—I am away from my children, in one way or another. Writing while they're awake means they're with someone else; writing while they're asleep means I don't clean the kitchen or plan tomorrow's menu or even get enough sleep to have energy for the next day. Every moment I take to write is a moment stolen from them. This is probably every writing mother's guilt, at one point or another, though there are other truths: that children need to be away from their mothers, that writing, in the end, makes us better mothers, or at least it should. Writing is exclusion; to write, I turn away from my children, but in writing about motherhood, we can find a new way of turning back toward them. Writing can be inclusion, too.

During my first semester in my Ph.D. program, when I told my dissertation adviser (right before I began showing) that I was pregnant, that indeed I had made the reckless move of starting a Ph.D. program pregnant, that I had in effect (in the eyes of many) condemned myself to failure in one form or another—either I would not complete the program at all, or I would be at best a mediocre student, or at any rate my allegiance would forever after be split between the altar of writing/ academia and motherhood—she, a mother herself, brought up none of these concerns, but merely offered a kernel of practical advice. "Well," she said, "You will learn to be an efficient worker." By which she meant—though I couldn't know it at the time—that during any free moment I had, I would have to plunge right into my work and get it done. No more sipping leisurely cups of coffee, browsing the shelves at Barnes and Noble for ideas, or the meta-analysis of writing about writing in my journal before doing the *actual* writing; no working eight-hour shifts to do four hours of work. It was a matter of jumping in and swimming for my life, even though the water might be freezing. There was no time to dip that toe in to check. The lesson was about time—and I learned it, slowly, wrenchingly, as I despaired, with my newborn wailing, of ever writing again. Still, I eventually got the hang of it. I learned to be efficient.

By the time my second child was born, I could write in fifteen-minute bursts, I could type around his sleeping form draped in a sling across my chest, I could write in bed while he nursed, typing one-handed on a laptop. Those were the conditions under which I wrote my book of stories. This was the nature of being efficient, of being a mother and a writer, the nature of mother time. And all of it was true for me: that I multi-tasked, that I used the material of my motherhood in my fiction and nonfiction, and that I felt guilty over the moments of time I stole back from my children, the moments I paid someone to watch them so I could disengage from them, so I could stop being their mother in the immediate physical sense long enough to become more deeply their mother in an emotional, spiritual sense, so I could be a mother in this other way too, to thoughts and language and ideas. And it is important to be a mother in this way, so that my children can look at me and say: yes, she is our mother, but she is also this other person. So that my daughter can look at me and say: she is, perhaps, something like the person I might become—which she already does. Even at age five, she would tell me, "I am going to be a paleontologist and a mom and a writer, only I'm worried about pumping milk for my babies while I'm digging for dinosaur bones." In her vision of the future, she has already integrated motherhood with work. Already she worries about her children. This, too, is why as a mother I am also a writer.

Paradoxically, even though writing seems to take time away from mothering, many mothers, I believe, write in order to be *better* mothers. Not only do they reflect on myriad mothering experiences in their writing—experiences that are often wholly overlooked in writing done by non-mothers—but they also, in taking that time to be self-reflective, model for their children an engaged and thoughtful mode of living. Being a writing mother goes beyond finding scraps of time to jot a few words down on a piece of paper. By being a mother to language, we learn more about mothering our children—and vice versa. The Senegalese writer Mariama Bâ, a mother of nine, expresses the purpose of motherhood in her novel *So Long a Letter.* "One is a mother in order to understand the inexplicable," she writes; "One is a mother to lighten the darkness. One is a mother to shield when lightning streaks the night, when thunder shakes the earth, when mud bogs one down. One is a mother in order to love without beginning or end" (2494). Yes, she is speaking of a mother's relationship with a flesh-and-blood child, but isn't this how we are mothers of language as well? Don't we tell stories to understand what cannot be explained in any other way? Don't we lighten the darkness with our words? Don't we shield and heal, and don't we love without beginning or end? Isn't the one act of creation akin to the other? Don't they both come out of love and toil, and don't they both leave a trace of ourselves in the world?

Woolf too recognized the importance of motherhood. "For we think back through our mothers if we are women," she wrote (76). And this is true both of literary mothers and the mothers who bear and raise us. My daughter will think back through me. She will look to me to learn how to be a woman, how to be herself. And I learned, in the months after her birth, that I could not be *myself* without my writing, my work, my *other* children. Contrary to the oft-repeated advice—if you have children, you can't be a writer—I would urge women to do both, at the same time. You *can* have it both ways. The world needs mothers and it needs writers, and it needs mothers who are writers, to give voice to this experience that is absolutely central to humankind. We can and should, in Woolf's words, "light a torch in that vast chamber where nobody has yet been" (84). We don't want to be in the position of Woolf's imagined eighty-year-old woman, who, when asked about her life, remembers nothing: "For all the dinners are cooked; the plates and cups washed; the children set to school and gone out into the world. Nothing remains of it all. All has vanished. No biography or history has a word to say about it. And the novels, without meaning to, inevitably lie. All these infinitely obscure lives remain to be recorded" (89). The world needs records of these experiences. And it needs mother writers—whether professors or authors of writing guides or mentors of another sort—who will stand up and say, *Yes, it can be done.* And I wish I had spoken out and said it to my MFA professor nearly a decade ago, but my words would have had no weight without the proof of lived experience behind them. They would have been the overly optimistic, ambitious words of someone who has neither borne children nor written very much. But now I—and others like Garrigues, Katz, DeMarco-Barrett, my dissertation adviser—say it. *Yes, it can be done.* And the truth is not in the words so much as is in our doing it, day after day.

The key to success in being a writer and mother, I think, lies in seeking and giving the kind of support that is most needed. Read Garrigues or Katz instead of John Gardner or Norman Mailer. Work with mentors like my dissertation advisor—who had experienced motherhood herself—rather than my MFA professor—who proclaimed children anathema to the writing life. And find other writing mothers who share the same concerns. Amanda, the woman who spoke up in class and talked of working on many projects at once, is now one of my dear writing friends. We are, as she likes to say, members of the same tribe. Even though her youngest child is now in college while my youngest has yet to start kindergarten, we are both walking down the same path. I have read a draft of her novel, and she has read a draft of mine. We both have a lot of pots going—she's teaching at a community college, writing, sculpting, mothering her grown children, while I'm trying to write and be a mother while recently going back to teaching full time—and we don't even live in the same state anymore, but we stay in touch. We share writing victories and defeats, drafts, and an unspoken knowledge of what this life—the writing and mothering life—entails.

Making such connections is particularly important, I think, because writing is unlike being a lawyer or a teacher or any dozens of salaried jobs. While I can justify having someone else care for my children while I go teach my classes at the university by the simple fact that the university gives me a paycheck every two weeks, I cannot shut my door and spend time away from my children writing literary fiction—or even this essay—with the same justification. Writing feels more selfish because often, there is no clear monetary reward attached to my efforts. Many literary journals don't pay at all, and the ones that do frequently pay so little that I am lucky to earn minimum wage (though I never even bother to calculate my hourly rate). And so putting my writing off until some amorphous "later" when I have "more time"—when the laundry is all done, the papers all graded, the children tucked into bed—is temptingly easy. And so a day, three days, a week, a month can easily slip by as I wait for that ideal "later," the mythical "more time" that never materializes. But as the writing mothers remind us in their guides, the time to write is *now*—during the half hour of sitting in the waiting room through ballet rehearsal, that extra fifteen minutes before bed. And having people like Amanda—people who want to see me succeed as a writer, who see my potential perhaps more clearly than I do, and who understand my unique challenges—helps to keep me writing, day after day.

So: Mother your children, and mother your words. Find your tribe, and tend to your pots. In the end, all those courses will get prepared.

ENDNOTES

[1]The interview appears on the blog of a writer named Cari Luna, who has developed a series of interviews with writers titled "Writer, with Kids." In her description of her project, Luna recounts an experience

during her MFA program when a classmate named Karla was told more than once that her chances of having a writing career while caring for young children were slim: "During a Q&A following a reading by one of our professors, a well-established author and mother of a then-teenage daughter, Karla asked if the professor had any advice for a mother who wanted to write. The professor's response? 'It's absolutely possible to be a mother and a writer, but you can only have one child.' Karla, her second child in her lap, said, 'Oh.' And the advice offered in conference by Karla's thesis adviser, herself a mother of three kids—one grown and two teenagers at the time—was that 'You can't expect to write when the children are very young. It just isn't possible. Put it away for now.'" Now a mother herself, Luna interviews writers to learn specifically about their parenting/writing strategies.

WORKS CITED

Bâ, Mariama. *So Long a Letter.* Trans. Modupé Bodé-Thomas. *The Norton Anthology of World Masterpieces.* Ed. Maynard Mack. 2 vols. New York: Norton, 1995. 2: 2440-2498. Print.

Cross, Michelle. "Writing in Public: Popular Pedagogies of Creative Writing." *Can It Really Be Taught? Resisting Lore in Creative Writing Pedagogy.* Eds. Kelly Ritter and Stephanie Vanderslice. Portsmouth, NH: Boynton/Cook, 2007. 67-76. Print.

DeMarco-Barrett. *Pen on Fire: A Busy Woman's Guide to Igniting the Writer Within.* New York: Harcourt, 2004. Print.

Gardner, John. *On Becoming a Novelist.* 1983. New York: Norton, 1999. Print.

Garrigues, Lisa. *Writing Motherhood.* New York: Scribner, 2008. Print.

Goldberg, Natalie. *Old Friend from Far Away: The Practice of Writing Memoir.* New York: Free Press, 2007. Print.

Katz, Christina. *Writer Mama: How to Raise a Writing Career Alongside Your Kids.* Cincinnati: Writer's Digest, 2007. Print.

Mailer, Norman. *The Spooky Art: Some Thoughts on Writing.* New York: Random House, 2003. Print.

Luna, Cari. "Writer, with Kids." *Cari Luna.* 5 March 2012. Web. 26 April 2013.

Luna, Cari. "Writer, with Kids: Jane Smiley." *Cari Luna.* 28 March 2012. Web. 26 April 2013.

"Ten Rules for Writing Fiction." *Guardian* 20 February 2010. Web. 10 March 2010.

Woolf, Virginia. *A Room of One's Own*. 1929. New York: Harcourt, 1989. Print.

3.
"A Long Private Letter"

Motherhood and Text
in the Works of Elizabeth Gaskell

MELISSA SHIELDS JENKINS

MY MOTHER wanted to be a poet, but gave up writing when she married at nineteen. She was twenty-one when my brother was born, and twenty-three when my twin sister and I joined my brother in the world. As my own nineteenth birthday came and went, with no prospects for marriage or children on the horizon, I dreamed of following the path that I and my siblings closed for my mother.

In my earliest days of teaching and writing for a living, I scoured my bookshelves for stories that differed from my own—stories of successful mothers who were also successful authors. I was a newly minted Ph.D. and a newlywed. As a child, I dreamed of a large family. As an adult, I worried. Almost all of my tenured colleagues were either childless or the parents of exactly one child. The parents of the singletons told me bittersweet stories of ultrasounds in which they prayed for a girl, or a boy, knowing full well that the tenure clock would only slow for them once. When I discovered that my first, perhaps only, daughter was on her way, I turned to these texts with a new urgency.

Two essays in Alice Walker's *In Search of Our Mothers' Gardens* treat the effect that human children can have on imagined ones. Part One of Walker's collection features the essay "A Writer Because of, Not in Spite of, Her Children." The essay opens with a conversation between Walker and another woman writer. Walker admits that the work she created during the first year of her daughter's life "sound[ed] as though a baby were screaming right through the middle of it" (66). Her friend argues that, even with "full-time help," her writing self "spent months in a stupor" (Walker 66). Because of these grim experiences, Walker was amazed to pick up *Second Class Citizen*, by Nigerian novelist Buchi

Emecheta, and notice a dedication to five children "without whose sweet background noises this book would not have been written" (67). Emecheta's novel begins with a girl's memories of a hectic childhood, lived within a vibrant, female-dominated community.

When recounting the growth and development of her own female-centered novel, *The Color Purple*, Walker found, to her surprise, that Emecheta was right. In "Writing The Color Purple" she describes the alternating periods of block and flow that accompanied her first days with the novel—days in which her daughter was living with her father—and the surprising bursts of creativity after her daughter's return (Walker 356, 359). Walker was relieved to find that her characters "adored" her daughter and that their experiences were enriched by her presence (359). One wonders, however, whether a different kind of novel—a novel that did not feature mothers and children losing and finding each other within a female community—could have emerged as easily.

Thoughts of busy, child-filled books born within busy, child-filled households recall Woolf's argument in *A Room of One's Own*. She claims that composition by fits and starts, interrupted by domestic noises and duties, is detrimental to certain kinds of female creativity and beneficial to others. In surveying her list of great Victorian women novelists—Charlotte Brontë, Jane Austen, George Eliot, and Emily Brontë—she notes that "not one of them had a child" (Woolf 114). Woolf was, of course, partly wrong, in that George Eliot was an active honorary "stepmother" for her lover's offspring—and tragically right, in that impending motherhood silenced Charlotte Brontë. Woolf says that motherhood has its genres—the novel and non-fiction prose, rather than the play or the poem—because "[l]ess concentration is required" for the former (115). Is Woolf right? Are there generic limits to the positive effects of motherhood on a writer? Is Walker right? Are certain kinds of books more welcoming of mothering than others?

I found surprising answers in the work of a Victorian woman whose life and writing challenge Woolf's account. Elizabeth Gaskell, a Manchester novelist who published her works as "Mrs. Gaskell," was the author of one acclaimed critical biography (of fellow novelist Charlotte Brontë), a few poems, a fragmented diary, several novels, and hundreds of letters. I begin with her private diary, which was published in a limited edition by Clement Shorter in 1923. The diary is a slim volume that she composed after the birth of her first daughter, Marianne. I then turn to Gaskell's engagement with mothering within other literary forms. This essay investigates the relationship between mothering and different "genres" of writing. The exploration reveals a closer tie between diary and novel than has been previously considered, which makes Gaskell's conclusions of interest to literary scholars who want to connect fiction with practices of life-writing. Her conclusions also speak to the sociological, psychological, and deeply personal questions raised for all mothers who are also writers. How might writing itself perform the work of mothering, while still serving as a cathartic antithesis to mothering? Can mothering men serve as sufficient surrogate parents when the world of work calls mothers away? The stakes are high for Gaskell, and for the women she hopes to touch through her writing. Gaskell's attempts to "de-gender" mothering within her writing speak to a hope for a presence that can compensate for her absence. She writes for her daughters, but she also writes for her life.

MOTHERHOOD AND MODES OF WRITING

Critical accounts of Gaskell focus on the connections between her work and her socio-political context (industrialization and the social problem novel), and on her identity as a wife (the implications of publishing as "Mrs. Gaskell"). Mothering is less often investigated as an aspect of her craft.[1] When texts do acknowledge her status as mother, they focus on the early death of her son Willie, rather than on the influence of her daughters (Payne 112). Gaskell's first child—a daughter—was born dead within a year of her marriage to William Gaskell, a Unitarian minister.[2] Gaskell refused to forget her stillborn daughter. One of her earliest creative writing projects, a sonnet called "On Visiting the Grave of My Still-Born Little Girl," is dedicated to her memory:

I made a vow within my soul, O child!
When thou were laid beside my very heart
With marks of Death on every tender part,
That, if in time a living infant smiled,
Winning my ear with gentle sounds of love,
In sunshine of such joy, I still would save
A green rest for thy memory, O dove!
And oft-times visit thy small, nameless grave.

Thee have I not forgot—my first born!—Thou
Whose eye ne'er opened to my wistful gaze
Whose suff'rings stamped with pain thy little brow
I think of thee in these far happier days—
And thou, my child, from thy bright heaven, see!
How well I keep my faithful vow to thee.[3]

Jenny Uglow notes that the poem is part of "a long tradition of women's poetry which goes back, for example, to Mary Cary's seventeenth-century poem 'Upon the Sight of My Abortive Birth,'" but that it is at the same time "unconventional" in directly addressing the dead child rather than speaking of it abstractly (92). I would add that the poem reads like a contract, an exchange of tokens between one who demands love and remembrance, and another who vows to deliver both. As with her descriptions of her living children in her diary, this description of her stillborn child is vividly, even eerily, embodied. Gaskell reminds her reader that the first months of mothering are largely physical—holding, stroking, and feeding a baby—and that death is most painful as a physical separation, as the wresting away of that small signifying body.

This poem resembles a diary entry in that it is dated to refer to a specific visit to her child's grave—Sunday, July 4, 1836. Yet, there are gestures towards the difficulty of containing the young girl's short life in that document or that day. The "vow" to her dead child contains the promise that she will be replaced by living children, yet that the health of the living children will always trigger thoughts of the first child's death. The vow, therefore, has strong threads of affection, but also hints of the macabre in its insistence on death in life. One manuscript copy of the poem, as preserved in the John Rylands library in Manchester, gains additional ghostly echoes because the hand in which the poem was written has not been identified. The archivists believe that the poem was transcribed by one of Gaskell's daughters. If this is the case, the vow to remember is pressed onto the page by one whose very presence signals the need to remember.[4]

Clement Shorter pushed for the publication of Elizabeth Gaskell's motherhood diary. His limited edition printing of fifty copies, in 1923, was part of the breathless race to publish the first definitive biography of Elizabeth Gaskell. Shorter was losing the race, as his attempt at a biography "fell victim to a fatal delay" in getting a draft to the editors of MacMillan's "English Men of Letters" series (Gaskell, *My Diary* 3). His panic was due in part to the mendacity he perceived in his literary opponent, Mrs. Ellis H. Chadwick. He noted that Chadwick had "written without new documents an interesting biography which has gone through at least two editions," despite the fact that his copy was "interleaved with the hundred-and-one correcting notes of Mrs. Gaskell's daughter Meta" (Gaskell, *My Diary* 3). Thus, his presentation of the diary was an announcement of his privileged access to Gaskell herself, and his right, as it were, to her life story. He argues that access to bodies of text does not trump access to the bodies themselves, re- minding readers of his preface that he visited Gaskell's daughters "at their mother's old home" (Gaskell, *My Diary* 4), and that he sought and obtained the permission of Gaskell's grandson in order to publish the diary. Gaskell's diary, then, authorizes Clement Shorter as the proper conveyer of the details of Gaskell's life. What value, however, did he see in the diary for readers?

In addition to exploring the relative use value of other texts about mothering, the diary tests a mother's ability or inability to write. She begins most entries with phrases relating to her failures within this par- ticular writing task, such as "I do not intend to be so long again without writing about my little girl" (Gaskell, *My Diary* 12). Gaskell opens the diary by dedicating its contents to her then six-month-old daughter. She declares, "if I should not live to give it to her myself, [it] will I trust be reserved for her as a token of her mother's love, and extreme anxiety in the formation of her little daughter's character" (Gaskell, *My Diary* 5). In dedicating the text in this manner, Gaskell may be thinking of her own mother, who died when Gaskell was thirteen months old (*Private* 11). She is thinking ahead to the day that her daughter may become a mother—a day that Gaskell fears she will not be alive to see—in hopes that the document she has created may compensate for this likely ab- sence. She also thinks ahead to the day when Marianne's questions will strain the limits of her mother's memory. Will she be able to respond when her daughter asks to "become acquainted with her character in its earliest form" (Gaskell, *My Diary* 5)?

The diary offers a space for Gaskell to digest contradictory advice about mothering, to conduct an empirical study of her own child, to challenge mortality, and to enhance memory. The form of the diary absorbs the weight—and shock—of all of these different uses. The "formation" of her daughter's "character" corresponds intimately with the construction of the material book. Gaskell records the development of her daughter's body and mind onto the pages of the book, relating the increased girth and complexity of the text to the corresponding growth of the daughter, and its movements to her movements. She writes early in the diary, "I have written a great deal tonight, and very unconnectedly. I had no idea the journal of my own disposition, & feelings was so intimately connected with that of my little baby, whose regular breathing has been the music of my thoughts all the time I have been writing" (Gaskell, *My Diary* 8-9).

The regularity of Marianne's breath—and the synergistic relationship between the peacefully writing mother and the peacefully sleeping child—is disrupted on almost every other page. After sporadic entries that contained gaps of months, Gaskell abandoned the diary before Marianne's fourth birthday. Some sections of the text have been removed, by either Gaskell or her heirs. Often, the omitted passages are prefaced by tantalizing hints. "Oh! I do hope and intend…" precedes one omission, and "Perhaps this is foolish, but I will put everything down related to her" precedes another (Gaskell, *My Diary* 10-11). The diary records the limits of record-keeping, and is full of memories about unreliable memories. Gaskell fills her earliest entries with regret about time lost. She writes on March 10, 1835, "The day after to-morrow Marianne will be six months old. I wish I had begun my little journal sooner, for (though I should have laughed at the idea twelve months ago) there have been many little indications of disposition &c. already, which I can not now remember clearly" (Gaskell, *My Diary* 5-6). Five months lapse between Gaskell's first entry and her second; she explains that "it is so difficult to know when to begin or when to stop when talking, thinking, or writing about [Marianne]" (Gaskell, *My Diary* 9-10).

The turns toward, and then away, from the diary involve an emotional need for free expression in a protected space, and for a select audience. But they also involve a perceived duty to the next generation. Both Gaskell and Shorter saw, in the diary, a contribution to the sociological and scientific understanding of childhood. The diary was meant to replace the flawed biography, and to satisfy the desire for access to Gaskell the woman as well as the novelist—a desire evidenced in the brisk sales of Chadwick's biography. Shorter also categorized it as a "very real addition to the literature treating the psychology of childhood" (Gaskell, *My Diary* 4). Therefore, the diary makes many "genre" shifts in a reader's hands. In all of these shifts, however, the diary falls short of readers' expectations. Those looking for a replacement biography would be frustrated by the piecemeal and partial nature of the diary. It offers insights into Gaskell's psyche as a mother, but offers few glimpses of her life beyond that role. As a "how-to" book, it also lacks coherence. Gaskell's references to contemporary childrearing texts include responses to Albertine Necker de Saussure's *L'Education Progressive* (1828-1832), and Andrew Combe's *Principles of Physiology* (1834). Her life with Marianne is a test of these accounts. Yet, in surveying the various texts, she demurs in her judgment of them, noting only that "Books do so differ" (Gaskell, *My Diary* 8). Combe's *Principles of Physiology,* for example, outlines how to "accusto[m] the mind to sound exertion, and not to fits of attention" (368). Gaskell calls "impatience" one of her daughter's "greatest faults" (*My Diary* 11-12). Gaskell's reluctance to retrain her into patience is, she thinks, in violation of "what every book says" (*My Diary* 11-12).

Those looking for the complete story of mother and daughters within the diary's pages will also be disappointed. When Gaskell abandoned the diary, she left many of its gaps unfilled. She continued to write, however. I argue that we find many of the missing words and phrases in her fiction.

FROM DIARY TO NOVEL

What is the relationship between writing in a diary and writing a novel, especially for the writing mother? How does confessional writing as a parent inflect fictional writing about parenthood? Critics have noticed the formal connections between diaries and novels. Judy Simons writes, in her study of diaries by women, "the sequential organisation of the diary, with its emphasis on the passage of time and the process of ageing confronts the writer with a simultaneous demonstration of her own continuity and her discontinuity" (12). Writing in a diary, even a diary not initially intended for outside eyes, is an exercise in the construction and delineation of character. In constructing herself in this artificial space, the woman diarist reveals the artificial nature of seamless characterizations and uninterrupted narrative, even as she tries to achieve the cohesiveness one would expect, supposedly, from a life well-lived. The diary straddles the line between the fragmented modernist representation of self in fiction, and the idealized march toward self-actualization found in the traditional bildungsroman. The shape of a fictional life is often more satisfying than the shape of a real one. Elizabeth Gaskell knew this, and wrote the conundrum into one of the most touching passages in her novel *Cranford*. In *Cranford*, a novel based explicitly on previously published true accounts, Matty describes a sad exercise that her father used to teach the divide between fact and fiction. Matty was told to "keep a diary in two columns" and on one side "put down in the morning what we thought would be the course of events of the coming day, and at night … put down on the other side what really had happened" (Gaskell, *Cranford* 107). The thought of separating one life into "ideal" and "real," and then documenting said separation on paper, moves the narrator to tears. Matty remarks, sympathetically, "it would be to some people rather a sad way of telling their lives" (Gaskell, *Cranford* 107). The pathos comes from the urge to turn messy lives into easily digestible textual experiences—to create, from fragments, an equation that adds up to something. The difference between the internal aspiration and the external final summary throws shortcomings into strong relief.

A diary is presumed to be a private text with an intensely limited circulation, if it circulates at all. Yet, diary writing rarely fails to make gestures toward the public world (Blake 51). Judy Simons cites Margo Culley in arguing that "the awareness of who might read the personal journal determines both its subject matter and its approach and consequently calls into question the whole status of the diary as a private literary construct" (2). The woman diarist is shaped by "seclusion and [her] response to it," but writing constitutes a desire to reach out, if only to have a past self speak to a future self. The diarist is in the unique position of shaping her experience as she lives it—perhaps telling herself "tales" or engaging in wish-fulfillment (Simons 8). A diary such as Gaskell's, which is addressed to an adult child while said child is still in her infancy, becomes like the first chapters of a literary bildungsroman. In writing her daughter's life as it is lived, she is not only trying to record her "character," but is indeed working to shape it.

As Marianne becomes "every day more and more interesting," so do Gaskell's observations about her daughter's growing ability to distinguish between the real and the imaginary (Gaskell, *My Diary* 6). An early description notes, with both pride and nostalgia, that Marianne "has a pretty good idea of distance and does not try to catch sunbeams now, as she did two months ago" (Gaskell, *My Diary* 6). In hoping that her daughter can distinguish between fact and imagination—between the solid and the ephemeral—she thinks about her imperatives to do so within the diary, if it is to be a true record of her child's development. Yet, empirical observation of an infant has its limits. When looking at her young child, she writes, "I wish we could know what is passing in her little mind" (Gaskell, *My Diary* 7).

Throughout this document, and others, Gaskell negotiates the tensions between writing as a way to alleviate a woman's anxiety, and writing as a barrier to fulfilling womanly duties. In *The Life of Charlotte Brontë*, Gaskell feels that she must divide her subject in two—the woman and the writer—in order to fully understand her (Stoneman 35). The most tragically moving passages in the biography record Charlotte Brontë's decline and death during her pregnancy, or, as Gaskell puts it in *The Life of Charlotte Brontë*, the "dreadful sickness" that silenced her prodigious talent (425). When a young writer, who is also a young mother, writes Gaskell for advice, she replies, "When I had little children I do not think I could have written stories, because I should have become too absorbed in my fictitious people to attend to my real ones" (*Letters* 694-695). She suggests, however, that motherhood has a positive, though delayed, effect on a woman's mature writing life: "When you are forty, and if you have a gift for being an authoress you will write ten times as good a novel as you could do now, just because you will have gone through so much more of the interests of a wife and mother" (*Letters* 695). A reader is reminded that Gaskell wrote her first novel to cope with the death of her young son, not to explore or celebrate his presence. Should we therefore separate the diary from her novels, thinking of the diary as the full expression of the young mother, and the novels as the full expression of the experienced one? Does a new mother do her children a disservice, or her writing a disservice, when she tries to tend to both at once? A full vision of Gaskell's evolving stance requires the introduction of husbands. In Gaskell's short story "Christmas Storms and Sunshine" (1848), the domestic tensions between two female neighbors, one with children and one without, is paralleled by the tensions between their husbands, who write for rival newspapers. But what happens when these two forms of rivalry are allowed to intersect, rather than to run parallel? What happens when the woman holds the pen and the man holds the child?

THE MOTHERING MAN?

As Marianne nears her fourth birthday, and Gaskell nears the end of her diary account, she frets over sending Marianne to spend half-days at a newly-formed infant school. She justifies her final decision via the language of shaping. She and her husband hoped "not to advance her in any branch of learning ... but to perfect her habits of obedience, to give her an idea of conquering difficulties by perseverance, and to make her apply steadily for a short time" (Gaskell, *My Diary* 34). These stated aims differ from those espoused by the proponents of infant schools. Three years before Gaskell commemorated the death of her first daughter, and two years before she started her diary, a popular *History of the Middle and Working Classes* had the following to say about the development of infant schools:

> The objects sought by these establishments are threefold: first, to preserve young children from the vice and mischief to which they are liable, from the neglect or inability of their parents: secondly, to instruct them in the rudiments of virtue and knowledge; by which they may be prepared for a more advanced state of education and improvement; and, thirdly, to accomplish both these ends by a more cheerful and natural mode of tuition than heretofore practiced in dame schools. (Wade 102-3)

Wade characterizes the schools as compensation for inept parenting and the insufficiency of nursery schools run by women. Gaskell's self-justification, in contrast, focuses on the improvement they anticipate as Marianne tackles the new challenges that come with separation from her parents. Sending Marianne away to school would be a sign of her and William's wise parenting, rather than of inept parenting. However, the anxiety that precedes the decision offers a different vision. The development of infant schools, and questions of their relative help or harm to young children, reveals a growing cultural anxiety about innate versus learned parenting abilities, and the nation's obligation to compensate for the shortcomings of individual parents.

Elizabeth Gaskell's husband, Rev. William Gaskell, shared her interest in the science surrounding human development, especially as relates to the development of literacy. In his *Two Lectures on the Lancashire Dialect* (1854), he writes at length about slang used by children, seeing it as indicative of larger forces of cultural evolution. He insists that "there are few things more permanent in this world than youthful games, many of which can be traced back several thousand years" (9). He finds comfort in the status of a child as repository of, and shaper of, culture. However, one wonders whether his desire to empower children was more theoretical than practical. Despite his insistence on linguistic flexibility in the abstract—his argument that slang words "are not vulgarisms," supported with reference to Shakespeare, Chaucer, and Milton—he is impatient when his young daughter diverges from the highest linguistic standards (Gaskell, Rev. W. 14). Gaskell records, with some anxiety, their joint decision that William would slap Marianne on the hand each time she refused to pronounce the vowel "A" correctly. She writes in retrospect, "I am sure we were so unhappy that we cried, when she was gone to bed. And I don't know if I was right. If not, pray, dear Marianne, forgive us" (Gaskell, *My Diary* 31–32). Jenny Uglow argues that the episode "sounds like more of a punishment to the parents than to the child," especially since Marianne's reading lessons ceased "until she decided to get out the reading-book herself" (97). Yet, the episode, as narrated in the diary, draws a distinction between the parents—between Gaskell's feelings about the act of discipline and her husband's. Gaskell writes that "we" shed tears, that "I" might have been wrong, and that Marianne should forgive "us." Her turn to the first person singular refuses to judge her husband, but the turns to "we" offer Marianne, and the reader, the option of providing the explicit judgment that she omits.

A letter from Elizabeth Gaskell to her sister-in-law Anne (or "Nancy") Robson, dated 23 Dec. 1841, introduces us to her husband's role in her life as a mother and writer. It also previews Gaskell's stance about the relationship between personal and professional writing, and writing in a community of women versus writing for both women and men:

> My dearest Nancy,
> I am sitting all alone, and not feeling over & above well; and
> it would be such a comfort to have you here to open my mind
> to—but that not being among the possibilities, I am going to

write you a long private letter; unburdening my mind a bit. And yet it is nothing, so don't prepare yourself for any wonderful mystery. In the first place I got y[ou]r letter today and thank you very much for it—I will send for the eggs on Sat[urda]y. I am so glad to say MA is better; …We have Mr Partington of course & he was very encouraging this morning and she certainly is better—but one can't help having 'Mother's fears'; and W[illia]m I dare say kindly won't allow me ever to talk to him about anxieties, while it would be SUCH A RELIEF often. So don't allude too much to what I've been saying in your answer. William is at a minister's meeting tonight,—and tomorrow dines with a world of professors and college people at Mark Philips—and the next day Xmas day it has been a sort of long promise that we all should spend at the Bradford's—by all, I mean W[illia]m, myself, two children & Eliz[abe]th and all stop all night—Yesterday this plan seemed quite given up—today Mr Partington seemed to think the little change might do MA good,—so it's on again—if all goes on well…

Now Anne, will you remember this? It is difficult to have the right trust in God almost, when thinking about one's children—and you know I have no sister or near relation whom I could entreat to watch over any peculiarity in their disposition. Now you know that dear William feeling most kindly towards his children, is yet most reserved in expressions of either affection or sympathy—& in case of my death, we all know the probability of widowers marrying again,—would you promise, dearest Anne to remember MA's peculiarity of character, and as much as circumstances would permit, watch over her and cherish her. (*Letters* 45-46)

Here, Gaskell links anxieties about motherhood to questions of audience. In these short excerpts from her long letter to William's sister, Gaskell thinks about the fate of her children upon her death, reflects candidly about the limitations of paternal feeling,[5] and reminds us of modern discourse about feelings of isolation and depression among young mothers. The letter raises the stakes for what the writing must accomplish—the creation of a virtual community that compensates for the lack of a real-time community. She also responds, with some anxiety, to the lack of control she has over the dissemination of her ideas and feelings once they are in written form. At another point in the letter she entreats, "let me open my heart sometimes to you dear Anne, with reliance on your sympathy and secrecy" (Gaskell, *Letters* 46).

More so than in her diary and letters, Gaskell's novels and short stories become thought experiments, opportunities to pursue the imaginative paths that she is wary to tread in life.[6] In the fiction, she thinks about what happens when the mother is absent through death or replaced through remarriage (*Mary Barton, Wives and Daughters, North and South,* and countless short stories). In the novels, as well as in the diary, she underscores texts about motherhood as spaces in which women speak to women, both laterally (to share stories), vertically (to impart or receive advice), and across time (speaking to daughters and to future generations of mothers). She sees her role as mother as related to her role as artist, as when she says of Meta, her second living daughter, "there are very fine materials to work upon I am convinced, if I but know how" (Gaskell, *My Diary* 33). She becomes even more explicit about the connection between her novels and her memoir when she says on one occasion of not being able to write in the diary, "I have no time to write about our dear little Meta tonight. I must devote my next 'chapter' to her" (Gaskell, *My Diary* 36).

The final entry of her diary, then, is only the beginning of her juxtaposition of motherhood and writing, especially as pertains to the ability for writing to insert men into the maternal sphere. Her fictional men often do what William Gaskell did not. The story "The Sexton's Hero," written to benefit the Macclesfield Public Baths and Workhouses, has as its agenda the cultivation of "maternal" feeling among working class men. The story's frame resembles Coleridge's "Rime of the Ancient Mariner" in that youth (two boys in this case) receive a sobering education by listening to a story delivered by a traumatized, aged man. The Sexton of the title is a man who never marries or has children; he is instead destined to save a child belonging to his lost love and his romantic rival. From the beginning of the story, his "maternity" is emphasized. Though he was mocked by adults for his refusal to fight, "the little children took to him … they'd be round him like a swarm of bees—them as was too young to know what a coward was, and only felt that he was ever ready to love and to help them, and was never loud or cross, however naughty they might be" (Gaskell 8). The baby he saves, at the cost of his own life, dies while teething, and his former love dies two years after the rescue of her child. So, the only tangible legacy remaining from this feminized man is a story. One gets the sense that the greatest productions of Gaskell's "maternal men"—who are surrogate fathers rather than biological ones—are the texts that will carry their influence beyond their limited, otherwise impotent, selves.

In other texts, she explicitly revisits some of the diary's conclusions about motherhood. For example, early in the diary she writes about keeping Marianne healthy, "I am going to clothe her in flannel waistcoats and long sleeves to her frocks this winter, and to keep her in well-aired rooms in preference to going much out of doors, unless the weather is very tempting" (Gaskell, *My Diary* 13). The idea comes from Combe's *Physiology,* among other places: "In infancy, and especially among the poor, want of proper clothing and the consequent exposure to cold are frequent causes of death, and still more frequent causes of sickness" (82-83). Combe provides the crucial caveat that overzealous mothers can overcorrect in the other direction, and "not only envelope infants in innumerable folds of warm clothing, but keep them confined to very hot and close rooms" (84). In *Cranford*, Gaskell re-genders the conversation, moving from the speech of a male expert to a space in which women speak with each other. One woman finds a document written by her grandfather, on behalf of her grandmother who was too ill to write, which provides "a severe and forcible picture of the responsibilities of mothers, and a warning against the evils that were in the world" (*Cranford* 55). Scribbled on the back of the document, though, in the grandmother's handwriting, is the advice to "wrap her baby's feet up in flannel, and keep it warm by the fire, although it was summer, for babies were so tender" (*Cranford* 55). Here, one woman looks for an exclusively feminine textual space, but finds it mediated by a male voice.

It would seem that the physical aspects of mothering—nursing a baby, for instance—could not be "mediated" by men. Yet, in Gaskell's novels, men find ways to compensate for the mother's physical absence, performing the same role that Gaskell's diary performed for her in life. In her first novel, *Mary Barton* (1848), Gaskell lingers on the image of John Barton caring for an infant and her desperately ill parents:

> So Barton was now left alone with a little child, crying (when it had done eating) for mammy; with a fainting, dead-like

woman, and with the sick man, whose mutterings were rising up to screams and shrieks of agonised anxiety. He carried the woman to the fire, and chafed her hands. He looked around for something to raise her head. There was literally nothing but some loose bricks. However, those he got; and taking off his coat he covered them with it as well as he could. He pulled her feet to the fire, which now began to emit some faint heat. He looked round for water, but the poor woman had been too weak to drag herself out to the distant pump, and water there was none. He snatched the child, and ran up the area-steps to the room above, and borrowed their only saucepan with some water in it. Then he began, with the useful skill of a working man, to make some gruel; and when it was hastily made, he seized a battered iron table-spoon (kept when many other little things had been sold in a lot), in order to feed baby, and with it he forced one or two drops between her clenched teeth. (61-62)

This haunting image of death-in-life tests the connections between the working man's labor and the mother's labor. Gaskell focuses on the strange relationships between the objects used by a father to construct the exterior of a home (bricks, iron, fire, mortar, water) and the tools used by a mother to maintain the interior of a home. The mixing of mortar is John Barton's training to mix gruel. Arranging bricks must replace fluffing pillows. "[B]attered iron" takes the place of the mother's breast (Gaskell, *Mary* 62). While in her diary Gaskell reveals the tensions between the work of writing and the work of mothering, here she uses her fictional representations of parenting to ask whether a man's work can relate, at all, to a woman's. This man finds a way to "make do" that may not be available to the solitary woman. Later in the same novel, in an odd and understudied scene of cross-dressing, a working man disguises himself in a woman's cap to soothe his orphaned granddaughter, shortly after they recruited a chambermaid to feed the baby:

I says: "See, Jennings, how women folk do quieten babbies; it's just as I said." He looked grave; he were always thoughtful-looking, though I never heard him say anything very deep.

At last says he: "Young woman! have you gotten a spare nightcap?"

"'Missis always keeps nightcaps for gentlemen as does not like to unpack," says she, rather quick.

"'Ay, but young woman, it's one of your nightcaps I want. Th' babby seems to have taken a mind to yo; and maybe in th' dark it might take me for yo if I'd getten your nightcap on." The chambermaid smirked and went for a cap, but I laughed outright at th' oud bearded chap thinking he'd make hissel like a woman just by putting on a woman's cap. Howe'er he'd not be laughed out on't, so I held th' babby till he were in bed. Such a night as we had on it! Babby began to scream o' th' oud fashion, and we took it turn and turn about to sit up and rock it. My heart were very sore for the little one, as it groped about wi' its mouth; but for a' that I could scarce keep fra' smiling at th' thought o' us two oud chaps, th' one wi' a woman's nightcap on, sitting on our hinder ends for half th' night, hush-abying a babby as wouldn't be hushabied. (Gaskell, *Mary* 106)

Old Job's story recounts his successful attempt to soothe a young child who had lost her mother. He tells the story in order to soothe an older child, Mary Barton. The girl is indeed asleep at the end of the story—proof that old Job did pick up some mothering skills, twice over, by turning mothering into a story about mothering.

Elsewhere, Gaskell is less optimistic. *Cranford* contains an extended investigation of the maternal man, again through a scene of cross-dressing. The wayward son, "Poor Peter," is a practical joker whose father tries to remedy this "in a manly way" (93) by educating him at home, but to little avail. The father flogs him after the following episode, here recounted by his sister Matty:

Well! he went to her [his spinster sister's] room, and dressed himself in her old gown, and shawl, and bonnet; just the things she used to wear in Cranford, and was known by everyone; and he made the pillow into a little—you are sure you locked the door, my dear, for I should not like anyone to hear—into—into a little baby, with white long clothes. It was only, as he told me afterwards, to make something to talk about in the town; he never thought of it as affecting Deborah. And he went and walked up and down the Filbert walk—just half-hidden by the rails, and half-seen; and he cuddled his pillow, just like a baby, and talked to it all the nonsense people do. (Gaskell, *Cranford* 95)

The father's extreme reaction leads Peter to leave the country for years. The father says, "Tell your mother I have flogged Peter, and that he richly deserved it" (Gaskell, *Cranford* 97). Gaskell's novel expresses ambivalence about the father's harsh reaction, in a way that recalls Gaskell's ambivalence about William Gaskell's strictness with Marianne. The beating indeed left "Poor Peter" "haughty as any man—indeed, looking like a man, not like a boy" (Gaskell, *Cranford* 96). Immediately after the beating, Peter puts a continent's distance between himself and his now grieving mother.

Gaskell's diary contains the seeds of John Barton, Old Job and Poor Peter. She says of Marianne at six months, for example, "She begins to show a decided preference to those she likes; she puts out her little arms to come to me, and would, I am sure, do so to her Papa" (*My Diary* 6). The words "I am sure" casts doubt rather than certainty, essentially saying of her husband, as she said of Marianne, that she wished she could "know what was passing" in his mind (*My Diary* 7). Perhaps William Gaskell hadn't yet spent enough time with Marianne to test Gaskell's assumption about Marianne's love for him, or perhaps Marianne hadn't "developed" enough to expand her affection beyond her mother. In either case, Gaskell is uncertain about her husband's role in her daughter's life, and her possible broaching of propriety in writing about it.

CONCLUSION

As her daughters aged, Elizabeth Gaskell tried to refine her sense of their personalities and interests. Meta was the most puzzling of the two children, which occasionally frustrated Gaskell, but often invigorated her. Gaskell wrote to Anne Robson on Sept. 1, 1851, praising Meta's ability to "appreciate any book" read to her by her mother. Gaskell continued, "Meta is untidy, dreamy, and absent; but so brim-ful of I don't know what to call it, for it is something deeper, & less showy than talent" (Gaskell, *Letters* 161). In this incompleteness—"I don't know what to call it" —her assessment of her daughter mirrors the form of her diary. Gaskell often includes statements such as, "I sometimes think I may find this little journal a great help in recalling the memory of my darling child if we should lose her" (*My Diary* 20). Gaskell doesn't often address her daughter directly in the diary, but when she does, it is a promise, as with the sonnet to her first stillborn daughter, to remember. One moment of direct address comes in her entry for "Monday evening, December 28th, 1835," in which she writes, "My darling little girl! How long it is since I wrote about you! But I have been ill, and perhaps lazy, which I certainly ought not to be in anything concerning you" (*My Diary* 17). Elsewhere, Gaskell speaks of the document as an aid to her daughter's memory rather than her own. We see this in her first entry after a year. Between the entry of Nov. 5 1836 and Dec. 9 1837, another daughter was born and a beloved aunt died. In trying to fill in the gaps of her fragmented record, to make the document catch up with life, Gaskell writes, "I have given this little account of the changes in our domestic relations that, if this book be given to Marianne (as I hope it will be) after my death, she may understand more fully anything I may have occasion to allude to" (*My Diary* 28-29). Here, Gaskell offers novelistic exposition of the kind not necessary for an exclusively private diary, but crucial to the story of a private life for public audiences.

Writing and literacy are often tied to the home, because the first lessons in both normally occur there (Blake 51). In Gaskell's work as a diarist, she showed all of the cracks and seams that are inevitable when trying to depict the chaos of motherhood. In her letters, she expressed suspicion and despair when thinking of her children's lives without her, due to the limitations in what she could expect from her "dear William" and from the wife who would replace her if she died. Her work as a novelist was a cathartic antidote to the maternal anxieties expressed in the other two spaces. She investigated alternatives to the model of the full-time mother—alternatives that depend on the bravely maternal man. Delegating the role of mother, to make room for the writer, is one of the most terrifying acts that Gaskell had to perform. There is an undeniable pleasure in thinking of the ways in which a mother is irreplaceable, ways in which no man, however well-meaning, can compensate for the emotional void left by her passing. Yet, in her novels, full of motherless children and creative male substitutes for mothers, Gaskell wrote her way into a freeing space. Elizabeth Gaskell's writing life offers a powerful vision of women writing as women, within a community of women. Her novels seem to revise her advice to young mothers who are also aspiring authors. On the one hand, writing stories while surrounded by "little children" may seem to be an impossible task. Perhaps all that will result is a halting diary full of omissions, gaps, and apologies. But the richness of the writing life that results should not be discounted. The "interests of a wife and mother" and the "gift for being an authoress" may have more to do with each other than we have previously considered. Or, at least, one can hope.

ENDNOTES

[1]There have been several good discussions of motherhood as a theme in Gaskell's novels and short stories, including two works by Barbara Thaden: "Elizabeth Gaskell and the Dead Mother Plot," and *The Maternal Voice in Victorian Fiction*. The relationship between maternity and the creation of narrative receives lighter treatment, and usually in individual novels rather than across Gaskell's oeuvre. For example, Anita Wilson's "Elizabeth Gaskell's Subversive Icon: Motherhood and Childhood in *Ruth*" investigates the relationship between art and life in that novel, and Margaret Croskery's "Mothers without Children, Unity without Plot" equates the absence of mothers in *Cranford* with a brand of narrative and personal freedom. One free-standing close analysis of Gaskell's diary, Anita Wilson's "Mother and Writer," closely analyzes the diary without connecting its method of composition to other texts by Gaskell.

[2]The death was followed by the birth of Marianne in September of 1834, and she would be joined by Willie and by three more sisters, Margaret Emily (Meta), Florence Elizabeth, and Julia. Julia and Meta never married, and became the caretakers of their mother's memory and literary legacy (Brill 105).

[3]Many versions of this poem are widely available, including a reprinting on page 91 of Jenny Uglow's biography, and a manuscript copy in the Jamison Collection in the John Rylands Library, University of Manchester. Almost all printings have slight variations.

[4]The poem resembles some of the diary's effusions about the imagined death of Marianne, as when Gaskell offers a short verse on Aug. 4, 1835, during a bad illness from which Marianne would recover:

> I did so try to be resigned, but I cannot tell how I sickened at
> my heart, at the thought of seeing her no more here
> Her empty crib to see

Her silent nursery,

Once gladsome with her mirth. (Gaskell, *My Diary* 11)

[5]In her reading of this letter, Patsy Stoneman refers to William Gaskell's "almost pathological avoidance of anxiety about his children's health" (29). Stoneman adds, in an aside that I pursue in this article, that the loneliness evoked here "was undoubtedly a personal source for Elizabeth Gaskell's insistent efforts to promote, through her writing, the closer involvement of men with the care of their children" (30).

[6]Here, I'm thinking about Andrew Miller's argument about counterfactuals, as laid out in his essay "Lives Unled in Realist Fiction." He sees the death of a child as one of the events that invites optative ("what if") imaginings.

WORKS CITED

Blake, Andrew. *Reading Victorian Fiction: The Cultural Context and Ideological Content of the Nineteenth-Century Novel.* Houndmills, England: Macmillan, 1989. Print.

Brill, Barbara. *William Gaskell: 1805-84.* Manchester: Manchester Literary and Philosophical Publications, 1984. Print.

Coleridge, Samuel Taylor. "Rime of the Ancient Mariner." *Selected Poetry.* Ed. H. J. Jackson. Oxford: Oxford University Press, 1997. 48-67. Print.

Combe, Andrew. *The Principles of Physiology Applied to the Preservation of Health and to the Improvement of Physical and Moral Education.* 11th ed. Edinburgh: McLachlan, Steward & Co. 1842. Print.

Croskery, Margaret. "Mothers without Children, Unity without Plot: Cranford's Radical Charm." *Nineteenth-Century Literature* 52.2 (Sept 1997): 198-220. Print.

Gaskell, Elizabeth. *Cranford/Cousin Phillis.* Ed. Peter Keating. New York: Penguin, 1976. Print.

Gaskell, Elizabeth. *The Letters of Mrs. Gaskell.* Eds. J. A. V. Chapple and Arthur Pollard. Cambridge: Harvard University Press, 1967. Print.

Gaskell, Elizabeth. *The Life of Charlotte Brontë.* Ed. Elisabeth Jay. New York: Penguin, 1997. Print.

Gaskell, Elizabeth. *Mary Barton.* Ed. Macdonald Daly. New York: Penguin, 1996. Print.

Gaskell, Elizabeth. *My Diary: The Early Years of My Daughter Marianne.* London: Privately printed by Clement Shorter, 1923. Print.

Gaskell, Elizabeth. *The Sexton's Hero; and, Christmas Storms and Sunshine.* London: Chapman and Hall, 1835. Print.

Gaskell, Rev. William. *Two Lectures on the Lancashire Dialect.* London: Chapman and Hall, 1854. Print.

Miller, Andrew. "Lives Unled in Realist Fiction." *Representations* 98.1 (Spring 2007): 118-134. Print.

Necker de Saussure, Albertine-Adrienne. *Progressive Education, Commencing with the Infant.* Trans. Mrs. Willard and Mrs. Phelps. Boston: W. D. Ticknor, 1835. Print.

Payne, Rev. George A. *Mrs. Gaskell and Knutsford.* Manchester: Clarkson & Griffiths, 1900. Print.

Private Voices: The Diaries of Elizabeth Gaskell and Sophia Holland. Eds. J. A. V. Chapple and Anita Wilson. Keele: Keele University Press, 1996. Print.

Simons, Judy. *Diaries and Journals of Literary Women from Fanny Burney to Virginia Woolf.* Houndmills, England: Macmillan, 1990. Print.

Stoneman, Patsy. *Elizabeth Gaskell.* Bloomington: Indiana University Press, 1987. Print.

Thaden, Barbara. "Elizabeth Gaskell and the Dead Mother Plot." *New Essays on the Maternal Voice in the Nineteenth Century.* Dallas: Contemporary Research, 1995. 31-50. Print.

Thaden, Barbara. *The Maternal Voice in Victorian Fiction.* New York: Garland, 1997.

Uglow, Jenny. *Elizabeth Gaskell: A Habit of Stories.* London: Faber and Faber, 1993. Print.

Wade, J. *History of the Middle and Working Classes; With a Popular Exposition of the Economical and Political Principles which Have Influenced the Past and Present Condition of the Industrious Orders.* London: Effingham Wilson, 1833. Print.

Walker, Alice. *In Search of Our Mothers' Gardens: Womanist Prose.* New York: Harcourt, 1983. Print.

Wilson, Anita. "Elizabeth Gaskell's Subversive Icon: Motherhood and Childhood in Ruth." *Gaskell Society Journal* 16 (2002): 85-111. Print.

Wilson, Anita. "Mother and Writer: A Study of Elizabeth Gaskell's Diary." *Gaskell Society Journal* 7 (1993): 67-79. Print.

Woolf, Virginia. *A Room of One's Own.* New York: Harcourt, Brace and Company, 1929. Print.

4.
Ekphrastic Mama

LORI LYN GREENSTONE

SPINNING A DREAM, WRITING A BOOK

YOU ARE A MOTHER of two young children. You must write a book in a day, the shortest day of the year, winter solstice. Can it be done? Or will you look for a Rumpelstiltskin-like muse to write it for you, in trade for your firstborn?

Midwinter Day, Bernadette Mayer's epic poem, may be the epitome of alternative motherhood memoir. Written in a single day (December 22, 1978) amidst mothering her two young daughters, it has been described as "the single strongest attempt to fold the experimental techniques of writing—free association, catalog, ekphrasis—back into the life from which it arises" ("Bernadette Mayer"). Using notional ekphrasis, in which art exists in an inchoate state of creation, Mayer records her first thoughts as she emerges from her early morning dreams....

> *I'm trying to find*
> *What I guess I'd rather not know consciously*
> *I'd like to know*
> *What kind of a person I must be to be a poet....* (Mayer 26)

On Halloween, after masked children stop ringing the doorbell, I fall asleep reading Shelley's work of ekphrasis, "On the Medusa of Leonardo Da Vinci in the Florentine Gallery," a verbal depiction of visual art so vivid the painting comes alive. On this eve of my 50th birthday, jumbled lines and a haunting image play in my mind: a trunkless head lies gazing on the midnight sky; horror, beauty and grace divine play upon its lips and eyelids, threatening to turn my gazing spirit into stone.[1] Like a dream track in a mythological mirror, Medusa shifts, the reflection mediating between this monster and me.

In the morning I awaken to circular shapes of shields swirling behind closed eyelids: Homer's shield of Achilles and Aeneas's shield by Virgil coalesce with Perseus's shield, all inspirations of ekphrasis, all possibly existing only within the mind of the authors, perhaps as dreams. Poet and author Fanny Howe describes the conundrum of dreaming and its effect on writing:

> ...[A] dream hesitates, it doesn't grasp, it stands back, it jokes, it makes itself scared, it circles and it fizzles.... A dream breaks into parts and contradicts its own will, even as it travels around and around.
>
> For me, bewilderment is like a dream: one continually returning pause on a gyre and in both my stories and poems it could be the shape of the spiral that imprints itself in my interior before anything emerges on paper. (Howe, *Wedding Dress* 9)

The circular shields disappear as I open my eyes, but out of the swirling shapes a vision materializes, moving me outside into the foggy November morning toward the barn with its upstairs art studio. The barn is set on our small hill below the house. A suspended bridge links the domestic space of home with this creative space built by my husband. At my feet the words "Art Ahead," formed of lavender glass shards I pressed into the cement foundation, point the way. I push through plum-colored doors, find large sheets of watercolor paper, and set the ball of my pen on the smooth surface. On this morning, inspired by Mayer, I will devote this day to drawing and writing. As freeform lines develop spiraling shapes of unplanned patterns, faces appear, off center. They are reminiscent of others I've drawn, gazing back at me from art around the studio, masks I've sculpted, portraits of other artists and mothers, and a self-portrait. Ideas surface, along with a title: *Shield of Ekphrasis*. Is this shield for protection, or battle, or reflection?

In early works of ekphrasis, where swords and shields were a prevalent theme, many scholars built on the connotations of these war implements by viewing ekphrasis as staging a battle for mastery between verbal and visual representations. However, the space between the verbal and the visual appears to me now as a liminal space between waking and sleeping where a creative voice flourishes; and while maintaining creativity is a battle, I find my mind returns to this dream space seeking solace. Pausing here allows the visual and verbal arts to flow together creating depth in the work, aptly described by scholar Michael Putnam:

> Ekphrasis … inevitably generates a pause in the narrative when art looks at and continues art, and when the artisan of words, who works on our imaginations by … verbal constructions, manufactures artifacts within (the) text for us to see with our mind's eye. As art describes art, we linger, not to escape the story's flow but to deepen our understanding of its meaning, to watch metaphor operating on a grand scale.… (Putnam 49)

Transcribing her dreams in a quest for personal knowledge of a private conundrum, Mayer lists people and props surrounding her, seeking clues to her question of identity. What kind of person must she be to be a poet, one who writes an entire book in a day while mothering two young children?

Following her early morning dreams, the second section of *Midwinter Day* opens with "Sophia likes a cup of coffee in the picture too. . ." (29), as if she is setting up a still life with her daughter. Her format becomes a framing device opening to reveal home as a stage with children's drawings as backdrops foregrounding real life: "curtains blue as ink I stare at, red Godard floor, white walls all crayoned, … from the walls a butterfly kite, a leaf on a ribbon from nursery school, … the stuck clock, the window faces south, laundry on it" (32). The ordinary details of everyday life are unfurled in a continual act of ekphrasis, the simplicity of listing household objects showing herself and others what kind of a person she must be, transforming the chaos of domestic life into art.

My eyes scan the piles of my own room searching for a still life in the mess: open books and journals scatter across the bed, neon notes stuck to pages, sheets and pillows. Alone in bed many nights, my husband at the fire station, I mix the luxury of a large bed with literary loves and writing projects. In the morning I awake, the small square notes stuck to my skin, an embodied list. If a still life resides in this chaos, writing motherhood is a lived aesthetic, an ekphrasis in itself.

Writing's married and fallen in with family,
Though it's more exhausting to love to write
Than to pursue what might have been described. (Mayer 116)

As Mayer presents snapshot portraits of people in her life, she makes a list of other mothers with whom she compares herself. Fanny Howe, American poet, novelist, and short story writer is on that list. In the late 1980s, I interviewed Howe for a writer's magazine. She had mentored me at UCSD. As a young single mother, Howe wrote at her kitchen table with three small children climbing across her feet, never letting the noise or interruptions become an excuse not to write. Her first drafts were hand-written as she curled up in bed. Contemporaries of the beat poet era, she and Mayer both write upon awakening, appropriating those bewildering moments beyond dreaming. When children become my excuse not to write, I evoke images of Howe. The excuses are many with children, the to-do list long, but the drive to write deepens.

On this morning I have only this on my list: draw and write whatever springs forth, Mayer-like out of the mist of motherhood. I spritz the drawing of the shield with water before the soluble ink dries. The blue pen lines disperse, transforming the drawing into a field of fluid dots, ink spidering out in thin veins. Touching the point of the pen to the wet surface again deepens the values, making the eyes appear to open and look back at you, then mutate, the mix of ink floating and dissolving, both mirroring and distorting my gaze.

I pause and wait for the surface to dry. The wooden bridge sways as I walk back to the house, to a life of mothering, a perpetual awakening, children spread across a twenty-five year span. An early morning fog hangs over the valley filled with blueberry bushes, a small sustainable farm project for the children. Last spring, as an experiment, we sent a large box of fresh blueberries from our small farm in Fallbrook to Fanny Howe at her home on Martha's Vineyard. She had just won the Ruth Lilly Poetry prize and shared our fruit with friends who gathered to celebrate, saying these were the biggest, sweetest, freshest blueberries ever. But we are not farmers, and the effort it takes to run this small agricultural project is one more wholesome distraction. One day soon we will leave this established life in southern California for somewhere in the Pacific Northwest where I will write by the wild warmth of a winter fire.

Figure 1: Lori Lyn Greenstone, "Shield of Ekphrasis," 2009, dispersible ink on hot press paper, 15 x 22 inches. Private collection.

To be irrationally married to words and produce
Wildness like a child or two, not grown up yet.... (Mayer 116)

Amidst raising children I have often turned away from writing, unable to reconcile the constant interruptions with the need to connect continuous threads of thought. In the process of exposing our first two children to art, taking them to draw and paint with artists in Yosemite Valley, I took up painting, a more compatible art form. We could draw and paint together, whereas writing is a more solitary pursuit. However, as I developed as an artist, moving from still life and landscape to figure work, my paintings seemed intent upon telling a story. My choice to paint rather than write created an internal battle. I evoked Howe's example of writing in the presence of children as inspiration, but for years I painted instead. Painting was play; writing was work, yet writing is more satisfying.

> As if love is not the food
> Of those of us satisfied enough to write. (Mayer 115)

Then one morning, in those first moments of wakefulness, I gazed at a painting I had recently done, one of many figure paintings modeled on our oldest daughter. In this painting a woman sat in a red dress, her stance wide, elbow on her knee, head resting on her fist, her gaze out of the frame. Emerging from that dream space of sleep, I began writing about a woman who turns away from the life in front of her, leaving her child, a modern day Anna Karenina, an act of ekphrasis engaging my own art.

Until that time, I felt I had to choose between creating visual art and writing. Painting was not only enjoyable, but it was self-supporting and it paid travel expenses, making the choice difficult. But ekphrasis uses art to foster writing, creating a space where I can privilege writing without letting go of painting. Illuminating what the eye might miss, ekphrasis pauses, pushing the space between seeing and saying, between painting and writing, a liminal space where confusion presages creativity. There, confusion is followed by a sense of anticipation and excitement. Drawing and painting reveal what I don't yet know, or what I would rather not consciously know. Writing brings those thoughts to the surface.

DRAWING ON CONFUSION

Anne Roiphe asks, "What are we to do with our confusions as mothers?" in her more traditional memoir *Fruitful: A Real Mother in the Modern World* (84). Like Mayer, she responds by creating lists, elevating the list to an art form, and using it to bring order to the chaos that thrives in the lives of mother writers.

Roiphe courageously lists things her children have done to make her angry—their rudeness, accusations, disdain. An inner emptiness and the constant demands of the child threaten to bring intense anger to the surface, hurling itself at the child. For Roiphe, putting pen to paper draws connections between anger and understanding, digging beneath the surface to deeper issues, the list providing a tangible link, a visible voice: "[A] voice inside keeps asking: Does having children strain or drain the creative force, does it weaken ambition?" (212).

Thinking back through early ambitions, motherhood has clearly diluted my efforts; periods of serious work alternate with no work, all my energy going to family. I find my way back to writing, often through art.

Sometimes life seems pared down to these two activities: mothering and writing, both immensely challenging and rewarding, also frustrating and disappointing, the conflicts and confusions of motherhood driving the writing response.

Back inside the house I sit down to write at my desk. I paint in the studio, but often write in the house, even though it means more interruptions. Being unavailable is inevitably followed by guilt. When I return to my desk, to an array of open books and drafts in the midst of revision, I often feel lost. To find my way back to the main ideas I make a visual map on a large sheet of newsprint I tape to the wall by my desk and fill it with notes, quotes, and images. I draw lines linking ideas, mapping my way through the chaos, forming my voice and taking flight.

Seeking to spin words into wisdom like straw into gold as I write, I find myself instead listening to children's voices upstairs. Distracted, I rise from my desk and go to the kitchen in search of caffeine.

My husband makes coffee and reminds me, "We're in this together," words echoing across our shared history. When we met in college I didn't want to get married. I was the fourth child born to my parents, "the straw that broke the camel's back" my mother often said, referring to her divorce when I was two. In the aftermath, we were often left in the care of my oldest sister, who was too young to bear the responsibility of three children. As the youngest, I feared the collective anger, passed down through the pecking order of my siblings, would pour out on my children, if I ever dared to have any.

In the late '70s, when I was beginning college, I tried to sort through the messages of feminism, that women didn't need men, and that marriage wasn't good for women. My mother's two marriages added weight to those claims. Her first marriage, to my father, ended in a nervous break-down with my mother on "vacation" in Patton State Hospital. The prescribed Lithium lowered her energy level, so she didn't take it. Hospital "vacations" cycled through my childhood, and my mother's mania, her energy focused on difficulty and complaint, left her largely unavailable.

...but a mother is never another/ She is still you, almost by rote. (Mayer 52-3)

I recognize my own mania, magnified by motherhood. I am the daughter of a difficult mother; I am the mother of a difficult daughter. Both mother and daughter, I am seamed into the middle space of this trifaccia, a tragic-comic mask linked by fury, pulled in both directions. The face on one side is old and wrinkled, the voice shrill, the life waning. On the other, the face is young and wild, full of promises broken, shrouding recognition. Painting my way through this role of artist-mother, I write myself into and out of surrounding stories, a manic mix the only mode of mothering I know.

I return to drawing the shield, letting the ink dry during pauses, between trips across the bridge. With the blue pen, unforced patterns emerge like spirals lifting up and swirling around, words filling the spaces with phrases of poetry written to deepen values. I spray the shield with water and raise it, sending fresh ink down the paper, drips ending in dots.

I draw part of Vincent Van Gogh's self-portrait off to one side of the shield, the point of my pen biting into the spiraling pinna of his ear, blue ink bleeding like crushed berries onto the smooth surface of his papery thin skin. Years ago, after studying Vincent's letters to his brother Theo, I began writing a story in the voice of the prostitute to whom Vincent handed his ear. Van Gogh's life was cut short by mania and a disapproving parental gaze. I draw his story into the lines made with my writer's pen, a tool that set my drawing hand free. While doing research in France, I attended a 150th birthday celebration for the artist featuring a rare exhibition of his original drawings. Inspired by his calligraphic marks, I stepped outside into a light rain and began to draw as a band came down the street in Arles. As a painter, I have been more comfortable with a brush than a pencil, my drawings suffering for my impatience to put pigment on paper. But in France, visiting this place where Van Gogh's story unfolded, I had only my writer's pen, resulting in fluid, confident line drawings, with no possibility of erasure.

The drawing was selected for *Strokes of Genius: The Best of Drawing*. Asked about my method, I wrote, "A breakthrough came when I tried drawing with my writing pen, a Pilot V7. With this pen, expressive lyrical lines and shapes seem almost to produce themselves, an elusive feat with graphite.... Spritzing the drawing with water disperses the line, bringing the drawing to life"(34). My pencil drawings, blatantly flat, do not find their way into art books. In writing or drawing, medium matters. Perhaps the permanence of ink demands wholehearted commitment, the story waiting to come out of a writer's pen, a fit implement for enacting ekphrasis.

Upstairs I hear our toddler awake. She is playing with her ten-year-old sister, Lily, as they come downstairs together.

"Are you talking, Mommy?" my youngest asks, seeing my door open. A closed door signifies I am unavailable, writing, not talking. But Lily wants me to listen as she prepares for an oral language fair at school. She plans to recite the first pages in *Secret Life of Bees* by Sue Monk Kidd, one of my favorite texts displaying strength in a community of women. Lily climbs up on the low dressing stool at the foot of the bed, making it her stage, and clears her throat.

"At night I would lie in bed and watch the show,"—she pauses and looks up at the ceiling—"how bees squeezed through the cracks of my bedroom wall and flew circles around the room, making that propeller sound, a high-pitched zzzzzz that hummed along my skin." She touches her wrist, and now I hear her alliteration of every "s" as her fingers run along her arm, putting herself into the text. "I watched their wings shining like bits of chrome in the dark and felt the longing in my chest. The way those bees flew, not even looking for a flower, just flying for the feel of the wind, split my heart down the seam."

I listen, trance-like. "You've made this your own," I say. I've done nothing to help her, except get out of her way. With my first daughter, I hovered, afraid she would destroy herself.

Meanwhile, my two-year-old has found a neon orange highlighter and is drawing on the newsprint map taped to the wall next to my computer. "Stop," I say, reaching for her arm.

"I have to," she says in her determined toddler voice, "I'm writing my thesis."

She is so serious that I let go and ask, "What's it about?"

"Pooh Bear. I like him … but he scares me." She continues with the orange highlighter, turning the phrases, quotes, and images into a game of connect-the-dots.

Can it be this simple—at a very young age, a girl sees and mimics writing as a way to explore a problem, making herself part of writing? I think of my struggling students, and my own challenges as a writer and mother. This movement, from the recesses of my mind down the length of my arm onto the page where thoughts take shape in the form of words and pictures yields clues to the mother-daughter conundrum, and the journeys between these two confusing roles. My daughters are my best chance to connect with my own close community of women.

What an associative way to live this is. (Mayer 35)

Mayer's life as a mother, partner, and writer are revealed as she lists the contents of the life around her. She catalogs each image, her community becoming a quick-sketch landscape her family walks through, seeing "the whole town every day," and "The house the mind but this still village is an embarrassing relative.… Behind their eyes the hideous secret of the emptiness of stuff"(49). In the background, the role of equal partnering in parenting plays itself out, the negative shapes pushing forward an inevitable conflict. During the writing marathon of *Midwinter Day*, Mayer was married to poet, Lewis Warsh. Knowing they later divorce, it is difficult not to read tension between the lines, or project the frustration many mothers feel over the unequal distribution of the parenting workload.

> *We are being quiet like the introduction to the opening theme at the beginning of the opera's overture.… Could it be this whole thing is only about children?… When will I begin?… Each word leaps in this way. I dream I've forgotten all about it, then I myself leap up. What shall I do?* (Mayer 87)

Having grown up in the '40s era of idealized domesticity, my mother believed children could define a woman's life. She discouraged my pursuit of an education. She got married to have children, she often said, and yet, clearly, we were not enough. We were often left with our grandparents, sometimes for months. Her energy leaps up at times, with nowhere to go. The manic-mother model was the only one I knew, and I didn't want to replicate it. But in the second year of marriage, I unexpectedly got pregnant.

> *The condition of motherhood demands that you learn to give birth to someone who won't last, to love someone who will leave, to teach a person who will suffer anyway, to put a life before your own.... To have a job that you can never quit.* (Howe "The Pinocchian Ideal" 266)

I didn't want that job; I wanted to continue my education. I didn't know how to mother. I was too young. I was scared.

I wanted to give up the baby, but my young husband wanted to keep the baby. Where was Rumpelstiltskin when you needed him?

"How many children did you want?" a friend asked when I was pregnant with our third. "None," I answered.

As poet Alice Notley says in *The Grand Permission*, "I didn't plan my pregnancies. I'm an experimentalist" (137).

In an attempt at order, I offer this maternal list:

> a married daughter, a son in college, one in high school, a pre-teen, one in elementary, a toddler, and a grandchild.

I'm experiencing all phases of motherhood simultaneously.

And no, I'm not Mormon or Catholic, and yes, I do believe in birth control (even if it doesn't always work). My three daughters are each born in different decades.

Falling down is a transition I offer you. (Mayer 88)

As I cross back and forth on the bridge between my studio and the house, I envision motherhood as an intertextual collage between the creative and the mundane. By working and living in a middle space between these modes, lost and found pieces are reaffixed into new patterns. Working through motherhood, I am drawn into a liminal space where everyday life both falls away and is reflected back to view from a distance. Writing becomes a shield like that of Achilles, simultaneous scenes staged around the center, a reflective lens fostered by a creative drive that thrives beneath the surface, and yet arises out of the mire of laundry, babies, and grown children gone wrong. Gone wrong? "*Can I say that?*" an echo of Mayer's refrain? "Those four words perfectly hit at the whole problem of the range of truth in language" (Coolidge).

A conflict between speaking out (ek = out + phrasis = speak) and remaining silent arises often in the life of a mother, and a daughter; in between lies an uneasy middle space. Which words that I utter or write, leaving a record, will return to haunt me? Confusion becomes an impetus for creating, the act of creation an attempt at resolution. Perhaps I am trying to find what I'd rather not know consciously—how have I contributed to my oldest daughter's confusion regarding motherhood and partnering?

At the age of seventeen, our oldest daughter trained with the Joffrey Ballet in New York City. After earning a scholarship to pursue her dreams, she let men distract her from her goal. "You can be foolish about a lot of things, but if you are foolish about men, it can ruin your life," I said, maybe too often, maybe not often enough.

As parents, we discouraged men we thought would use her. We encouraged a man who valued her as an equal partner, a friend of her brother's who not only loved her, but loved us as a family. While he finished his education, she moved to Denver to dance with a modern company. Three-and-a-half years after they met, they got married; all their siblings were in the wedding. Our son-in-law held our two youngest daughters when they were newborns. He was the best man in our oldest son's wedding.

After they had been married for five years, our daughter said she wanted a baby. She had been trying to conceive for awhile. Yet in some cosmic economy, where anti-oxidants (from eating so many organic blueberries) override contraceptives even late into middle-age, and a great sense of humor reigns, I got pregnant. I didn't tell anyone, except my husband. "We're in this together," he responded, a reassuring reminder. Then, as if cast in a comedy, my daughter and I were pregnant together, our babies arriving five months apart.

Her husband shared the parenting load, helping her go back to school not long after they had their first child. She studied acting and played the silent paramour in a college production of *Anna in the Tropics*, based on *Anna Karenina*. As if life can get away with imitating art, she had an affair with the lead actor, an aspiring make-up artist, who used her as a model for his final exam. He wanted to make something beautiful into something ugly, he said, as he transformed her into a werewolf with blood dripping down a fanged and hairy face, masking recognition, except for those blue eyes gazing directly out from Facebook. It was not her first affair, but it was the one that ended the marriage and her newly formed family.

> *I am ... focusing on the common shared experiences of bearing and raising children in these fragmented times.... [F]eminism ... needs to be tempered with connection and love, for partner and child....*
> (Roiphe x)

Our son-in-law's parents divorced when he was two. He wanted to avoid that fate for his family. "I think I fell in love with the whole picture," he says, looking back, piecing together parts of a shattered portrait. "I wanted to be part of your family."

Letting go is difficult. I was two, too young to remember, when my parents split up. The latent two-year-old in me now rises up, a panic-stricken, tantrum-throwing mini-Medusa. This is the mother I have become as I watch my daughter throw away her family. "Who are you?" I yell, looking at the "bad-boys" she chooses, unable to recognize the daughter I thought I raised, the mother I thought she would be. Writing is my only semi-safe means of reflection, mediating between horror and self. Anne Roiphe addresses the fear that accompanies this anger:

> We fear the destructiveness inside ourselves. Most of us are afraid that if we caught our true face in the mirror we might see ... the Medusa who turns her enemies to stone. This makes us feel guilty.... Anger bestows on you a portrait of your soul. It is often followed by guilt. The portrait is more detailed if you have children. (Roiphe 74-75)

"You were never there for me," my oldest daughter said when I asked her what role I played in the break-up of her marriage. I look for the truth in her statement. I put my education on pause when I had her, then started again when she was in school. Later, I taught her at home so she could study dance and we could travel as a family. Yet, in other ways there must be some truth in her statement. I was impatient with the constant needs and demands of the child.

"I didn't choose him," she says, about her ex-husband, "You chose him." Did I have that much influence? Or do we restructure our memories to fit the life we are left with?

Sometimes the story changes in remembering. (Mayer 86)

Later, I tell my oldest daughter we are moving. We have talked about it for a long time, but now the house her grandfather helped build is sold, along with the blueberry farm and the art studio. Tired of empty stuff, I'm making a list of things to get rid of—does she want her designer wedding dress? It still hangs in her old closet, encrusted with $300 worth of Swarovski crystals I sewed onto Italian peau de soie. I'd like to sell it.

"You were a horrible mother," she says, then comes when I am gone and takes the dress.

It was only a sentence formed of phrases left by a dream. (Mayer 85)

I return to the shield of ekphrasis and gaze at the faces staring back, at my half-self embedded in the swirls of blue ink. In portrait classes we were urged to look carefully at the model. Otherwise, we draw our own familiar features into every face, seeing only ourselves in others. Looking closely at my reflection in the mirror, I draw a hand with fingers folded into the palm, a wrist running down, propping up the chin, lines connecting to the borders of the shield, to words I carry with me to help me find my way, words I inscribe for safe keeping around the border of the shield.

Hanging above my work space is a portrait of myself as a mother reading to my middle daughter. The watercolor painting of the child is fresh, but the watercolor of the mother quickly became overworked, losing its transparency as I sought to get it right. Self-portraits are often unflattering, but I didn't want it to be murky as well. I put the painting aside for eight years, the span between my middle daughter and my youngest. Every time I looked at the painting, I wanted to obliterate the mother, but leave the child untouched. One day I began tearing up old letters and art catalogs, layering the pieces over the large figure, covering her with a collage of transforming words. As she read to her child she was made of words, Ekphrastic Mama.[2]

In a language made up of idiom and lyricism ... Mayer's ... search for pattern woven out of small actions confirms the notion that seeing what is is a radical human gesture. (Howe, "Review of *Midwinter Day*" 16)

Memoir is an empowering myth, the blue pen my sword in this battle to be both mother and artist. As I write in my studio now, my youngest comes in, asks if she can "work," gets up to her place and begins to draw. She is quiet, but she watches to see when I will stop working and be with her. This last child feels like an unlikely and welcome gift.

"You're the best mom in the world," she says, when I stop writing and look at her drawing of a planet with moons and stars. "No, you're the best mom in the universe... even better than an alien mom." No one loves me like this, and yet I know it won't last.

At the place where feminism and motherhood intersect the fires still burn ... [W]hen I started this book I wanted to see what mothering does ... to our souls, to our ambitions.... [My stories] reflect the way history runs through all of us digging craters in our hearts. Just as political puzzles are half-understood clues to private life, so private life, with its ever moving currents, carries the answers to political puzzles. (Roiphe ix, x)

For me, being a mother is both too little and too much, a paradox driving artistic expression and authorial voice. It is too little fulfillment to base a life on, and too much responsibility to bear alone. In this middle space between generations, between my mother and my daughters, between undefined waves of feminism and a backwash of confusion, I am defining my feminism within motherhood, within writing, within art—all forms of speaking out.

I thought I was going to write
A story of my theories tonight
Not this desirous essay on art and home. (Mayer 117)

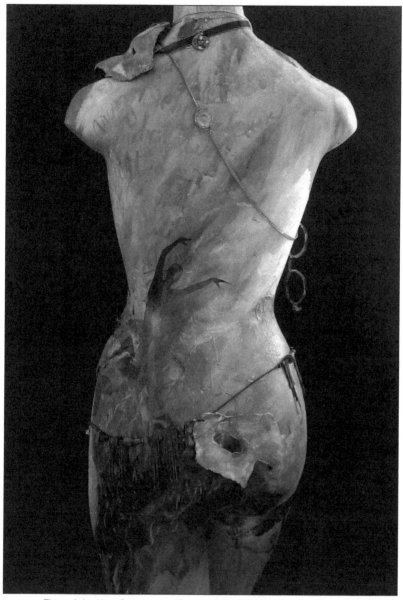

Figure 2: Lori Lyn Greenstone, "Truncated Soul," 2008, mixed media sculpture, 13 x 40 inches. Private collection.

Night falls in the art studio where a sculpture stands, cathartic art made from lost and found pieces of our oldest daughter's early life—her dog tags from a Smithsonian trip, a mask of her face cast when she was ten, a pair of broken glasses, an old watch, a tarnished ring, a paper casting of my hand across her heart. The trunk-style mannequin appears to me now as Medusa's severed body, svelte and attractive, even with no head, no hands, no feet. Still, as you enter the gallery studio the curves are alluring. It is a torso only, a sculpture whose life began as the inanimate armature of high fashion, a truncated soul. It draws you in and sends you circling around its hollow, shapely form. The neck rises, but slides off at an angle. Shoulders round and drop, but no arms fall to its side or reach out. Slender thighs extend down, but meet an abrupt end. Tap on any part and you are met by an echo.

Onto this form the artist inscribes words she cannot say to ears that cannot hear. Rich quinacradone gold layered next to thick, dark gesso creates a lacquered garment for an undomestic body. Into the wet, black paint the artist carves a message with the soft rubber tip of a dull implement, a love letter letting go, moving torn layers aside, revealing jaded greens and dull lavenders, flecks of deep red. A strip of black lace is laid into dark gesso, then stripped away, leaving its mark, the imprint of a delicate garter appearing in bas-relief across the rise of one thin thigh.

A body must have a head, even if it is only a mask to hide behind. The hollow form of the sculpted mannequin awaits a face in the form of a mask to animate its soul. Masks conceal. Behind the mask, you pretend. Without it, who are you?

In writing memoir we create our own myth, our personal story of creation. Reflecting upon my daughter, my mother, myself, I raise my shield, polishing it with each line. Next to the mannequin I put down my pen, the drawing complete on this first day of 50, my life a tumbling conundrum—life as art, art as energy; poet as mother, mother as writer—drawing in dispersible ink across a paper-thin shield.

ENDNOTES

[1]A paraphrase of lines 1,4,5,9 from the poem
[2]Editors' Note: This piece of art graces the cover of our collection, with our thanks to the artist.

WORKS CITED

"Bernadette-Mayer." *Style of Negation*. Word Press. 7 Apr. 2008. Web.

19 December 2012.

Coolidge, Clark. Letter to Bernadette Mayer. 21 January 1980. MS. Collection of the University of California, San Diego Library. San Diego, CA.

Howe, Fanny. "Review of *Midwinter Day* by Bernadette Mayer." *American Book Review* 6 (1984): 16. Print.

Howe, Fanny. "The Pinocchian Ideal." T*he Grand Permission: New Writings on Poetics and Motherhood.* Eds. Patricia Dienstfrey and Brenda Hillman. Middletown, CT: Wesleyan University Press, 2003. 263-266. Print.

Howe, Fanny. *The Wedding Dress: Meditations on Word and Life.* Berkeley: University of California Press, 2003. Print.

Kidd, Sue Monk. *The Secret Life of Bees.* New York: Viking, 2002. Print.

Mayer, Bernadette. *Midwinter Day.* New York: New Directions, 1999. Print.

Notley, Alice. "Doublings." *The Grand Permission: New Writings on Poetics and Motherhood.* Eds. Patricia Dienstfrey and Brenda Hillman. Middletown, CT: Wesleyan University Press, 2003. 137-144. Print.

Putnam, Michael C. J. *Virgil's Epic Designs: Ekphrasis in the Aeneid.* New Haven: Yale University Press, 1998. Print.

Roiphe, Anne Richardson. *Fruitful: A Real Mother in the Modern World.* Boston: Houghton Mifflin, 1996. Print.

Rubin Wolf, Rachel. *Strokes of Genius: The Best of Drawing.* 1st ed. Cincinnati, OH: North Light Books, 2007. Print.

Shelley, Percy Bysshe. *Poems Selected from Percy Bysshe Shelley.* London: C. Kegan Paul & Co., 1880. 163. Print.

SECTION TWO
WHAT THE OTHER BOOKS DON'T TELL US

5.
Milkmother Memoir

PAMELA DOUGLAS

Let women's experience serve as a fresh revelatory source.
—Grace Jantzen, *Becoming Divine* (253)

A T THE AGE OF THIRTY, I, too, became a mother.
From then on, stories of pregnant, birthing and breastfeeding women flooded my days, told both by the mothers of young children whose company I kept, and by the patients I saw in my work as an Australian general practitioner. But I noticed that on my bookshelves at home, an imaginative silence about the transfigurative maternal body prevailed. I certainly had access to a weighty genre of non-fiction self-help written by "experts," but why, I wondered, was there so little literary writing available that was "concerned with the subject, the mother as site of her proceedings" (Kristeva 237)?

In the twenty-two years since my daughter's birth, fiction and creative non-fiction by Australian women writing as mothers and daughters have flourished. But there are still relatively few Australian women writers who have dared to foreground the body of the reproductive female, and to defy an entrenched cultural prejudice against writing frankly about maternity. World-wide, women writers are only just beginning to contest the belief that stories of a woman's embodied experience in pregnancy, birth, breastfeeding, and caring for small children, are tedious and peripheral. This essay argues that the new subgenre of the milkmother memoir is a powerful strategy for the demedicalisation of the transfigurative maternal body, and for the elaboration of the milkmother in a new feminine imaginary.

In using the term "transfigurative maternal body," I am referring to the female body which is becoming, or has recently become, two bodies. In using the word "medicalisation," I refer to a particular set of largely unconscious values and assumptions employed by my own profession as we relate to mothers, and which mothers internalise in their relationship with their own bodies. Access to high quality medical care protects women and babies from death and illness, and is a fundamental human right not yet attained in many parts of the world, including by disadvantaged populations in Australia.[1]

Yet early on in my career as a GP, it became clear to me that *unnecessary* medicalisation of a mother's body has the potential to impact negatively on a mother and baby's well-being, causing distress and incurring unnecessary and expensive interventions. Whilst ensuring the safety of every mother and baby in all countries must remain everyone's primary concern, even wealthy countries such as mine increasingly confront limits to their health budgets, and a public debate about the costs and potential negative outcomes of unnecessary medicalisation has emerged.

Maternity is inevitably and profoundly embedded in cultural practices and understandings of gender and the body. As corporeal theorists have argued for the past two decades, all knowledge about the body, including the so-called "objective" knowledge of science and medicine, is value-laden, and determined by historical, sociocultural and political discourse. In the midst of my sometimes terrifying, often tumultuous and exhausting early experiences of maternity, I coined the term "milkmother" to denote the pregnant, birthing, and physiologically or metaphorically lactating woman.[2] But invention of the term "milkmother," and using evolutionary biology to justify the choice of milk as metaphor for this phase in childbearing, is far from a moralistic prescription for "the natural" or a revival of essentialism.

As the Australian corporeal theorist Alison Bartlett argues in *Breastwork*, her pioneering study of breastfeeding, even concepts of "the natural," commonly employed by breastfeeding advocates, are political ideologies, shaped by histories and cultures (789). Instead, agreeing with Bartlett, I suggest that "the milkmother" is a particular way of performing mothering, significant because of its differences to the way mothering is performed with older children. Breastfeeding, for example, can be framed as just one of many ways of performing the milkmother; formula feeding is another. The metaphor of "milk" in "milkmother," then, reminds us of the kind of maternal performance that is demanded by the developmental dependence of children up to three or four years of age, with their need for constant monitoring and interaction, for feeding, bathing, cleaning, carrying, rocking, picking up, putting down, entertaining, nappy changes, toilet training, and for facilitation of play and adventure even as safety is ensured. These tasks are physically demanding, extraordinarily time-intensive, and usually specific to the care of very young children. The milkmother has a set of biopsychosocial needs that are different to those of the mother of older children, and in the absence of a separate category by which to refer to this unique stage in many women's lives, it becomes difficult to articulate her special needs, for example in the workplace, and to advocate for her.

And a milkmother, as I was learning myself, is in biological transition, from the pre-maternal years into a lifelong state of maternity; her physiological transfiguration is accompanied by a profound psychological rite of passage.

I also use the term "feminine imaginary," borrowed from translations of the work of French post-structuralist philosophers. In English, the word "feminine" has typically connoted conventional and socially acceptable expressions of femaleness. The *Macquarie Dictionary* defines "feminine" as "1. pertaining to a woman. 2. weak; gentle. 3. effeminate." This essay invests the word "feminine" with a different, and much more powerful, meaning. Hélène Cixous writes in her 1975 manifesto, "The Laugh of the Medusa": "A feminine text cannot fail to be more than subversive. It is volcanic; as it is written it brings about an upheaval of the old property crust, carrier of masculine investments; there's no other way" (258). For Cixous, and for this essay, asserting the feminine is a feminist act. A feminine imaginary would contain images of the valorised woman in all her life-stages; it would include representations of men; and it would include representations of diverse racial and sexual orientations and life-choices, including the choice not to have children. However, this essay focuses on representations of the milkmother in Australian women's memoir, and how they contribute to a feminine imaginary.

In this essay, I also discuss the process of writing *Bone Mother: a memoir in milk*, a milkmother memoir telling the story of my own vulnerable body, as well as the disguised stories of my patients. *Bone Mother* was a shared winner of the 2009 Queensland Premiers Literary Awards (Emerging Author) and remains unpublished as yet, for reasons I discuss later. Because *Bone Mother* offers a gendered, insider's critique of medical representations of the pregnant, birthing and (literally or metaphorically) breastfeeding body, located at the intersection of the personal and professional, it illustrates the subversive potential of this new subgenre. I examine the relative under-representation of the milkmother in Australia women's writing, looking more closely at the way the small number of milkmother memoirs that have emerged here in recent years, including Susan Johnson's *A Better Woman*, take steps to demedicalise the gestating, birthing and metaphorically or literally lactating body.

In this essay, as in my life, I move between discourses. Though each discourse is in fact complex, contested from within and without, and constantly dynamic, I will simplify my positioning in the following way. Professionally, I write and work in three discourses: the medical or scientific discourse, with its masculinist and positivist conventions concerning knowledge and the body; the discourse of feminist and corporeal theory, that interrogates ideas of female knowledge and of the female body; and popular discourse, by which my patients and I speak about their personal knowledge of their bodies. Because I speak these three discourses, the tone of my essay—and my life—may seem uneven as a result.

Yet none of these discourses adequately describe my own experience in my encounters with patients or in my personal life; in order to try to do this, I have written a memoir. At first I called the various drafts of *Bone Mother* fiction, and looked to other Australian writers' representations of the milkmother in fiction, noting the subgenre's relative paucity, subversiveness, and, wherever I could find it, the milkmother's *jouissance*. Finally, I realised that memoir is the genre most suited to my emergent voice, and drew courage from the few other Australian milkmother memoirists that I could find.

Out of the three discourses, out of the complex influences of each, out of their dynamic inter-relationship over time; through the research, writing and re-writing of this and other essays; and through the intermittent drafts and shifting genre of *Bone Mother* over many years, my own synthesis emerged, in my own embodied, uneven, vulnerable voice.

THE MEDICALISED MILKMOTHER

> I am completely overwhelmed. Overwhelmed by fear and bewilderment. No one ever warned me it would be like this.
> —Fiona Place, "Apocalypse Now" (61)

An assumption that the maternal body is untrustworthy and inadequate to the task of reproduction profoundly shapes medical practice during pregnancy, birth, and the first weeks and months postpartum. A doctor's necessary vigilance, our necessary readiness for catastrophe, blurs into a pervasive belief that the gestating, birthing and lactating body is unruly, capricious, and dangerous. I have participated in my profession's struggle to contain its anxiety about the maternal body. I have participated in our tendency to represent her in a medicalised language heavily reliant upon metaphors of machinery, electrical circuitry, and engineering.

Beginning in childhood, women learn from the stories they hear that their bodies are unfit to meet the frightening physiological or psychological demands of this time of life. This in turn promotes a woman's mistrust of her own bodily function, and she, too, becomes anxious and afraid. Her imagination is a biological event: the immune, neuroendocrine and neuromuscular systems of the body alter in response to imagined disasters and associated emotions, mediated by a host of hormones, neurotransmitters, and immune factors. These physiological effects of fear and anxiety, and unnecessary and intrusive medical practices that interfere with normal physiological processes, trigger costly cascades of preventable technological or pharmaceutical intervention. It is not surprising then, that the milkmothers I see in my work often imagine their body throughout pregnancy, childbirth, and the early years of childraising to be unreliable, unpleasant, and "not enough." Throughout my twenty-five years in general practice, "not enough" has dominated the narratives of my pregnant, birthing, and breastfeeding patients: I wasn't dilating, the baby was too big for my pelvis, I didn't have enough milk, nothing I do can settle him. If the popular discourses, the narratives of women, are alive with the belief that the maternal and infant bodies are incompetent or inadequate or unable to be relied upon, a belief mostly based upon physiological misconceptions and medicalised representations, that belief becomes a self-fulfilling prophecy.

In the texts of Western philosophy, psychoanalytic theory, and literature, as Michelle Boulous Walker observes, "the maternal body occupies the site of a radical silence" (1). We find "readable absences," which in their absence speak to systemic denial (2). Our cultural imaginary, despite the extraordinary complexity of contemporary western societies and the relative autonomy and equality that contemporary western women enjoy, remains fundamentally masculinist, dominated by stories and images of heroic quests for power and status; of war and of conquest; and of the female body as object for the satisfaction of the masculine gaze. Our cultural imaginary offers us representation of the pregnant, birthing, and (physiologically or metaphorically) breastfeeding woman in just one main figure, the Virgin Mary, ideal of purity and devotion. But the Virgin is the mother without a body. In the representations of her that have come to us over the past one thousand years, she has no sexual desire, no morning sickness, no screams in childbirth, no lochia. She has no engorgement, or difficulty attaching the baby to the breast, no sleep-deprivation, no resentment. She has an ethereal beauty, and is asexual, since she is—as in the "Litany of Loreto"—"Mother most pure, Mother most chaste, Mother inviolate, Mother undefiled." She is the product of a patriarchal imaginary: acted upon, not an agency of movement or flux. I see images of her, young eyes downcast, head slightly inclined, and imagine her anxiety and depression. She is the Mater Dolorosa, Our Lady of Sorrows. The Virgin Mary—the most dominant archetype in the history of Western civilisations, as Kristeva reminds us in her groundbreaking essay, "Stabat Mater"—is necessarily cleaned up, with her body hidden so that she herself remains pure.

We lack a mythopoeic story for the extraordinary bodily transformation of pregnancy, birth, and breastfeeding. We lack empowered and empowering narratives about this rite of passage. Even in the twenty-first century, the milkmother has little in the way of a feminine imaginary to guide her through the physical and emotional ordeal that is associated with her transformation, her initiation. This means that her rite of passage becomes, as feminist scholar of religion Grace Jantzen argues, if not completely impossible, "at least fraught with ambiguity and partiality" (128). In my consulting room, new mothers frequently repeat the words of author Fiona Place, as she writes of her experience of childbirth: "I am completely overwhelmed. Overwhelmed by fear and bewilderment. No one ever warned me it would be like this" (61).

Women flee their bodies psychologically, and disown or even fail to identify their somatic experience. Why would we not be afraid?

The relative absence of empowered images of the milkmother in the cultural imaginary has allowed the medical profession to co-opt the way she is represented. As Janemaree Maher writes, "the healthy body in pregnancy is, in our culture, primarily defined through medical knowledge" ("Rethinking" 146). The masculinist imaginary then inscribes itself into the milkmother's body. We need only look as far as the Australian corporeal theorists, including Bartlett and Elisabeth Grosz, to find the argument that the milkmother's body remains colonized by the discourses of biology and medicine, with tangible if unintended effects on the patient's body. These theorists remind us that for all its life-saving, health-improving power and technologies, the biomedical discourse is just one narrative among many about the body. They contend that doctors and public health advocates adhere to biomedical advocacy scripts as if these were the only legitimate way to communicate knowledge; and that medical advice oversimplifies bodies, which are complex sites of histories, cultures and structures of knowledge. They contend that biomedical scripts are delivered within an asymmetric power relationship, which is stripped of subjectivity and imagination, and unaware of the way evidence itself is constructed by political and sociocultural contexts.

Bone Mother aims to confront these problems, by exploring my experiences both as a doctor who is consulted by milkmothers, and as a milkmother who seeks help from the medical institution.

Bone Mother, then, can be understood as a counter-narrative, which disrupts traditional scripts about the body of the pregnant, birthing and literally or metaphorically breastfeeding woman. It is a reflexive exploration or autoethnography in memoir, by a doctor who is, in the writing, also a milkmother. My positioning complicates oppositional discourses of female agency versus medicalisation of the female reproductive body, so that *Bone Mother*, when published, may be considered "volatile" (to use Grosz's term—unpredictable, unstable, with boundaries that are difficult to discern, therefore dangerous) by my colleagues. However, as physician Rita Charon writes, "only sophisticated narrative powers will lead to the conversations that society needs to have about its medical system" (1900). *Bone Mother* attempts such a conversation with respect to the reproductive maternal body: it aims to bring, by virtue of its genre, a new, more complicated, more subjective, disruptive and self-aware positioning of the doctor in relation to her own body and society. It aims to radically expand notions of what constitutes legitimate inquiry by a doctor, and in particular, inquiry by a doctor concerning the pregnant, birthing, and metaphorically or literally breastfeeding woman.[3]

THE RISE OF MEMOIR

The words are being spoken now, are being written down, the taboos are being broken, the masks of motherhood are cracking through.

—Adrienne Rich, *Of Woman Born* 25

Virginia Woolf was working on her groundbreaking memoir, "A Sketch of the Past," in 1941, just four months prior to her suicide. When she presented this account, which included a description of her sexual abuse at the hands of her half-brother, to her Bloomsbury friends, she was met with a terrible silence. "Only autobiography is literature," Woolf claims, predating the trend to narrative non-fiction in women's writing by forty years. "Novels are what we peel off, and come at last to the core, which is only you and me" (Nicolson 142). Sixty years later, the memoir has flowered into a remarkably popular and lively genre internationally, and is dominant in Australian women's creative non-fiction. It is longer than the essay, stylistically flexible, and, unlike conventional concepts of autobiography, interested in the meaning of ordinary, often marginalized, lives.

With the advent of second wave feminism from the 1970s, Australian women's fiction did begin referring to the mother's body, but wrote her as abject in order to subvert the dominant sentimentalisation of motherhood. For example, dark, rapacious mothers feature prominently in Elizabeth Jolley's fiction, but the milkmother, the body of the pregnant, birthing and breastfeeding mother, appears much more rarely. The subjective milkmother body is still a last frontier in Australian fiction: there are only a handful of novels in which she is foregrounded.[4] In 1996, Sue Woolfe complained to Bartlett: "there are no stories about us.... I don't mean, how to mother, I mean the imaginative experience of mothering" (Bartlett *Jamming* 236).

However, from 1996 onwards, the reading public had its first taste of Australian mothers writing about themselves in creative non-fiction as subjects. Introducing *Motherlove*, her edited collection of short stories about mothering, Debra Adelaide writes of her contributors' shared belief "that at the heart of the birth experience lies the ineffable: *that there is no word for it*," and how these writers "wrestled with words to describe the indescribable" (5). Also that year, Stephanie Holt and Maryanne Lynch edited *Motherlode*, a collection of poems and stories about mothering. In the opening segment, her text interwoven with lyrical sequences about her experience of childbirth, Marion Campbell reflects on the difficulty of writing: "If a mother tries to speak out, as herself, people are embarrassed. They say she is making a spectacle of herself" (1). The following year, Susan Maushart declared in *The Mask of Motherhood* that a conspiracy of silence surrounded mothering in Australia, and Adelaide's second collection of short stories written by Australian women about mothering was published.

BONE MOTHER: A MEMOIR IN MILK.

Bone Mother *is concerned with the reclamation of the interior authority of a mother's body.*[5]

As a young mother, I began to keep the notes that eventually became *Bone Mother: a memoir in milk*. I knew that many new mothers struggled with loneliness, isolation and shame, yet there was a serious lack of representations of the milkmother in women's fiction and creative non-fiction. I also knew that Australian women had very low expectations that anyone would be interested in their experiences as milkmother (Maushart 339). In *Bone Mother*, I was determined to write the detailed subjective physicality of pregnancy, abortion, birth, lactation, and the raising of small children. I didn't have the time to create a narrative more distant from myself, but made meaning of those long, often tedious days caring for my little daughter and son by imagining that my story might someday have value for others. The journal writing gave my life meaning beyond the exhaustion and invisibility of caring for small children. I remained confident that the experience of becoming a mother was no more or less able to be expressed in words than female sexual desire, or mystical revelation, if only a woman could find the time (or the money that bought time) to put words to paper. Many years later I read Cixous' "The Laugh of the Medusa," and realised that I, too, had been trying to write in "white ink," "that good mother's milk" (251).

As my children grew older and I had more time to create a structured narrative, I wrote my story as fiction. I began to think that perhaps my work had lost any claim to autobiographical accuracy, and I knew from various literary scandals that readers are intolerant of inaccuracies when a work is marketed as a "true story." Yet the manuscript drew from my journals, and addressed real events and intimate physical and emotional truths.

By 2009, I referred to *Bone Mother* as "fictional memoir," influenced by Australian writer Drusilla Modjeska's decision to call *Poppy*, a story about her mother's life, a "fictional biography." My problem of genre mirrored a broader trend in the evolution of Australian women's writing from the 1980s. Women writers experimented with genre as they claimed their private, radical truths in the public domain, blurring the boundaries between fiction and non-fiction. Finally, from the 1990s, women not only found the courage to reach their own reality in fiction, but also to claim their transgressive, generative bodies in the public domain unmediated by fiction. Helen Buss, in *Repossessing the World: Reading Memoirs by Contemporary Women*, claims that memoir is the ideal genre for bringing women's highly relational lives into the public domain. Each woman's personal counter-narrative re-claims silenced or distorted histories in our society. In 2010, I found the courage to re-write *Bone Mother* as memoir.

Thomas Larson, in *The Memoir and the Memoirist*, argues that memoir deals inevitably with relationship. Memoir is, in his view, defined by its focus on the emotional immediacy of a singular relationship between the memoirist and an event, or a person, or an idea: memoir is characterized by a chosen thematic centre.

In *Bone Mother*, and in the subgenre that I call "milkmother memoir" more generally, this thematic centre is the experience of the pregnant and birthing woman, and the metaphorically or literally breastfeeding woman. A milkmother memoir writes the body of the mother, writes of the birth-pain and the lochia and the let-down of milk and the waking in the night to an infant's cry; it writes the taste and the scent of a child and the mundanely physical acts of care as if they *mattered* to the world.

A PROFESSIONAL WOMAN

Memoir offers a mode to repossess ways of knowing the world
and the self that does not divide the heart from the head.

—Helen Buss, *Repossessing the World* (xxv)

Buss argues that contemporary female memoirists "make possible
through their 'balancing acts' the solutions individuals perform to avoid
the dichotomies of traditional identity patterns" (63). Memoir allows
women to avoid "sacrificial logics," in which identity must be forged out
of the repression or sacrifice of other parts of the personality (Weir).
I see women around me striving to succeed as doctors, and caring a
great deal about their female patients, without seriously questioning the
fundamental masculinist assumptions upon which the profession and
its approach to illness, and in particular, women's health, has been built.
I, too, believe with Modjeska that it is "the role and contribution of
women as intellectuals and writers to work against splits, for it is often
women who are best in a position to understand the consequences of
psychic and social fractures" (37). I, too, believe that the future of humanity depends on this. So in writing *Bone Mother* I wanted to reclaim
a feminine perspective on the practice of medicine from within the
practice of medicine, something that has scarcely been attempted as yet.

Buss argues that in memoir, women re-possess "a female identity
from male-based disciplines of medicine and psychology, history and
literature that had 'possessed' femaleness" (xii). I aimed to bring the
relational, gendered self to gaze at medical research, at medical practice,
and re-vision it. I wanted to perform myself as a woman who challenged
the scientification, the medicalisation, of the transfigurative reproductive
body, so that other women could gain from my exploration. Milkmother
memoir is the genre for this task.

JOUISSANCE

Hero: a man, now also a woman, distinguished by the performance of extraordinarily brave or noble deeds [and] a man, now
also a woman, admired and venerated for his or her achievements
and noble qualities in a field.

—*New Shorter Oxford English Dictionary*

Emily Martin gathered metaphors for giving birth that appealed to women, in contrast to the often machinery-based, or "not-enough," language of medical professionals. She found, for example, that women preferred to describe labour as a river or a ripening fruit, and contractions as rushes or bursts of energy (157-58). Such descriptions contrast with the self-fulfilling, "not enough" representations of the pregnant, birthing, or lactating woman in the masculinist imaginary, and contrast with representations of the maternal as abject. Young women have trouble recognising the extraordinary heroism involved in birth and infant care, because heroism remains associated with masculinist definitions that reference war. As a result, women are frequently unprepared for their own often shocking physical transfiguration.

In the new subgenre of the milkmother memoir, experimentation with a new use of language is inevitable. I felt we lacked a language that names—that valorises—the heroism of the transfigurative female body. And I was eager to write of a moist abundance specific to the body and psyche of the milkmother that is rarely named or celebrated, as another counterweight to the medicalised, "not enough" discourse of my patients. I decided that the particular kind of flourishing specific to the transitional maternal body that I attempt to write in *Bone Mother* is most aptly suggested by the French word, *jouissance*, rich in connotation. Later, I discovered Bartlett's use of jouissance, this "resplendent" term, in her discussion of "milk time:" "I can't help but think of juice, juice-ance, wet and sticky, tasty, sweet.... It seems perfect for describing breastmilk" (*Breastwork* 184).

Whilst "pleasure" is the simplest translation, the noun comes from the verb "jouir" that has no exact English equivalent but means something like to enjoy, to have an intensity of feeling that takes one to the edge, or to revel in without fear of the cost. It also means to have an orgasm. The French feminist theorists suggest that jouissance is a re-experience of the pre-oedipal physical pleasures of infancy and later sexuality, which are repressed in patriarchal culture (Jones 368). While they extend definitions of sexuality to include a diffuse consciousness that involves every part of a woman's body, I aim to step beyond considerations of the sexual, to claim a jouissance that is specific to the physical transfiguration of maternity: jouissance as the flourishing, flowering, and vivification that accompanies the experience of pregnancy, birth, lactation, and tending of small children. Jouissance, an embodied fullness of experience, embraces both joy and difficulty. In my use of it, jouissance implies a surging fruition, which must inevitably yield to senescence. Jouissance is sensual, even in pain. Jouissance is soulful, even if unremittingly physical. Jouissance is ravishingly moist.

When milkmothers write from their jouissance, they represent themselves in ways that challenge phallocentric discourse. Jouissance is a nuanced, complicated, deeply lived celebration of the transformative maternal body, even out of the pains of childbirth, even out of difficulty and exhaustion.

MILKMOTHER MEMOIR AS SITE OF INTERNAL TENSION

Larson proposes that memoir is characterized by fertile tensions that operate within a central thematic focus, and which open up opportunity for reflection. The memoirist is able to carry the reader through these tensions because of the feelings of sympathy and compassion—the intimate bond—she establishes with the reader. I consider two kinds of internal tension that characterize the milkmother memoir: tension between the "I-then" and "I-now;" and between myself and the life I didn't lead (or myself and the baby that didn't live). I also consider milkmother memoir as a site of tension between self and the world.

I-THEN AND I-NOW

In writing her trailblazing memoir, "A Sketch of the Past," Woolf reflects on the tension between what she calls "I-then" and "I-now," between the rememberer and the remembered self, interconnected but different. This friction in memoir gives rise to nuanced reflection and the making of meaning. Memory is constantly revised, shifting sand even in the writing of it, subject to the alchemy of life experience, personal maturation, other people's recollections, events in the wider world, and personal values.

The relationship between the memoirist and the remembered inevitably evolves as the story is written. This has been particularly evident in my own work, as the writing has spanned twenty years, and the revisions have marked different stages in my own maturation as a woman, as well as generic transformation. Having come to understand the importance of the pull between the rememberer and the remembered, I considered ways to strengthen the tension between "I-now" and "I-then" as I finally re-wrote *Bone Mother* as memoir. I located the "I-now" on an overseas trip shortly after my children had left home, looking back on and reflecting upon "I-then," in my milkmother years.

Buss and Larson argue that memoir may, in fact, be a therapeutic process. I agree that despite the integrity of my desire to give something to other mothers with young children, my memoir has been, at heart, what Larson names as "a devotional and therapeutic practice," by which I have inquired into the truth of my life (9). As a young ex-Methodist mother predisposed to silence by devastating internalised voices of judgment, writing to an imagined reading public as I cared for small children became integral to my psychological survival. I wrote *Bone Mother* to save myself. I'd been writing it for no less than seventeen years when I realised that part of the reason I wanted to fictionalize my narrative lay in my fear of being seen as self-obsessed, or self-indulgent. Memoir sounded less like a work of creativity, I thought, and more like a therapy session. It is a relief to allow that the writing of memoir for personal benefit may also be a legitimate gift to others.

Another important site of internal tension for the memoirist lies between fact and memory, fertile opportunity for reflection and analysis since the memoir can only ever be one version or variation of what happened. Because I want to maintain the reader's trust, in *Bone Mother* I either discard the magical realism of my fictional draft, or make it clear that certain strange events are imagined. The testing of memory against significant known facts may be revealing of both the memoirist and of those with whom the writer shares her private selves and who remember differently. Importantly however, many women were raised to accommodate immense cultural pressure by allowing the dominant discourse to frame or erase their stories and memories. This may occur, for instance, in those who contested patriarchal paradigms or dysfunctional family dynamics, whose lives have borne the awful wound of a family's negative projections. For these women, claiming memory without justification, apology, or shame, despite the differing constructions of truth by those around them, may be a vital and therapeutic task.

There is also tension in memoir between reflection and the need to tell a good story. The need to "show," then, is in tension with the reflective voice, who "tells." The art of memoir is to braid a compelling story with the narrator's reflection on and analysis of the evolution of that story, in a way that keeps the reader engaged, or even in suspense. The writer wants the reader to keep turning the page, and necessarily draws on techniques of plot, character development, pacing and description. In my own re-write of *Bone Mother*, I aimed to strengthen the tension between both the "show" and the "tell," bringing both into sharper focus.

MYSELF AND THE LIFE I DIDN'T LEAD
(OR MYSELF AND THE BABY WHO DIED)

Up until the time I re-wrote *Bone Mother* as memoir, the narrator was named "Genevieve." I wrote in the first person, yet maintained distance by pretending she wasn't me. I heard my motives for the use of this device spoken by a patient of mine, an intelligent, well-groomed woman in her early forties. She was, in effect, apologising to me for her desire to continue with an unplanned pregnancy in very uncertain circumstances. *This is not*, she said, *the life I planned for myself.* She was afraid that I would misread her, or judge her, though I felt only an understanding and a desire to offer support. But I felt ashamed of *Bone Mother*, despite a conviction that women needed intimate, jouissant milkmother texts. I felt ashamed of my constrained enthusiasm for medical practice. I felt ashamed of the prejudice directed towards me after giving birth, of the way I let my milk run free, of the exhaustion I felt tandem feeding, even as I refused to wean. I felt ashamed of my chaotic emotional life, of my disastrous first marriage, of my poverty. *This is not the life I planned for myself.* To some extent, in that version, I tried to sanitise my life in the writing of it, so that I would be seen as a real doctor, with something credible to say. If I invoked "Genevieve," distanced myself, I could pretend the narrator wasn't me. For Rosamund Dalziell, "the emotion of shame constitutes a driving force in many Australian autobiographies published since 1960" (253). She observes:

> Autobiographical confrontation with shame has the potential to open up festering wounds within society, overcoming denial and facilitating healing, tolerance and reconciliation. Shame is deeply embedded in Australian culture and confronting this painful emotion is difficult, individually and socially. (11)

In re-writing *Bone Mother* as memoir, I needed to come to terms with that life I didn't lead, the stable one, the overtly successful career, the successful marriage. My memoir is re-written in the tug between the life that was, and the life that wasn't; in the tension between who I am, and who I wanted to be. Re-writing as memoir demanded that I face this with deep compassion for myself.

Related to the theme of "myself and the life I didn't lead" is another theme specific to milkmother memoir: the theme of "myself and the baby that died." The first two milkmother memoirs published in Australia both appeared in 1991, both in diary form and about the loss of a baby to Sudden Infant Death Syndrome (known as cot death at the time); neither remains in print. Donna McDonald's memoir, *Jack's Story*, blends descriptive narrative, reflection, dreams, and poetry as she tells of her son's cot death at six months and its effects upon her marriage. On a website promoting her other publications as a physiotherapist, Sarah Key discusses *Freddie: A Diary of a Cot Death*, in which she tells the story of her ten week old son's cot death: "I could hardly bear, for instance, that his lips were wet when I found him but when I wrote it, some of that horror began to fade." These two heroic women, writing the devastating force of their loss, broke through the silence that shrouded the milkmother's personal experience in Australian women's writing.

Another Australian milkmother memoir about the death of a baby, published in 2007, is characterised by a chronological, material realism, and a more popular style. The first part of this memoir, in particular, as Jane Hansen describes her life in the "brutal, blokey world of television" (39) is decidedly colloquial. Hansen lays bare her turbulent emotional and physical experiences as she miscarries, has a stillbirth, and then a very premature baby who dies after a harrowing eight months. The experiences recounted by this author are by necessity painfully embedded in and defined by the medical. Hansen observes: "Grief over the loss of a child is life-threatening. For weeks I chastised myself for not having the foresight or courage to 'go with him'" (209). Hansen continues to give voice to her depression and suicidal thoughts after her premature baby's death, even through the pregnancy and infancy of her first living son. The reader is less able to dismiss Hansen's ravaging grief as self-indulgent, maternal obsession, because Hansen has already been seen to hold her own in the male-dominated world of war correspondence, facing the regimes of both the Taliban and Saddam Hussein with courage. Her demonstrated worldly competence helps the reader accept that Hansen is neither weak nor maudlin, but a normal woman transfigured body and soul by the birth and death of her babies.

These three brave milkmother memoirs challenge the belief that mothers are unnatural and diseased when their emotional state differs from that homogenous, tightly constrained perinatal state that the masculinist culture calls "normal."[6] But it is as if the volcanic thrust of an unspeakable grief is required, in order for a milkmother to make her appearance in an Australian memoir, to break through the taboos into the public domain undisguised. Refusing to be ashamed of the madness of their grief, these three courageous mothers write for their own sake, and for the sake of all of us.

SELF AND THE WORLD

In *Bone Mother*, I aim to explore how roots from my topside world of professional and public life plunge deep down ravaged, dreaming, interior wildernesses. The memoir is an ideal genre for representations of the milkmother as she performs her multiple, complex, radically relational identities—as she performs her various kinds of work, transcending the limiting oppositional discourse of the "stay-at-home" or "working" mother. Milkmother memoir allows women to avoid the danger of sacrificial logics, in which identity must be forged out of the repression or sacrifice of other parts of the personality. It allows us to explore the ambiguities in the creative, hybrid, dynamic, and adaptive identities we inhabit. This fertile tension between multiple and contradictory selves can be developed, not as a source of crippling anxiety, conflict and guilt, but as a richly textured, empowered, and generative complexity, offering powerful potential for the creation of a new feminine imaginary.

The cognitive dissonance I have struggled with as I inhabit the masculinist paradigm of my own profession (Douglas "The Rise"), and my witness of patients' struggle with discordance between their lived milkmother experience and the cultural expectations around them, have motivated me to write creatively. Memoir, and therefore the milkmother memoir, is a culturally disruptive practice, a counter-narrative, and as such, is powerfully suited to my task. Fiction veils and protects; memoir carries the power of an identifiable individual willing to bear witness in the public domain; willing to invite the reader's identification, in the hope that she will help free others from the corrosive effects of loneliness, shame and secrecy.

In *Bone Mother*, I am what Gillian Whitlock calls the "disobedient subject," who subverts sentimentalized and medicalised representations of herself. I take the culturally intelligible and authorized performance of medical identity, and contest this. In *Bone Mother*, I am the recalcitrant, non-compliant, leaky milkmother body. I draw the reader into my world and my identity, then resist the dominant frames of interpretation, hoping to change the reader's mind. In Buss's words, I have found in memoir the perfect medium to embroider my own rebellious discourse (xv).

THE ETHICS OF WRITING IN MILK

The right of every woman to tell her story—even if she becomes a mother—has been hard-won.[7] But our stories inevitably intersect and intertwine with the stories of others. To write about oneself is also always to write about others. So how can we tell our story without intruding upon others, without exposing or exploiting them? How can we tell our story without causing distress to those we love?

I was acutely aware, as I wrote my "memoir in milk," of the absolute need to maintain professional codes of confidentiality: in that, there is no ethical ambivalence. But beyond professional considerations, relational responsibility remains acutely problematic in milkmother writing, and demands wise navigation through the borderlands of fact and fiction, of silence and speaking out. Until now, much of the debate about the ethics of life writing in the media and critical literature has concerned the author's right to artistic expression—her right to a creative voice—in tension with the reader's right to veracity. In the past fifteen years, this debate has changed the way memoir is written, so that now writers are careful to notify the reader when a good story may be incongruent with the facts. Memoir, however, also asks us to consider the rights of those whose stories we tell.

A teenaged child, for example, is unable to give adequately informed and independent consent for use of her story in a parent's memoir, since she is still too young to comprehend the potential implications of publication. The problems of story ownership are even more pronounced in milkmother memoir because of the extreme vulnerability and dependence of young children in the first years of life. How do we write in milk, as Cixous asks of us, and still protect a child's right to privacy? The father is fundamentally important to the child, even when he has not been kind to the mother or responsible in his relationship with his child. To what extent should the mother protect resisting subjects who are identifiable due to their shared relationship with a child? Should the mother abandon her right to tell that part of her story that intersects with an irresponsible father?—who, by virtue of irresponsibility or obdurate unkindness or worse, may have painfully affected much of her life as the child grew up?

For many years I dodged the complex ethical dilemmas that milkmother memoir poses because of my own powerful desire to write and make sense of my life as a younger woman. I came to terms with defamation laws, which protect an individual's right to a positive reputation, when I re-wrote my children's father as an unrecognisable fictional character. Imagination, confabulation, and the deletion of aspects of my experience now disguise him. I put my writing of *Bone Mother* aside for long periods in part because of my concern to protect my children, and to avoid further complications in my relationships with both the children's father and my family of origin. The ethical problems often seemed too hard to solve.

Beyond respect for legal constraints, there are no definite solutions to the ethical problems posed by milkmother memoir. The only certainty is that an ethical writer will make a considered response to the issues. I've formed the view that writing about highly relational lives in a way that protects loved ones' privacies means that there will be some parts of my text that are difficult to discern, some stories that can never be told. Milkmother memoir demands that I abandon any desire for revenge, that I allow the anger to wash away with the years, that I allow parts of my story to be swallowed in silence, perhaps forever. This silence is both an act of self-respect, and of love for the children.

My children enjoyed reading about their younger selves (or at least how I, their mother, perceived their younger selves) on the back of scrap paper when they were growing up. Allowing them to access selected parts of my writing became an extension of my mothering, positively reinforcing their developing sense of self. They felt they must be important to be in print like that, even if only we three read the stories! However, an intention to publish these stories in the public domain challenges my private maternal role as custodian of stories and identity. Willa McDonald discussed the ethical problem of parent memoir as she grappled with her own commissioned memoir concerning her adopted child. In the end, she put her responsibility as mother first, her identity as writer second, and shelved the memoir.

Even as adults, children remain vulnerable to hurt in a conflicted family situation. My daughter, settled permanently in New York, has told me directly and kindly, when I asked if she would like to see it in preparation for publication, that it is my story, not hers, and she wants to wait until she is over thirty before she reads it. My son, studying and playing volleyball in Canada, has gamely said he'd like to read it "one day." He's actually very busy at the moment, he points out. Although they both trust me to be fair, and protective of their interests, they know my story will refer to their father in ways that are likely to be uncomfortable for them, even if he is radically disguised in the text. Both say they are keen to see me publish soon, but have they given me adequate consent? I don't believe so. Can I go ahead anyway? Although they live overseas at the moment, and perhaps would never have to confront the public implications of their mother's writing, I have made, for now, a decision to publish only after they are ready to read it.

Though a milky ink is sometimes hard to read, it is no longer merely a palimpsest. The painful re-writing of *Bone Mother* as I grappled with my concerns about others' shared privacies over many years, has significantly strengthened my story. Using milk as ink offers the writer opportunities for a more complex and imaginative engagement with her lived experience than would otherwise be necessary. As I've worked creatively with the acutely relational substrate of my life in *Bone Mother*, writing in milk has demanded of me a sensitive, complicated, and intensely moral intelligence.

THE BODY EXTREME

Johnson's *A Better Woman*, published in 1999, is a groundbreaking innovation in Australian women's writing, a pioneering example of milkmother memoir. Johnson declares on her website: "I couldn't find any books which told me what it felt like to be a mother," and locates this book as a direct response to the milkmother's silence, a courageous step towards the creation of a feminine imaginary: "I wanted to give a voice to the voiceless, to the thousands and millions of stories of motherhood which had never been told" ("A Better").

In her introduction to *A Better Woman*, Johnson addresses the complex relationship between fact, memory and a good story, stating that her book, "like all books, is composed of half truth and half lie" (xii). She claims her power to withhold: "As the teller of the tale I have revealed only those details I wish you to know" (xv). She declares that any self she reveals is inevitably conditional, contingent, and subject to artifice: "Although this book is not fiction, it shares fiction's pruning and shaping and therefore cannot hope to offer you my naked self laid bare" (xii). I learnt from Johnson that readers tolerate "fiction's pruning" in memoir if the writer is honest about dishonesty. Her memoir is, nevertheless, a daring foray into her interiority. Johnson warns us that we will receive enough of her truth to be shocked. She throws down a challenge to any sentimentalized, Virginal ideas of motherhood with the audacious words: "Here I stand anyway, your worst nightmare" (xiii).

A Better Woman tells the story of how Johnson's children's births, and an unusual and distressing complication, a recto-vaginal fistula, affected her life. Bad things do happen to maternal bodies sometimes that cannot be predicted or avoided. She shows us her intimate injury and her medicalisation without shame (or shows us her initial shame and her decision to transcend it), contesting romanticised ideas of perfect childbirth and happy outcomes. Of birth, Johnson says: "I tried to remember a baby was coming but the thought kept escaping me and I kept finding only pain to remember, pain to dwell in, pain that was me. … 'I need an epidural,' I shouted, beginning to scream" (30). But most importantly, Johnson lays her experience of illness and injury alongside the bliss, grit and satisfactions of her milk years. The heroism of this refusal to be defined by the abject, the sentimental, or the medical moves the reader. Instead, we admire her enduring jouissance, her indomitable spirit—and the wisdom that emerges out of the poetic physicality of her love for her babies.

Of breastfeeding, Johnson writes: "When he is awake he wants only your arms to hold him, only your milk to swallow, only the smell of your breath" (59). Of the blurring of time: "He lived mainly in a cot by our bed and when I wasn't feeding him I rocked his cradle with one hand to try and get him to sleep. I would rock until my hand slipped in exhaustion and every time he woke again crying to be fed I was sure

I had just that minute finished feeding him" (46). Johnson concludes her writing—her other work—with the relief and astonishment of any mother completing a project, or dealing with illness, or both, at the same time as she cares for small children: "And listen to this: reader, I made it to the end" (254). Here, she names what has been her central task: the writing of her milkmother story, a professional writer's performance of work, which has occurred alongside her performance of work as milkmother. In the phrase "I made it to the end," she addresses us in a pleased tone, reminiscent of Jane Eyre in Charlotte Brontë's novel: "Reader, I married him"(498). There was no story beyond marriage that Jane, or Brontë, could speak. Now, a hundred and fifty years and half a dozen generations of women later, Johnson not only writes a stunning memoir that speaks herself as milkmother, but writes it at the same time as she cares for young children.

Modjeska observes that Johnson faced significant problems in writing her memoir: "There was an ethical minefield to weave through" (197). These ethical dilemmas are, I contend, the specific problems of any milkmother memoir, and promise a fertile complexity and restraint. Johnson herself deals bluntly with relational ethics: "While I am free to write about myself I am not free to write about my husband or sons" (xv). She does, however, still manage to describe her young family with a writer's precise eye for detail, at the same time as she conceals individual personalities and identities.

In her discussion of Johnson's memoir, Modjeska re-iterates the word "extreme," describing it as an "extraordinarily intimate memoir" (197) that deals with "extreme intimacy of bodily malfunction," and "extremities of physical disintegration" (198). She recognises Johnson's writing of the body as an uncommon act, deep and exposing. It's my privilege to inhabit this intimate world of the extreme body, every working day. Familiarity with the body, and in particular, with the female body, is a gift given to me by a profession that has often caused me to despair. In writing my own manuscript, *Bone Mother*, I find in milkmother memoir a genre that enables me to normalise profound bodily intimacy, so that we can speak of the body of the milkmother without disgust, without anxiety, without shame. I hope the reader will then understand that the milkmother is not "extreme." Or, if she is, then each of us is extreme in our bodily reality, because our fragile flesh is forever poised on the edge of death, even as we give forth life, and this is ordinary. It's not that we shouldn't be afraid, exactly, since bringing new life into this chaotic mortal world is inevitably frightening, but milkmother memoir teaches us that we can draw strength from another woman's story, that we can celebrate our jouissance and our heroism, and that we are not alone.

ENDNOTES

[1]Infants are many times more likely to die in developing countries than in countries like mine; less than one percent of the half a million women who die each year in childbirth are from more developed countries ("Maternal Morality"). However, the Australian Bureau of Statistics reports that the maternal mortality ratio for Indigenous women in 2003-2005 was almost three times higher than for non-Indigenous women, and in 2006-2010 the Indigenous infant mortality rate was twice that of non-Indigenous infants (Australian Indigenous HealthInfoNet).

[2]Caring for a disabled child may remain milkmother work for the whole of that child's life, and applying this term may help to communicate the particular, often overwhelming, problems these families face. Fathers and other male carers may capably perform the work of the milkmother, but because my own experience is female, and because around the world women are still predominantly responsible for the care of their young children, this essay limits itself to female experience. (Across cultures, small children have been principally cared for by women, although only rarely exclusively by a mother in the absence of other involved adults or older children.) A woman may become a mother without passing through a milkmother phase, by caring for older children who are not her biological offspring, but she may also become a milkmother by caring for or adopting a child still in his or her milk years. Many women, having once conceived and become a milkmother, identify as mothers for the rest of their lives, regardless of intervening miscarriage, stillbirth or death of a child. Milkmothers are not necessarily heterosexual, and belong to the many diverse cultures and the entire spectrum of class and socioeconomic positioning which characterise human societies.

[3]I am currently contracted to write a book about unsettled babies, which aims to make sense of this often distressing problem by applying strategies similar to those I employ in *Bone Mother*. In my crying baby book, I tell stories about and reflect upon my experiences as an older

woman, a clinician, and a researcher, in order to lay open the evidence.
[4]These include Sue Woolfe's *Leaning Toward Infinity*, and Amanda Lohrey's *The Philosopher's Doll*.

[5]Extract from a thesis prospectus that I delivered in 2003 to my fellow students and staff at the University of Queensland, in the School of English, Media Studies and Art History.

[6]That's not to say that early diagnosis and treatment of perinatal anxiety and depression is not important, because maternal suffering, adverse effects on the infant, and even loss of life can be avoided with appropriate intervention. It's just that we should also be careful not to pathologise unnecessarily, because of the negative effects this may have upon a woman's sense of self and empowerment.

[7]The capacity to write one's story requires a degree of material comfort and leisure, privileges not available to women in many parts of the world.

WORKS CITED

Adelaide, Debra, ed. *Motherlove: Stories about Birth, Babies and Beyond.* Milsons Point, NSW: Random, 1996. Print.

Australian Indigenous HealthInfoNet. "Mortality." *Health Info Net.ecu. edu.au.* 8 April 2013. Web. 13 May 2013.

Bartlett, Alison. *Breastwork: Rethinking Breastfeeding.* Sydney: University of New South Wales Press Press, 2005. Print.

Bartlett, Alison. *Jamming the Machinery: Contemporary Australian Women's Writing.* Canberra: Association for the Study of Australian Literature, 1998. Print.

Brontë, Charlotte. *Jane Eyre.* 1847. London: Penguin, 1996. Print.

Buss, Helen M. *Repossessing the World: Reading Memoirs by Contemporary Women.* Waterloo: Wilfrid Laurier University Press, 2002. Print.

Campbell, Marion. "Spectacular Motherhood." *Motherlode.* Eds. Stephanie Holt and Maryanne Lynch. Melbourne: Sybylla Feminist, 1996. 1-10. Print.

Charon, Rita. "Narrative Medicine: A Model for Empathy, Reflection, Profession, and Trust." *Journal of the American Medical Association* 286 (2001): 1897-1901. Print.

Cixous, Hélène. "The Laugh of the Medusa." *New French Feminisms: An Anthology.* Eds. Elaine Marks and Isabelle de Courtivron. Brighton, Sussex: Harvester, 1981. 245-64. Print.

Dalziell, Rosamund. *Shameful Autobiographies: Shame in Contemporary Australian Autobiographies and Culture.* Carlton: Melbourne University Press, 1999. Print.

Douglas, Pamela. "The Rise and Fall of Infant Reflux: The Limits of Evidence-Based Medicine." *Griffith Review* 32 (2011): 241-254. Print.

Grosz, Elizabeth. *Volatile Bodies: Towards a Corporeal Feminism.* St Leonards: Allen and Unwin, 1994. Print.

Hansen, Jane. *Three Seasons.* Sydney: Pan Macmillan, 2007. Print.

Holt, Stephanie, and Maryanne Lynch, eds. *Motherlode.* Melbourne: Sybylla Feminist, 1996. Print.

Jantzen, Grace M. *Becoming Divine: Towards a Feminist Philosophy of Religion.* Manchester: Manchester University Press, 1998. Print.

Johnson, Susan. *A Better Woman, A Memoir.* Sydney: Random, 1999.

Johnson, Susan. "A Better Woman, A Memoir." *Susan Johnson: Australian Author, Website and Blog.* 2005. Web. 4 Aug. 2005.

Jones, Ann Rosalind. "Writing the Body: Toward an Understanding of L'ecriture Feminine." *Feminisms: An Anthology of Literary Theory and Criticism.* Eds. Robyn Warhol and Diane Price Herndle. 2nd ed. New Brunswick, NJ: Rutgers University Press, 1997. 357-70. Print.

Key, Sarah. "Freddie: Diary of a Cot Death." *SarahKey.com.* n.d. Web. 10 May 2013.

Kirkby, Joan. "The Call of the Mother in the Fiction of Elizabeth Jolley." *Journal of the South Pacific Association for Commonwealth Literature and Language Studies* 26 (1988): 46-63. Print.

Kristeva, Julia. "Motherhood According to Giovanni Bellini." Trans. Thomas Gora, Alice Jardine and Leon S. Roudiez. *Desire in Language: A Semiotic Approach to Literature and Art.* Ed. Leon S. Roudiez. New York: Columbia University Press, 1980. 237-70. Print.

Kristeva, Julia. "Stabat Mater." *The Kristeva Reader.* Ed. Toril Moi. New York: Columbia University Press, 1986. 161-85. Print.

Larson, Thomas. *The Memoir and the Memoirist: Reading and Writing Personal Narrative.* Athens: Swallow Press/Ohio University Press, 2007. Print.

"Litany of Loreto." *A Prayerbook for Adults.* Homebush, NSW: St Pauls, n.d. 256-58. Print.

Lohrey, Amanda. *The Philosopher's Doll.* Sydney: Vintage Random House Australia, 2004. Print.

Maher, Janemaree. "Rethinking Women's Birth Experience: Medical

Frameworks and Personal Narratives." *Hecate* 29.2 (2003): 140-51. Print.

Martin, Emily. *The Woman in the Body: A Cultural Analysis of Reproduction*. Boston: Beacon Press, 1992. Print.

"Maternal Mortality." World Health Organization, May 2012. Web. 3 July 2013.

Maushart, Susan. *The Mask of Motherhood: How Mothering Changes Everything and Why We Pretend It Doesn't*. Milsons Point, NSW: Random, 1997. Print.

McDonald, Donna. *Jack's Story*. Sydney: Allen and Unwin, 1991. Print.

McDonald, Willa. "Letter to My Daughter: Ethical Dilemmas in the Writing of a Memoir." *Text* 14 (2010): 1-12. Print.

Modjeska, Drusilla. "Apprentice Piece." *Timepieces*. Ed. Drusilla Modjeska. Sydney: Picador, 2002. 3-40. Print.

Nicolson, Nigel, ed. *The Sickle Side of the Moon: The Letters of Virginia Woolf*. London: Hogarth, 1979.

Place, Fiona. "Apocalypse Now." *Motherlove: Stories about Birth, Babies and Beyond*. Ed. Debra Adelaide. Milsons Point, NSW: Random, 1996. 43-70. Print.

Rich, Adrienne. *Of Woman Born: Motherhood as Experience and Institution*. London: Virago, 1977. Print.

Walker, Michelle Boulous. *Philosophy and the Maternal Body: Reading Silence*. London: Routledge, 1998. Print.

Weir, Alison. *Sacrificial Logics: Feminist Theory and the Critique of Identity*. New York: Routledge, 1996. Print.

Whitlock, Gillian. "Introduction: Disobedient Subjects." *Autographs: Contemporary Australian Autobiography*. Ed. Gillian Whitlock. St Lucia: University of Queensland Press, 1996. ix-xxx. Print.

Woolf, Virginia. "A Sketch of the Past." *Moments of Being: Unpublished Autobiographical Writing*. Ed. Jeanne Schulkind. London: Sussex University Press, 1976. Print.

Woolfe, Sue. *Leaning Toward Infinity: How My Mother's Apron Unfolds into My Life*. Boston: Faber and Faber, 1997. Print.

6.
"Where's the Funeral?"
Maternal Silences in Memoirs of Postpartum Depression

JUSTINE DYMOND

> A recognition of women's unquenchable creativity—contained
> so often within domestic limits, yet astounding in its diversi-
> ty—has been one of the deep perceptions of a feminism which
> looks with fresh eyes on all that has been trivialized, devalued,
> forbidden, or silenced in female history.
> —Adrienne Rich, "Motherhood: The Contemporary
> Emergency and the Quantum Leap" (262-263)

ON A RED-EYE FLIGHT from San Francisco to Dallas on my way home to Massachusetts more than four years ago, I sat next to a mother and her two-month-old baby. When I guessed her baby's age correctly, she was impressed. I told her my little one was almost two and apparently my age-guessing abilities hadn't yet faded. What was most poignant to me as I sat next to this first-time mother was how calm and easy-going she was for a new, nursing mom traveling alone by plane with her newborn in the wee hours. Her appearance, at least, seemed unruffled. At one point, I held up a blanket for her to have some privacy while settling her little boy into nursing, and at other times I cradled him in my arms while she gathered her things. I marveled at how small he was. I asked her how he slept and she said, "Wonderful." And to top it off, she was flying to D.C. to visit her sister, also a new mom with a one-month-old. Two newborns in one house: it made me shudder to imagine.

While I had trouble recreating the sense-memory of the weight of my daughter as an infant (even though I remembered holding her so much in those first few months that my arms ached), I could recall vividly my own very ruffled self from those first months. Nursing hurt like hell, and I felt like a milking cow with my daughter breastfeeding every two hours. Worse, my daughter didn't sleep soundly for more than an hour—two, if we were lucky—at a time. I recently remarked to someone that I realize now how much lingering trauma there is in sleep-deprivation. For nearly eleven months, my husband and I got four hours of uninterrupted sleep only once or twice a week. Though our daughter has been sleeping through the night now, at five, for nearly a year, I still have trouble sleeping soundly myself and will wake sometimes two or three times during the night. But the more lasting effect is that I am hyper vigilant about her sleep schedule and my bedtime habits, beyond what is necessary now. If something threatens to disrupt her nighttime routine by even a half-hour, I'm anxious and fearful that she won't sleep. The anxiety in turn makes it difficult for me to relax and enjoy time spent with her or social evenings out with my husband and friends.

On top of sleep deprivation, I developed pregnancy-induced carpal tunnel syndrome that lasted about 18 months after my daughter's birth. The constant holding and the ridiculously difficult-to-maneuver baby equipment exacerbated the pain. There I would be, driving around Amherst and Pelham with my arm braces on, trying to get the baby to nap for 45 minutes, effectively giving up the 20 minutes of naptime I might be able to extract for myself between rocking her to sleep and when she woke up screaming in her crib.

Besides exhaustion, the effects of severe sleep-deprivation include depression and irritability (though my husband, who suffered as much sleeplessness as I did, never developed depression). "Depression" and "irritability" seem like understatements. If I wasn't too tired to think, I was usually smoldering with repressed anger, at anything and anybody. This situation was not helped by my precarious employment. Between teaching appointments, I did not have access to maternity leave, paid or unpaid. Seven weeks and change after my daughter's birth, I went back to work, teaching 2/3rds time as a postdoctoral fellow. If I hadn't signed the contract while I was still pregnant, I would have most likely turned it down. And I was fortunate enough to contemplate this—my husband's job provided our health insurance and enough income to support us all if need be.[2] But instead I worried about my CV, my future employability, etc. And I gritted my teeth and stepped back into the classroom and discovered the joys of a mechanical breast pump.

What I didn't know at the time was that, in addition to the physical adjustments to motherhood, I was depressed, and very likely experiencing postpartum depression (PPD).

I am drawn to examining three motherhood memoirs about PPD by women who were writers before they were mothers—Marrit Ingman's *Inconsolable: How I Threw My Mental Health Out with the Diapers* (2005), Heather Armstrong's *It Sucked and Then I Cried: How I Had a Baby, a Breakdown, and a Much Needed Margarita* (2009), and Adrienne Martini's *Hillbilly Gothic: A Memoir of Madness and Motherhood* (2006)—in particular because of my own identity as a writer whose experience with PPD manifested itself in writing, or, I should say, not writing. A longtime journal keeper, I have huge gaps of months and even years when I could not write about my experience with PPD. Even while I write this, I fail at adequately recreating the experience in words. Mostly, I remember that we had a hard time and the reasons why. Of course, the sudden change in lifestyle that usually accompanies new parenthood kept me away from the pen and the computer. But when I was able to find time to write, the anxiety and anger was so deafening that when the words did come out, I found myself unable to face the negativity of my own thoughts. Where I had once found solace in writing, I found no refuge from my own rage. Where I once rehearsed language to represent experience and find insight, my language seemed to close down rather than open up possibilities of meaning.

That these memoirs were written by women who identified as writers *before* they became mothers was important to me, but initially these memoirs drew me in because I wanted to find at least a glimmer of a reflection of my own experience. What these writers do is make clear that PPD requires medical attention and treatment. However, as I will also explore here, these memoirs to different degrees acknowledge the cultural contexts that create silences even within the narrations of women's experiences with PPD. These silences—both inside and outside the memoirs—at times expose what is the limit of the speakable in a culture that still idealizes motherhood. In other words, as in all literature, the *what* of our stories is shaped by *how* we tell those stories, but illness, perhaps especially mental illness, doesn't always fulfill the narrative expectations readers bring to memoirs. In particular, the confessional dynamic of the memoir genre privileges the individual's revelation of "sin," i.e., madness, and movement to "redemption" through institutionalization and/or medication, but PPD doesn't always follow such a clearly demarcated narrative path.

In a radio interview on NPR-affiliate WAMC,[3] Rebecca Wolff, from whose poem I borrowed the first half of this chapter's title, "Where's the funeral?",[1] discusses her poem as an expression of "a really really bad postpartum depression that I experienced." The title, as she explains, is meant ironically, in the voice of another person asking, "'Why are you looking so glum, new mom?'" In the interview, Wolff also discusses her use of blank spaces on the page to express what "literally there are no words for" or, alternately, what might be more "satisfying" for the reader to fill in.

In this way, the elliptical and paratactic form of poetry lends itself to the expression of what isn't said, and the novel has long been a genre where the unspeakable can appear on the page.[4] I am not ready to suggest that the kinds of silences that burrow through memoirs of PPD offer comfort, enlightenment, or resistance. But by speaking and writing from, through, and out of silence, Armstrong, Martini, and Ingman lay down a foundation for the more deliberate and strategic silences we see in poetry and fiction to happen in memoir.

SILENCES OF OMISSION

The *Diagnostic and Statistical Manual of Mental Disorders* describes PPD as not differing from other depressions except for the timing, "within four weeks after childbirth" (422). PPD symptoms include "fluctuations in mood, mood lability, and preoccupation with infant well-being, the intensity of which may range from overconcern to frank delusions" (422). The DSM is a clinical reference book, not usually consulted by postpartum women. The books for expecting and new mothers that I read while I was pregnant and early in my mothering, as well-intentioned as they try to be, often offer minimal information on PPD, or worse, information that could be easily misunderstood. La Leche League's *The Womanly Art of Breastfeeding*, which I consulted frequently while learning how to nurse my daughter, devotes one-and-a-half pages to PPD, most of which is focused on encouraging the mother to continue to breastfeed regardless of what help she seeks for depression. While in no way does the book suggest that mothers *not* get help for depression, the implied message is that breastfeeding is the main priority, as in these sentences:

"Ending the breastfeeding relationship can be very difficult for a mother emotionally and sudden weaning may cause hormonal changes that intensify her depression. Any decisions about how to treat postpartum depression should take this into account" (336).

The Nursing Mother's Companion (whose cover boasts, "Over 750,000 Copies Sold!") devotes just over three pages to "Depression and Anxiety" (137-140), and, unlike *The Womanly Art of Breastfeeding*, does include an extensive list of symptoms and of "coping measures." Perhaps it's not fair to expect manuals on breastfeeding to give a lot of page space to PPD. Though I have not conducted a systematic study of these manuals, the ones I did read while pregnant and a new mother lacked the information I needed to recognize what I was experiencing.

In one of the books I primarily consulted during pregnancy, Dr. Miriam Stoppard's *Conception, Pregnancy and Birth*, the description of PPD symptoms includes "hopelessness and despondency ... lethargy, anxiety, tension, panic, sleep difficulties, loss of interest in sex, obsessional thoughts, guilt feelings, and lack of self-esteem and concentration" (361). I recognize my postpartum self in only two of the symptoms: anxiety and tension. (I exclude "sleep difficulties" only in that it is hard to discern which came first, sleep difficulties as a result of PPD or PPD as a result of sleep difficulties, though there might be no distinction of origin in my case.) Most descriptions of symptoms, including the narrative example on the next page in Stoppard's book, focus on the mother not wanting to get out of bed and crying constantly. My symptoms seemed almost the opposite of those: I could barely keep still, and I was angry nearly constantly, crying only occasionally. The image of a disturbed bee comes to mind, buzzing anxiously and vigilantly around the baby.

Penelope Leach's *Your Baby & Child* ("More than 2 Million Copies Sold") devotes one paragraph to "The blues" and not quite one page to "Postpartum depression." During my worst hours, I never even thought of consulting Leach's book, perhaps because the title suggested to me that it was exclusively focused on the needs of the child (which, of course, now strikes me as illogical—the mother's *needs* are not easily separable from the baby's). If I had read Leach, I might have welcomed her saying, "Depression is a real illness," "Depression drains everything of joy and color, saps your self-confidence and energy and turns you in upon yourself in anxious spirals," and "So, if you should suffer from postpartum depression, you will need practical and emotional, and possibly medical, help quickly and as much for your baby's sake as for your own" (52-3). Reading these sentences now, I do wonder about the hesitation in "possibly" in the second sentence. How easy it is to deny the severity of PPD, especially by the person experiencing it.

For me, there was a silence in the popular medical literature about PPD, a silence of omission—my experience didn't seem to match, so I did not consider that I was depressed. Instead, for a year, I consulted and tried every possible strategy for getting the baby to sleep, except the oh-so-demonized Ferber method. And I kept my serious doubts about my "naturalness" for mothering quiet. I silenced myself.

SILENCING MEDIA IMAGES

I also did not recognize myself in the popular media's narratives of PPD. It was, and still is, a phenomenon understood by many through the filter of sensationalized media images: Susan Smith's racist testimony that a black man hijacked her children when she had drowned them herself, Andrea Yates's drowning of her five children,[5] or Melanie Stokes's suicidal jump from a hotel's twelfth floor. These kinds of sensationalized public images silence meaningful conversation about PPD. Who wants to be in the same category as Andrea Yates?[6]

Even when women in the public eye have brought thoughtful attention to PPD, there has been a media firestorm. In 2005, Brooke Shields released her memoir *Down Came The Rain: My Journey Through Postpartum Depression.* This public revelation of an experience many women keep private was met with an immediate backlash; most publicized was Tom Cruise's claim that Shields's use of Paxil was a mistake and that she should have used vitamin supplements.[7] At the time of this tabloid debate, which I glimpsed in headlines while waiting in grocery checkout lines, I was experiencing my own struggle with PPD, but, still, while I scoffed at Cruise's ignorance, I didn't identify with the experience of a superstar model and actress. Most women, like me, do not experience PPD in these extremes, or in front of news cameras. Instead, postpartum depression most often feels like the slow burn of the 1950s housewife melancholia: everything looks perfect, why doesn't it feel perfect?

The truth of the physical experience of motherhood is not frequently represented in mainstream culture, except as an alarmist narrative (e.g., the television show "Pregnant"), or a saccharin coated image of the peaceful, loving, caring mother gazing at her newborn. It's also hard to find the truth about pregnancy and birth, which can be a physically distorting and crippling experience.[8] In her chapter on "milkmother" memoirs in this collection, Pamela Douglas notes, "I noticed that an *imaginative* silence about the transfigurative maternal body prevailed upon my bookshelves at home" (105). Despite our medical technology, what happens to a woman's body is more akin to *Aliens* than a *National Geographic* special on the birds and the bees: nausea, heartburn, swollen ankles, vaginal tearing, hemorrhoids at best; diabetes, high blood pressure, fistulas, toxemia, and worse, at the other end of the spectrum. Like Douglas, Carroll Smith-Rosenberg argues that the medicalization of pregnancy and childbirth has historically "reflected and helped shape social definitions of the appropriate bounds of woman's role and identity" (59), which can invasively and alarmingly contribute to a woman's sense of inadequacy. The lack of truthful representation of women's pregnant, birthing, and lactating bodies in popular culture and literature can further compound women's unrealistic expectations of what motherhood *should* be like.

Given that the sentient experience of motherhood is rarely represented with much accuracy, then it comes as no surprise that truthful representations of the mental health experiences of mothers are even rarer. As with most, if not all, mental health disorders, the public discussion of PPD is masked by fear, social repression, and a basic reluctance to see PPD as part of a larger cultural problem rooted in images and narratives of "perfect" mothering, the "othering" of mental illness, and the criminalization of illness.

As a result, those with PPD suffer the silence that accompanies the stigma of mental illness in general. Mental health disorders are still whispered ailments. Like cancer used to be. Or AIDS. In her memoir *Inconsolable*, Ingman bluntly notes, "I'd discovered from my own experience socializing with other mothers that we could talk about just about anything other than mental illness. We could eat braised puppy and defecate on each other before the topic of PPD would come up" (39). The costs (or punishments, if you want) for coming out about PPD are evident. Shields's experience is a case in point. Why was Tom Cruise allowed a public platform for his blatant ignorance? I commend Shields[9] for paving the way for us lesser mortals. Most of us are not celebrities, but that doesn't mean we have less at stake; in fact, as Hilary Clark points out, Shields had some control over the effect of her "coming out": "While celebrities are not likely to accept lucrative endorsement offers from the makers of Paxil and Effexor, narratives of mental illness do sell; celebrities like Shields can gain positive exposure—and, to some extent, control over the consequences of publication—from doing interviews and appearing on talk shows" (452).

For the rest of us non-celebrities, the stigma of mental illness—notwithstanding the near banality of Prozac-popping—is still alive. But PPD has the added stigma of "bad" motherhood, another avenue for blaming women for not being perfect. Rich was one of the first feminists to speak about this double-bind of motherhood:

> A society which penalizes some children because they are not white, others because they are not male, indoctrinating in them a sense of worthlessness, can still lay the blame for the waste of its young on the 'bad' mothers who have somehow failed to be superhuman, who have somehow failed to rear, in a callous and ruthless social order, well-adjusted, obedient, achieving, nonalienated children. ("Motherhood" 364)

More recently, Jocelyn Fenton Stitt argues that, following Catherine Kohler Riessman's work, "The medicalization of negative reactions to motherhood as 'postpartum depression' has served to let women defend themselves against accusations of being bad and uncaring mothers" (345). While the recent surge and relative openness in memoirs about postpartum depression perhaps reflect this "defense," I contend that stigma surrounding mental illness combined with the deeply entrenched ideologies about motherhood continue to restrict and shape what women can say about experiencing PPD. The social strictures, cultural expectations and assumptions of what can be said by mothers about their own experiences—and, let's face it, the fear of *blame* for what is out of our control—create pages of silence, even when there are words on the page.

MEMOIRS BREAKING THE SILENCES

I didn't find another narrative that came close to what I experienced until I read Heather B. Armstrong's memoir. Blogger and author of *It Sucked and Then I Cried*, Armstrong writes, "The depression came and went and then came again, but the anxiety was constant. I could barely eat anything and couldn't sleep, even though I'd tried every sleeping pill available at the pharmacy. I wanted to commit suicide if only because then I wouldn't have to feel the pain of being awake anymore" (190). Armstrong uses the words "pain" to describe the experience of PPD. By identifying that depression hurts—whether physically or psychologically, or both—Armstrong allows those who haven't experienced it to understand PPD as a medical concern. I've never had a migraine, but I've had headaches, and so I can imagine how crippling the pain might be.

And PPD *is* a medical condition. I emphasize the medical nature of PPD because the myth that PPD is merely "baby blues" or raging hormones that just need time to settle down still circulates. Recognizing that PPD is a serious condition requiring medical attention is imperative if we want to see mothers *and* children lead healthy lives and not waste their lives (or lose their lives) in undiagnosed suffering.

Armstrong's memoir humorously recounts the tedium of new parenthood and how the anticipation of the tedium can exacerbate anxiety: "The expanse of the day unfolded before me and I couldn't comprehend how I was going to distract my cranky baby for the next twelve hours. There'd be walks and more walks and books and rattles and moving from the porch to the sidewalk and back to the porch to delay her disappointment just a few more minutes" (168). For a healthy parent, taking care of an infant can be at various times tedious, overwhelming, frustrating, and terrifying; with depression, these feelings remain constant or almost always constant.

In Chapter Nine, when we get the first extended discussion of Armstrong's PPD, she describes her daughter Leta's increasing "fussiness," refusal to nap during the day, and her screaming:

> My daily life felt like torture. I struggled to make it from hour to hour. I felt like I didn't know what I was doing. I was trying to find the humor in all of it, but I couldn't ignore the crushing misery any longer.
>
> There were many things about parenthood that I understood intellectually. I knew that this period of her life was only temporary and that things would eventually get better. I knew that I was a good mother and that I was meeting her needs as a baby. But depression isn't about understanding this intellec-

tually. It's about an overshadowing emotional spiral that makes coping with anything nearly impossible. (Armstrong 123)

Armstrong's account of PPD is curiously a double-narrative, of the experience itself and of the experience of blogging it. In both streams of her narrative, she includes a frank description of institutionalization. If there's anything this memoir does—and it does a lot—is tell Armstrong's story of PPD unplugged, to use rock-star parlance. And for those of us who have experienced PPD, Armstrong is a rock star. She has a huge fan base on her blog *dooce.com*, and her blog entry that announced she was admitting herself to a psych ward was probably one of the bravest, most honest[10] pieces of writing I have ever seen on the Internet.

Writing in retrospect in her memoir, Armstrong maintains her honesty, sometimes shockingly so:

> I kept thinking that my depression would go away, that my self-medication was going to work. But I should have known better than anyone else that this just doesn't go away. In fact, it festered and grew until one morning I found myself throwing things in the general direction of loving and wonderful people who did not deserve to have things thrown in their general direction. It had entered my blood stream and was systematically choking me to death. (168)

The virus-strangler metaphor notwithstanding, Armstrong does not shy away from identifying her anger as a central symptom of her illness. Festering anger is bound to erupt in violence, and, yet, anger can be a productive tool for individual and cultural change. Armstrong finds her "salvation" in the correct combination of medications and makes individual change. After committing herself to a hospital, she sees a psychiatrist who "had treated hundreds of women just like" her and promised that what he would prescribe her would work (196). She writes:

> I cannot express how much I liked this doctor. I felt a huge sense of relief and safety in being under the care of someone who knew so much about how to treat postpartum depression. At one point in our conversation he set down his pen and paper, paused, and then looked at me and said, "You poor woman. I

am so sorry for what you have been through." And I cried. I cried hard. My God, what I had been through. (196)

The doctor's recognition of the pain and suffering of PPD is an extraordinary moment, one that recreates in me my own sense of relief, now that I am no longer experiencing PPD. However, there is a part of me that sees in this scene a parallel to the confessional with the priest offering salvation: "*My God*, what I had been through."

Armstrong's frankness appears to be—and *is* in many ways—a clear voice breaking through the silence and stigma about PPD. And yet Armstrong's willingness to lay herself bare, almost literally, on the page (e.g., grisly detail about her battle with constipation) might be seen as a kind of masking, in the way that tell-all memoirs aim for shock value rather than insight. Armstrong's insight is often delivered obliquely through humor. For example, two weeks after the baby's birth, she and her husband:

> ...decided that it was time to face my new worst fear ... the fear of taking Leta to a public place. I was frightened of the diseases that lurked in public places, viruses that could have wreaked havoc on the immune system of a fourteen-day-old baby, but I was more scared of being that woman with the screaming baby that I'd so often wanted to choke or beat with a wooden club. I had to keep reminding myself that the worst thing that could happen would be that she would start crying and either Jon or I would pick her up and comfort her while the other stuffed groceries into the shopping cart. It wasn't like Leta would all of a sudden stand up in her car seat, pull out a machine gun, and open fire on unsuspecting grocery shoppers. (91)

Armstrong's humor seduces me as a reader, especially as it implies how absurd one's mental state can become with PPD. (Or even without PPD; how many new mothers and fathers fear their own newborn's power to protest in public?) This self-deprecating humor is reassuring to a reader who has experienced the same anxiety; I can laugh at myself too, through the prism of time and sanity.

Though Armstrong's honesty and humor allow for an empathic response, she never explicitly reflects on the cultural contexts for PPD and her writing is almost purely narrative, that is, never interrupted by analysis or supplemented by outside research. The memoir remains focused on the "I" to the extent that Armstrong says in the preface that "I don't think I would have survived it [PPD] had I not offered up my story and reached out to bridge the loneliness" (xi).

Similar to Armstrong, Adrienne Martini, author of *Hillbilly Gothic: A Memoir of Madness and Motherhood*, uses a blunt, ironic humor to write about PPD and to confront cultural stigma: "I wasn't the first of my generation to log some time in the loony bin" (3). The heart of the memoir is Martini's breakdown and voluntary hospitalization in Tower 4, the psychiatric ward of a Catholic hospital in Knoxville: "[A] plastic bracelet is slapped on my wrist. Should I lose my mind enough to forget my name, it is helpfully attached to the end of my left arm. I sign enough forms to make paper-company executives dance with unbridled joy at the profits" (128).

This kind of sarcastic wit is familiar in narratives about madness, and, as with Armstrong, humor becomes, paradoxically, a shield against too much intimacy with the reader. Instead, the most powerful aspects of Martini's memoir are when she describes her emotional state and her unwillingness to put up with cultural straitjackets, such as the Supplemental Nursing System, a contraption that her doula puts on her when she can't breastfeed (92). The baby has to be fed every two hours, it takes 45 minutes for her to nurse, and then it takes 15 minutes for the SNS to be cleaned between feedings. Even with her mom and her husband helping out, it's a nightmare for Martini. The lack of sleep becomes excruciating. "But," Martini explains, "the larger problem is just the wrongness of three people involved in this whole endeavor. It shouldn't take a village to feed one newborn" (94-5). After more than 24 hours of sleeplessness, she finally tells her husband that she "'can't do this anymore'" (95). They buy more formula and "Life moves on. For the first time in days, I nap while someone else feeds the baby. It is wonderful" (96).

While Martini's first experience as a parent is reflected through the prism of postpartum depression, she is, like Armstrong, clear-eyed in the details, and this approach magnificently explodes sentimental myths about newborns and motherhood:

> Everything happens randomly. One minute she is starving; the next unconscious, or shrieking. I never know how long anything will last. She could be asleep for five hours or five minutes. There

is just no way to tell. If she is awake, she wants to be rocked or held or cooed at. I can't actually do anything that is not related to these mommy duties. Most of the day, I sit on the couch and wait for whatever comes next, my hands folded in my lap, like a preschooler waiting for the next set of directions. (98)

Martini mentions several times that silence is a tradition in her family. In regards to her "great-grandmother Elizabeth Flowers Hendershot Cain, who abandoned her three kids—one of whom was Nell, my grandmother—under mysterious circumstances," Martini works hard to break the silence open (110-111). She finds a front-page obituary in a local W.VA. newspaper that no one else in the family had seen and which sheds some light on Elizabeth's death, but not on her life. Martini writes:

> It angers me, frankly, this denial of a woman's life. Times were different, I know, and I'm approaching this from a twenty-first-century perspective where better living through chemistry is possible. I know the temptations of denial, of wanting to push away everything that hurt you in the past in order to preserve yourself. Still, I'm pissed that I never got the chance to know any of this, to have this decision [to silence her great-grandmother's story] made for me because someone else was scared. (114-115)

To further break the legacy of silence, Martini gives room in her memoir to the story of her cousin Julie, who also suffered severe postpartum depression and bipolar disorder.

While Martini's approach borrows self-consciously from the stereotyped images of crazy backcountry yokels (hence the title *Hillbilly Gothic*), Martini pummels myths about mental illness: "[T]here are millions of women like me, mothers who have some problems now and again but who are more or less okay. We are not freaks. We are your neighbors and your friends and your family. We are responsible, reasonable adults who need to be less ashamed to admit that we struggle sometimes" (218). The story of Elizabeth also provides a historical longview on the lack of choices mothers have had, whatever Elizabeth's suffering was, and how silencing that history creates a vacuum of silence—medically and culturally—for the mother experiencing PPD now. How much more might we know and understand about PPD if our grandmothers and their grandmothers before them had felt free to speak?

The recent surge in PPD memoirs thus breaks a long silence. That Armstrong and Martini often use humor to articulate the double-bind of silence also follows in a long tradition of comedy as cultural criticism. Provoking laughter to express what cannot be said otherwise without retribution at the very least allows the topic of PPD and cultural myths of motherhood to enter the realm of public discussion. But more than that, humor can reflect the return of sanity. When I imagine some of my low moments of depression, such as when I found myself yelling into my cell phone in my driveway at an innocent Virgin Mobile customer rep because that was the person I could scream at without repercussions, I can see myself from a distance and point at that self and say, "What a basket case." This critical and temporal (and medicated) distance allows for laughter that is both a means of survival and also the privilege of the survivor.[11]

Like humor, self-consciousness in memoirs about PPD can be a strategy of deflection or insight. Self-consciousness is a prevalent trait across the genre of memoir as a whole, but in PPD memoirs, self-consciousness can, like humor, allow what is uncomfortable or even unbearable to speak to be spoken. In Armstrong's memoir, she deflects her self-consciousness onto her family:

> When my friends and family said that they couldn't believe I was being so open about this, I wanted to ask them WHY NOT? Why should there be any shame in getting help for a disease?
>
> If there is a stigma to this, let there be one. At least I was alive. At least my baby still had her mother. At least I had a chance at a better life. (194)

In Armstrong's deflection she expresses a defiant posture, in effect saying to her reader, "Go ahead and stigmatize me," which is refreshing in light of media sensationalizing of PPD. I do admire Armstrong for confronting that stigma—acknowledging that the problem doesn't lie with her but with cultural attitudes—and yet Armstrong's memoir is a narrative of redemption through medication and therapy. Healed, she does not direct anger at the silencing social codes of motherhood.

Humor is not a panacea, and the lack of discussion of cultural factors that contribute (or even cause) PPD means that some memoirs reinforce the "self-help" ideology of treatment as resolution both to the crisis of PPD and to the narrative of PPD memoirs. Armstrong's prevailing message advocates for the efficacy of medication or redemption by psychiatry, which, as Marrit Ingman notes, may only tell half the story:

> Because cultural and economic cofactors complicate mental health, I take exception … with the popular notion that a woman's postpartum depression is concentrated entirely within in her endocrine system and can be successfully treated by a gynecologist—a too-rosy and sexist (but persistent) ideal of recovery that rarely matches real women's experiences. A mother's mental illness—just like any other human being's—is a day-to-day struggle with a possible whole range of emotional, physical, and behavioral symptoms. To assign blame solely to our hormones smacks of the "hysteria" for which women and mothers have long been blamed. ("Mom, Interrupted" 35)

In her memoir *Inconsolable*, Ingman also notes the "life-saving" quality of writing her story: "Writing this book kept me alive—creatively, spiritually, and literally—during the most difficult episode of my life so far" (vi). And while Ingman, like Armstrong, unapologetically chronicles her use of medication, unlike Armstrong, she details the many ways that PPD is not merely a problem of hormones or neurological chemistry. She writes, "I suspect that when we talk about PPD, we're actually describing a variety of conditions, one of which may actually be the condition of motherhood itself. Some maternal depressions are situational in origin—from exhaustion, from emotional depletion, from being alone with a baby, from being supported inadequately" (2-3). Ingman also discusses the observed phenomenon of PPD in parents of adopted children and in biological fathers, facts that point to cultural factors and social structures, that is, non-biological causes, of PPD (3). Ingman thus opens up a larger context for understanding her experience and PPD memoirs in general. Traditionally, memoir privileges the individual as agent in her story, rather than highlighting the longview of historical and cultural factors that shape experience *and* that create the possibility for the story to be told.

Adrienne Rich, writing more than 30 years ago, understood that there was a larger cultural problem underlying women's experience of parenting: the institution of motherhood in which mothers themselves were silenced. In *Of Woman Born,* Rich articulates how the perception of mothers experiencing severe PPD as "bad" helps to perpetuate the myths of motherhood that silence all mothers. Rich writes:

> The scapegoat is also an escape-valve: through her the passions and the blind raging waters of a suppressed knowledge are permitted to churn their way so that they need not emerge in less extreme situations as lucid rebellion. Reading of the "bad" mother's desperate response to an invisible assault on her being, "good" mothers resolve to become better, more patient and long-suffering, to cling more tightly to what passes for sanity. The scapegoat is different from the martyr; she cannot teach resistance or revolt. She represents a terrible temptation: to suffer uniquely, to assume that I, the individual woman, am the "problem." (283)

What permeates the public discussion of PPD is the careful tiptoeing around the possibility that motherhood can constitute a violence—on the mother herself no less.

This double-bind of silence—mothers afraid to speak their experience; motherhood as a silencing institution—has become heightened in our current era when the medical, cultural, and legal surveillance of motherhood is at a peak.[12] In her article, "Mom, Interrupted," Ingman describes this surveillance as a "double burden":

> Beyond the stigma already associated with mental illness—which is itself a political topic—mothers face a double burden. Because we inevitably involve our children in our struggles simply by being alongside them, a mother's mental illness is perceived to be harmful to her children.
>
> …We need not apologize for our efforts to recover: when we struggle with the beast, we send our children messages of self-respect—that we are people, and people matter. We show them how to survive as surely as we show them how to put food in their mouths and how to drink from a cup. (36)

Ingman's words are a relief to read, and yet in writing this essay, I feel as though I am confessing a sin—fear, shame, and plain old embarrassment well up in me as I consider how many people—family, colleagues, friends, acquaintances, neighbors—don't know that I had PPD. When I mentioned this project to one colleague and my reluctance to speak publicly about it, she suggested that I was a part of the silencing problem. She was both right and wrong: right, in that, yes, my hesitation contributes to the silence—the lack of stories that other mothers might find helpful; but also wrong in that women who experience PPD have a lot at stake—why should we be responsible for the stigma against us?

But I am speaking, and I look forward to the day when women no longer feel shame for what they experience. The shame stems from the idea—conscious or unconscious—of inadequacy and wrongdoing. And thus PPD memoirs often come across as confessional, but memoirs such as Ingman's also shatter sacred cultural images of the "super mom" and "maternal instinct," thus moving beyond the conventional structure of the confession that progresses from shameful secret (the "sin" of mothers with depression) to recovery (redemption through religious faith, therapy, and/or prescription medication). In her Afterword, Ingman muses about whether she will be depressed again:

> I can't live my life waiting for the other shoe to drop. It will or it won't.
>
> More likely, I'll remain on the slippery slope of motherhood—frustration, depletion, exhaustion, boredom—between sanity and madness. We all live here. In so many moments I've wondered why we even make reference to "postpartum depression" when life with young children is so self-evidently crazy-making. Love is not enough to keep you happy. Why do we tell mothers this lie? (*Inconsolable* 249)

Indeed, "we all live here." When we can tell our stories truthfully, perhaps then we can also start to change a culture that both creates impossible standards of motherhood and simultaneously undermines the work of parenting. Here, I'm thinking of how many states still ban breastfeeding in public; how few women have paid maternity leave; how few of us have access to affordable, quality child care; and the list could go on. Ingman acknowledges the larger structural problem when she coins the term "postpartum *oppression*—the grind of getting by in a culture that systematically devalues women and their mothering" (*Inconsolable* 249).

This cultural inability to acknowledge and hear "postpartum oppression" in narratives about PPD means that memoirists confront another kind of silence, one created by the structural expectations of narrative, particularly the memoir genre. Interestingly, Armstrong's and Ingman's memoirs are broken into self-contained or nearly self-contained chapters, while Martini's follows a more or less chronological narrative arc. Martini's chapters are numbered; Armstrong's and Ingman's chapters are all titled. This difference may be explained merely as a circumstance of writing: Armstrong's memoir is made up of revised versions of her blog entries. Several of Ingman's chapters were originally published separately in various periodicals. Armstrong's and Ingman's stories, unsurprisingly, are recursive, circling back to various key moments. And yet all of the memoirs have key moments, those experiences that stand out from all the other seconds and minutes and can be plucked and shaped into stories. And there are lots of good stories in these books, entertaining, funny, heart-breaking ones; everyone likes a good story of someone going off the deep end.

What doesn't make a good story are all those seconds and minutes that the writer has shaved away from the narrative arc, and yet it is in those unwritten moments that depression pools.

I wish I had some crucial moment to narrate in which self-realization occurred for me about my depression. Certainly there was a breaking point, when my anxiety and exhaustion sent me to the doctor, but it was complicated (or should I say "masked") by a work situation with an abusive boss and it took a while to recognize under the layers of stress that part of my condition was depression. And even then, once I started medication, I went through a few therapists and went off medication and then back on. There is a lot that I can't remember, too. This jagged narrative, rather than a moment of crystallization and then redemption, characterizes the PPD experience (and perhaps parenting). The memoir genre's dependence on narrative structure itself imposes a silencing of the fragmented experience of motherhood and PPD.[13] Perhaps the elliptical and paratactic quality of poetry is more suited to the experience of PPD.

In Tillie Olsen's *Silences*, she famously gathers a compelling range of reasons for why women of the nineteenth and twentieth centuries were silenced as writers—either before the pen was ever grasped or after or between the writing that did manage to be written. I recently went back to this book to find mention in it of the silence brought on by

PPD. Though Olsen doesn't discuss PPD specifically,[14] she does mention Harriet Beecher Stowe, who wrote while her many children were still young and who "had a near-breakdown" (204). In a separate section, she mentions breakdowns again, though this time not necessarily in connection with mothers who are writers, though Sylvia Plath and Anne Sexton are mentioned in her list of writers who committed suicide (227). It is very likely because Olsen took the time and had the insight to write *Silences* that the idea for this chapter could have happened—a feminist inheritance from one mother to another. And, standing on the shoulder of this giant, I extend her idea of what can silence women to the experience of PPD.

But even within the memoirs about PPD, there is a self-imposed silencing, one that Olsen might have attributed to Virginia Woolf's "angel in the house," that inner self-criticizing perspective fostered by generations of masculinist criticism which still can create hesitancy and self-doubt in women writing about their own mental health.

Yes, let's acknowledge that women are writing openly about PPD, but let's also keep our ears attuned to the continued silences.

ENDNOTES

[1]"Where's the Funeral?" is the title of a poem by Rebecca Wolff in her collection *The King*.

[2]I want to emphasize my good fortune in the question of employment. Now, on the other side of PPD, I am concerned about the women who suffer from PPD but who do not have access to a livable wage or work conditions that allow for paid sick leave.

[3]See Paul Elisha, "Bard's Eye View: Rebecca Wolff."

[4]See, for example, *Listening to Silences* (Hedges and Fishkin).

[5]Marrit Ingman's memoir has a chapter titled "The Inevitable Remarks about Andrea Yates."

[6]Indeed, PPD is a different category of illness than postpartum psychosis. As Tracy Thompson notes, "Women with postpartum psychosis (which is extremely rare) usually operate under a delusion they firmly believe in, and are often unable to tell right from wrong" (68).

[7]For example, see "Cruise Clashes on TV Over Drugs." See Jocelyn Fenton Stitt for a fuller discussion of the implications of this public debate.

[8]As this book goes to press, the British television series "Call the Mid-

wife" has made a welcome intervention with more realistic images of women in labor and childbirth.

[9]I don't mean to ignore Marie Osmond's 2002 memoir, *Behind the Smile: My Journey Out of Postpartum Depression*, which I acknowledge also took courage to publish, but Shields's "coming out" provoked a lot more media attention.

[10]I realize that I may be painting too fine a portrait of Armstrong's integrity here in the wake of her more recent controversies. See Sarah McAbee's piece, "Mother Huckster: How Mommy Blogs Became a Brand" in *bitch* for an account of Dooce.com's Maytag controversy.

[11]Many thanks to Professor Rebecca Lartigue for pointing out that humor is the prerogative of those who survive.

[12]See Susan J. Douglas and Meredith W. Michaels, *The Mommy Myth: The Idealization of Motherhood and How It Has Undermined Women*, especially the chapter titled "Threats from Within: Maternal Delinquents." Historically, who is allowed to be a mother has been policed in various ways in the U.S., perhaps most egregiously (outside of the history of racial slavery) in the form of forced sterilization programs targeting Native American women and low-income women of all backgrounds. Rich notes, "Already by 1968, 35.3 per cent of Puerto Rican women of childbearing age, two-thirds of them under 30, had been sterilized— under funding by the department cynically termed Health, Education, and Welfare" ("Motherhood" 265). These eugenicist policies may no longer have official sanction but the notion that certain people should not have children, or too many children, still persists, especially in the recent backlash against so-called "welfare mothers." This shameful history complicates what might otherwise be life-saving potentialities. For example, a bill in the Massachusetts legislature mandating postpartum screening for depression attracted opposition from progressive organizations, in part from the fear that individual women might be blamed for their own medical conditions. See "Searching for Consensus" by Maureen Turner in *The Valley Advocate*.

[13]Of course, many memoirists have explored the "problem" of memory and its tension with the requirements for narrative, such as Mary McCarthy's classic *Memoirs of a Catholic Girlhood* and more recently Mary Karr's *The Liars Club* and *Lit*. Scholars have also explored the complexity of memory and the fragmentation of self; see, for example, Helen M. Buss's *Repossessing the World: Reading Memoirs by Contemporary Women*

and Jeanne Perreault's *Writing Selves: Contemporary Feminist Autography*. I am not suggesting that my assertion about the fragmentary nature of memory is an original one; rather, I am suggesting that the institution of motherhood and the cultural intolerance for mental illness exacerbate the challenge to shape the experiences of PPD into narrative.

[14]Perhaps this is because PPD was not a known psychiatric disorder in 1965, when the book was published.

WORKS CITED

Armstrong, Heather B. *It Sucked and Then I Cried: How I Had a Baby, a Breakdown, and a Much Needed Margarita.* New York: Simon Spotlight Entertainment, 2009. Print.

Buss, Helen M. *Repossessing the World: Reading Memoirs by Contemporary Women.* Waterloo, ON: Wilfrid Laurier University Press, 2012. Print.

Clark, Hilary. "Confessions of a Celebrity Mom: Brooke Shields's *Down Came the Rain: My Journey through Postpartum Depression.*" *Canadian Review of American Studies* 38.3 (2008) 449-461. Print.

"Cruise Clashes on TV Over Drugs." *BBC News* 25 June 2005. Web. 22 July 2010.

Diagnostic and Statistical Manual of Mental Disorders. 4th ed. Arlington, VA: American Psychological Association, 2000. Print.

Douglas, Susan J. and Meredith W. Michaels. *The Mommy Myth: The Idealization of Motherhood and How It Has Undermined Women.* New York: Free Press, 2004. Print.

Elisha, Paul. "Bard's Eye View: Rebecca Wolff." WAMC Northeast Public Radio, 5 August 2009. Web. August 5, 2009.

Hedges, Elaine and Shelley Fisher Fishkin, eds. *Listening to Silences: New Essays in Feminist Criticism.* New York: Oxford University Press, 1994. Print.

Ingman, Marrit. *Inconsolable: How I Threw My Mental Health Out with the Diapers.* Emeryville, CA: Seal Press, 2005.

Ingman, Marrit. "Mom, Interrupted: Toward a Politics of Maternal Mental Health." *The Maternal is Political: Women Writers at the Intersection of Motherhood and Social Change.* Ed. Shari Macdonald Strong. Berkeley: Seal Press, 2008. 30-39. Print.

Karr, Mary. *The Liars Club: A Memoir.* New York: Viking, 1995. Print.

Karr, Mary. *Lit: A Memoir (P.S.).* New York: Harper Collins, 2009. Print.

Leach, Penelope. *Your Baby & Child.* 3rd ed. New York: Alfred A. Knopf, 2003. Print.

Martini, Adrienne. *Hillbilly Gothic: A Memoir of Madness and Motherhood.* New York: Free Press, 2006. Print.

McAbee, Sarah. "Mother Huckster: How Mommy Blogs Became a Brand." *bitch* (Spring 2011): 30-34. Print.

McCarthy, Mary. *Memoirs of Memories of a Catholic Girlhood.* New York: Harvest/HBJ,1957. Print.

Olsen, Tillie. *Silences.* 1965. New York: Feminist Press, 2003. Print.

Osmond, Marie, Judith Moore and Marcia Wilkie. *Behind the Smile: My Journey Out of Postpartum Depression.* New York: Grand Central Publishing, 2002. Print.

Perreault, Jeanne. *Writing Selves: Contemporary Feminist Autography.* Minneapolis: University of Minnesota Press, 1995. Print.

Rich, Adrienne. "Motherhood: The Contemporary Emergency and the Quantum Leap." *On Lies, Secrets, and Silence: Selected Prose 1966-1978.* New York: W.W. Norton & Company, 1995. Print.

Rich, Adrienne. *Of Woman Born.* New York: Bantam Books, 1977. Print.

Shields, Brooke. *Down Came the Rain: My Journey Through Postpartum Depression.* New York: Hyperion, 2005. Print.

Smith-Rosenberg, Carroll. "Puberty to Menopause: The Cycle of Femininity in Nineteenth-Century America." *Feminist Studies* 1.3,4 (1973): 58-72. Print.

Stitt, Jocelyn Fenton. "Tom vs. Brooke: Or Postpartum Depression as Bad Mothering in Popular Culture." *Mediating Moms: Mothers in Popular Culture.* Ed. Elizabeth Podnieks. Montreal: McGill-Queen's University Press, 2012. 339-357. Print.

Stoppard, Miriam. *Conception, Pregnancy and Birth.* New York: Dorling Kindersley Publishing, Inc., 2000. Print.

Thompson, Tracy. *The Ghost in the House: Real Mothers Talk About Maternal Depression, Raising Children, and How They Cope.* New York: Harper, 2006. Print.

Turner, Maureen. "Searching for Consensus." *The Valley Advocate* May 20, 2010: 12-15. Print.

The Womanly Art of Breastfeeding. Seventh Revised Edition. La Leche League International. New York: Plume/Penguin, 2004. Print.

Wolff, Rebecca. *The King.* New York: W.W. Norton & Company, 2009. Print.

7.
Lost and Found

Intimacy and Distance in Three Motherhood Memoirs about Autistic Children

RACHEL ROBERTSON

WHEN MY TEN-YEAR-OLD son started a new school, he was asked to complete a brief questionnaire to help the teacher get to know him. Whereas most of the questions were specific, like "what is your favourite subject?" one simply said "your family." My son wrote: "My family are people I can rely on and I love them also. I like doing odd jobs for them." I'm guessing that the teacher expected information about who he lives with, if he has any siblings or grandparents and so on, but I love Ben's answer.[1] It seems complete. What else do we need to know about family except that we love them, we can rely on them and they can rely on us?

It is especially moving to see Ben write this comment because at three years old he was diagnosed with autism,[2] and autistic people are often considered unable to form close relationships with others, unable to self-reflect, and unable to empathise or consider the needs of others. Having known Ben ten years, I know that he is capable of love, empathy and self-reflection, though the way he experiences and expresses these things is likely to be very different from how I and other neurotypicals do.[3]

Reading his comment about family makes me realise that Ben is the person I feel most connected to in the world. I'm not talking about the fact that I love him most—which I do—but about intimacy. The fact that this has not always been the case, and that our intimacy is often disrupted and fragmented, that distance often co-exists within the space of this intimacy, does not diminish my sense of connection to him. But it does complicate things, so that we do a continual dance of closeness and separation, with me feeling that I have to do most of the fancy footwork while Ben wanders about only half recognising the dance.

I have no idea whether this is a common feeling for mothers, especially single mothers, because Ben is my only child. I've had to work hard to get to know my son and so perhaps it is only that I am therefore made aware of things that other mothers—mothers of typically developing children—don't notice. But certainly, the mother of an autistic child will be forced to reflect on issues of intimacy and distance because of the differences in communication, interaction, and preoccupation that autistic people demonstrate. When your toddler pushes you aside like a piece of unwanted furniture in order to spend hours alone gazing rapt at a row of different coloured tea bags, then all your unexamined assumptions about intimacy, about reciprocity, about love, all are shattered and tossed into the air. This is when the real work of mothering begins. Your child is two, you have weathered 730 sleepless nights, changed 6000 nappies/diapers, breastfed through cracked and torn nipples, pored over 25 child development books, mashed numerous pumpkins and apples, tried to turn the baby's cries down with the television remote control.... In short, you have done what all mothers do, and yet you haven't even started to learn how to mother your child, because your child appears to be changing in front of your very eyes, won't even meet your eyes, seems to be disappearing off into a parallel world, a mysterious place you soon realise you must try to go yourself, although you can never really get there. This is the start of the dance of intimacy with an autistic child.[4]

Because I am a writer as well as a mother, my attempt to become as close as possible to Ben has involved writing about my experiences and reading the stories of other mothers. It was only when I neared the end of writing my own motherhood memoir that I realised that a central—although not always acknowledged—theme of all the memoirs I've read about autistic children, including my own, is the issue of intimacy. How does the mother write about the intimacy of motherhood when the expected act of mothering has been so challenged? How can she portray the challenges of her child's neurological difference—the child's distance from her—in a way that also represents her closeness to him or her? If she feels that her child, as she once knew the child, is lost to her, how does she express both the loss and the accommodation of that loss? Is the motherhood memoir in fact the result of a desire for reconnection, a desire to "find" her child once more? Does the act of writing a motherhood memoir create, or recreate, the intimacy between mother and child that the difference of autism may have disrupted?

There are no simple answers to these questions, nor is there a single model for how mothers write about autistic children. Indeed, the literature on mothering indicates the wide range of approaches women take, as well as the prevalence of maternal ambivalence[5] and the complexity of representing mothering in literature generally. But in working on my own book and reading others, I see that the choices a writer makes about how she addresses the issue of intimacy have implications both for the way her child is represented and for the representation of difference and disability in her work. In this essay I will explore the way three mothers have written about their autistic children in published works of memoir, looking at the play of distance and intimacy—how the child is lost and then found again—and linking this to the way the children and autism as a condition are represented. By comparing the different paradigms for understanding disability used by the authors, I demonstrate that both symbolic and medical paradigms lead to a representation of autism (and autistic people) that is stigmatized and distances the reader from the autistic character, whereas a socio-cultural paradigm of disability allows for a more accepting view of autism and brings the reader closer to the autistic character. This is not to suggest that the *representation* of a child in a maternal memoir is the same as the mother's personal view. Nor is it to suggest that there is one correct way to represent disabled children in memoir (or one correct way of mothering). Analysing the play of intimacy and distance in these memoirs allows me to explore the level of complexity and ambivalence around mothering and difference within each text. My own experiences of the dance of intimacy in living with, and writing about, my son has led me to value memoirs that are both progressive and complex in their representation of autism and the relationship between autistic child and non-autistic mother.

> *Anne-Marie had now become a source of unmitigated pain. She was going so fast into some shadowy space, and I didn't know how to reach her. As each day passed she seemed to fade more and more into herself, into a private dreamy world where she wandered alone. We were losing her.* (Maurice 44)

This is how Catherine Maurice describes her daughter, Anne-Marie, at one year old in her memoir *Let Me Hear Your Voice: A Family's Triumph*

Over Autism. First published in 1993, the book tells the story of how two of Maurice's children were diagnosed with autism (Anne-Marie first and then Michel) and her five-year journey to move them into "recovery" through the use of intensive behavioural therapy.

Maurice describes how Anne-Marie began to "slip quietly away from us" (4) and was "wandering into darkness" (20). She notes, "I was in a race against time, and either I found something that truly helped or I had lost Anne-Marie forever" (57). As her daughter exhibits more "autistic mannerisms," Maurice increasingly feels she is losing her daughter and all possibility of genuine intimacy. Autism itself—which is, after all, simply a medical term to describe what is considered to be a neurological condition but is observable only through behavior—begins to have a character in this book, being described as a "black cave" (57), a "jagged hole" (21), a prison, a concept that "gave meaning to the phrase 'death in life'" (57). Maurice often uses religious imagery (she is a committed Catholic), contrasting God with "this evil," autism (60).

Maurice sets up a dichotomy between the "autistic self" and Anne-Marie's "real self," working to "bend, break and ravish her autistic self" in order to get to the true "Anne-Marie spirit" (81). Using the fortress and siege metaphors long associated with autism, Maurice determines to "besiege" her daughter, destroy the autistic self and drag her "into the human condition" (81).[6]

In this way, Maurice establishes a symbolic equivalence between autism and distance or the lack of humanity and between what she terms "recovery"—the non-autistic self—and the possibility of family intimacy and connection. At one point Maurice writes, "Anne-Marie would be whole and normal. She would talk and smile and grow and love" (67), thus suggesting that autistic children aren't whole, don't develop and can't love properly. Like any mother, Maurice wants her daughter to love her and wants signs of this love. When she doesn't receive these signs—smiles, eye contact, desire to interact—she conflates the lack of evidence of Anne-Marie's love with a lack of love, again relying on the autistic self/real-self dichotomy to understand this.

In fact, Maurice admits in her memoir that she is using the terms "autistic self" and "real self" in a symbolic way and that this approach can be questioned. She says that while she now (at the time of writing her memoir) disagrees with the notion that there is a normal child locked within an autistic shell, parents who are "fighting" for their child need this fictional construct. And in many ways, her memoir relies on this, because without the notion that she is recovering her true daughter from the ravages of autism, the type of story she is writing would change completely. By constructing this dichotomy of autism versus true self, of the lost child versus the recovered child, Maurice creates narrative tension and motivation. Her story becomes what Arthur Frank in *The Wounded Storyteller* calls a "restitution narrative," where an illness or disability is viewed as an assault on the normal order and the narrative arc entails a journey to return to the pre-disability order. Maurice's underlying premise is that autism is the enemy which must be fought and vanquished so that the family can return to normal life. As with many restitution narratives written by parents, the struggle of restitution is performed by a number of heroic characters, including clinicians and parents. The child becomes the ground over which these characters act rather than a heroic character herself, and the sign of success is that the child becomes like other children, what Maurice describes as "normal."

Near the end of her book, Maurice notes that the "black-and-white" approach to "recovery/nonrecovery" is probably no longer useful (302); however, she never questions her primary assumption that "recovery" is better than "nonrecovery" or that a "normal child" is preferable (for parents at least) to an autistic child. In this way, Maurice views autism solely as a medical condition without any value, an individual deficit with no social or cultural dimension.

G. Thomas Couser has outlined three different paradigms of disability which may be used by writers in their representation of disabled individuals. In the symbolic paradigm, "impairment serves as a trope for a moral or spiritual condition" (22). In the medical paradigm, impairment is viewed as a dysfunction or medical problem. In the socio-cultural paradigm, disability is "located at the interface of particular bodies with particular societies"; that is, disability is a socio-cultural construction (22).[7] As Couser notes, writers may use more than one paradigm in their work, and Maurice uses both symbolic and medical paradigms. In the symbolic paradigm, autism becomes the opposite of God, "the human condition," and the loving family. The "triumph" of the family over autism represented in the book means that Anne-Marie and Michel are "redeemed" (290): "We walked through the valley of the shadow, and now we walk in light" (291). Couser notes how the symbolic paradigm, as well as commonly presenting disability as negative, "always generalises, stereotypes, essentialises," erasing "individual differences within the group" (23). Thus, all autistic children—and all aspects of autistic children—are represented by Maurice, through her use of the symbolic paradigm, as damaged.

The medical paradigm views disability as an issue of medical deficit or defect. The disability is seen to reside in the individual, with medical technology the key way to change or normalize the individual to the extent they can function within society. As Couser notes, one may accept the value of medical interventions in real life without accepting the medical paradigm as an appropriate mode of representation of people with a disability. Mitzi Waltz (2005) argues that parent narratives about autistic children are often ambivalent about medicalised notions of disability, juxtaposing both acceptance and subversion of the medical paradigm. Maurice, however, appears to accept the medical paradigm and to have no qualms about identifying the specific form of intervention that she believes "recovered" her children from autism. In fact, her story of "recovering" her children becomes a kind of advocacy for behavioural modification intervention, even to the extent of including an Afterword by Dr. Ivar Lovaas, one of the key proponents of behaviour modification for autistic children. Maurice does admit that not all children "recover" in the way her two did. This doesn't change her approach; she still maintains the medical view of disability as a defect that should be righted. Those children who don't "make progress," as she puts it, are "still there, left behind" (302). Her children have been found, but others are still lost.

In Maurice's book there is a linear journey from mother-child intimacy (pre-autism) to distance and then back to intimacy through behavioural intervention. Autism itself is unequivocally represented as the enemy of intimacy and there is no space for the co-existence of intimacy and distance.

> *I couldn't see Ben. I couldn't find him through the lens I was looking through. And through my tears, I knew that to find him, to see him, to have him the way I needed to ... I'd have to take off the lenses I'd been wearing. I'd have to wipe them clean.* (LaSalle 264)

The dynamic of the search for the lost child also features in Barbara LaSalle's book *Finding Ben: A Mother's Journey Through the Maze of*

Asperger's, albeit in a very different way. LaSalle's memoir, published in 2003 when her son was thirty-four years old and incorporating short contributions by him, is the story of LaSalle's journey towards "finding"—that is, accepting—her son.

In a shocking Prologue, LaSalle paints her son as irredeemably "other" and herself as an unnatural mother for her reactions to him. Ben is thirty-three and LaSalle is helping him with his shopping:

> Thirty years of advising, commenting, suggesting. What *hasn't* been said in that much time? It's enough for both of us. I'm fed up with trying to change my son. I'm tired of how it feels to look at him and see layers of fat, to listen to him and hear a constant low-grade wheeze, to flinch at his flat feet, at the fixed, unchanging expression on his face, at his glazed, vacant eyes. I'm tired of trying to get a straight answer from a crooked person, even though that crooked person is my son. (1-2)

LaSalle deliberately describes her son in pejorative terms that highlight his medical conditions and his difference from the idealised American young man. By distancing herself from him, labelling him as "crooked" and "other," and using language that links disability with the monstrous, the incompetent and the immoral (crooked), LaSalle is harnessing the symbolic paradigm to establish the beginning point of her quest to reconnect with her son. At the end of the book, she once again goes shopping for Ben and delivers the food to his apartment, but this time, she stops in her task of putting away the food and turns to her son: "I look at Ben and I see my son. He is beautiful in his green T-shirt. He is beautiful in his slippers. He is beautiful in his own smile" (270). She has "found" Ben and says she now loves and accepts him as he is (271). Although her journey as mother has been over thirty years, the journey of the quest has actually been the time it has taken her to write her book. Both LaSalle and Ben describe the process of writing this memoir as one of the key reasons for LaSalle's change of heart and their improved relationship. In an epigraph to the final chapter, Ben says, "Here's the big secret: I never changed. I'm still the person I was when I was little. The world just caught up to me" (263). It's hard to escape the conclusion that when he says "world," he actually means his mother.

Whereas Maurice uses the fortress/siege metaphor of autism, LaSalle uses, and then subverts, the maze or puzzle metaphor. Mitzi Waltz argues that the puzzle metaphor arises from the medicalisation of autism which locates autism as a "'problem' within the affected person" and calls for a medical hero as saviour or puzzle-solver (6). Initially in *Finding Ben*, it appears that LaSalle endorses this view as she continually looks for "a real little boy" (5), fighting the notion of his "anomalies" (15) and trying to work out whether Ben is "better or worse" than other, more "normal" children (45). However, by the end of the book LaSalle has changed and it becomes clear that it is not Ben who is lost in the maze, but rather LaSalle. Instead of retrieving Ben through normalising him, the retrieval is achieved through LaSalle's re-education. The "maze of Asperger's" is not the conventional puzzle of autism that must be medically solved in order to return the autistic child to normal life, but rather an alternative way of living and thinking that neurotypical people must learn to decipher. The child doesn't learn to be normal; the mother learns to connect to difference. Whereas at the start of the book, Ben's difference results in distance from his mother, at the end, she embraces him and his difference. Ben, with Asperger's in his messy kitchen, and his mother, her eyes finally open to her actual son rather than her idealised son, are allowed intimacy.

While LaSalle uses the symbolic paradigm in her work in order to make her point about her own previously held negative views of disability, she avoids the trap of generalising, essentialising, or stereotyping him. Unlike Maurice's representation of her pre-recovery children, Ben is always presented as an individual with his own characteristic approach to life. Ben is the most realised character in the text, while LaSalle comes across as an obsessive single-minded woman, unable to look beyond her own obsession. This is particularly interesting in a book about someone with Asperger's Syndrome, because of the so-called obsessive behaviour that the literature claims characterises the condition. From as early as three years old, Ben is portrayed as having agency. When a nurse asks Ben to show her colleagues how he can read the newspaper at only three years old, Ben replies: "I don't have to read it. I did that already this morning in my own newspaper. I'll just tell them what it says" (37). As well as illustrating Ben's remarkable reading and language skills and his lack of understanding of other people's intentions (not realising that he is being asked to perform), this exchange demonstrates

Ben's ability to make choices and follow his own logic. There are many similar descriptions throughout the book, as Ben chooses his own reality over LaSalle's (and society's) reality. As well as including descriptions of Ben and his dialogue, LaSalle has incorporated Ben's own words about the different periods of his life, giving her representation of him greater depth and showing how Ben has developed and grown over the years. In this way, the book reinforces that people with Asperger's grow and develop just as neurotypical people do.

By the end of *Finding Ben*, there is a suggestion that Asperger's Syndrome can't be "cured" and that Ben's choices and preferences are a legitimate way to live. The medical paradigm is therefore contested to the extent that LaSalle questions the desire to "cure" or "normalize" Ben and argues that it is society's views on difference—in this case represented by LaSalle herself—that resulted in Ben's most debilitating experiences. While gesturing here towards the socio-cultural paradigm, LaSalle's memoir doesn't fully embrace it. Many of LaSalle's reflections on Ben are comparisons—he is always seen as either smarter or less competent than other children or young people. She assumes that there is a norm that exists and is represented by "regular" children, and she constructs Ben as other to that norm. She fails to deconstruct the normal/abnormal and non-disabled/disabled dichotomies, using the terms as though they were absolute rather than unstable and relational categories which depend upon each other for their existence and on opposition for their meaning.

It is clear that LaSalle would much rather that Ben were what she describes as a "regular" kid (27). The stigma of his difference affects her deeply: "If my son didn't fit in, how would I? This was my worst nightmare" (41). Ben, too, in his contributions to the book, reflects his own sense of shame about himself and his inability to achieve certain goals. In spite of the book's ending, where LaSalle notes that she now loves and accepts Ben "as he is" and comments on his brilliance, courage and inspiring attitude, there is no attempt to explore how she or others might re-conceive disability as diversity rather than deficit.

Nor does LaSalle explore the wider cultural and medical issues that have helped to construct her own views on disability. She appears to write the book to indict herself for her inability to love and accept Ben unconditionally as well as to help other mothers with similar experiences. She takes all the blame for her culture's ableism onto herself and constructs the journey of healing as an individual quest, albeit one she can share in print with others. Given that the book shows Ben being treated harshly and unfairly by educational, judicial and medical institutions and individuals within these institutions, it is odd that LaSalle doesn't explore how the community in which she and Ben live has contributed to their experiences and attitudes.

This focus on the mother-son relationship and the construction and understanding of difference within that relationship results in Ben becoming a kind of yardstick for his mother's moral and social development. Although Ben is given his own voice in *Finding Ben* and has a strong presence, the trajectory of the story is that of his mother's journey to acceptance. Ben acts as a barometer for his mother's character, keeping the stigmatisation of disability as a moral issue within the family rather than a social and political community-wide issue. While *Finding Ben* reflects the growth of LaSalle's moral development, it does not reflect a larger social or political awareness. LaSalle as lost mother and Ben as found child form the limits of the book; issues of intimacy and distance in the wider community are not explored.

> *A common belief among people not deeply familiar with autism is that there is a normal child trapped inside, struggling to get out. That's a false belief. I reiterate that Sam has no "normal" core. He is autistic through and through.* (Moore 136)

In *George and Sam: Two Boys, One Family, and Autism*, British author Charlotte Moore writes very differently from Maurice and LaSalle about distance and intimacy with her children. Here, the only time a child is represented as lost is when Moore recounts the way Sam literally gets lost, for example after wandering away from his mother on a visit to Hereford Cathedral to be found dancing on the bank of the river Wye. The reader of *George and Sam* may feel something is lost from the book, but it is not the children so much as their mother's emotional responses. Moore's children were born several years after Maurice's and were young teenagers when the book was published in 2004. Her memoir describes her experiences parenting three sons, two of whom are autistic, using a structure that is part chronological and part thematic. In 2012, an updated edition of the book was released, containing a postscript (which replaces the previous final chapter) and an appendix with copies of Moore's *Guardian* columns from 2001-2003, which were the genesis of her book.

Unlike Maurice and LaSalle, Moore uses no central metaphor for autism and never appears to represent her sons using a symbolic paradigm. Her portrayal of George and Sam is always specific, detailed and grounded in their actions or (less often) their words. They come across as highly unusual, interesting, and frustrating to live with. As Moore notes:

> What makes me smile is the way that every single thing they do is so utterly characteristic. Never imagine that a child who doesn't talk or play much lacks character. "Autism" is an umbrella term; the condition in no way reduces individuality. The boys express their characters in their every tiny action, and individuality is something I'm inclined to celebrate. (274)

Here, Moore values her sons as individual personalities, rather than a series of medical deficits or the sum of a diagnostic label.

While the book does include moments of celebration like this, there is no shrinking from the difficult realities of the boys' experiences and of Moore's own life as a mother. She writes about smeared faeces, boys climbing the roof in the rain, locked cupboards, flooded bathrooms, obsessions with blackberries, washing machines and Walt Disney characters, breakfasts consisting solely of chocolate mints, and failed therapeutic and schooling trials. In this memoir, difference and disability appear to be accepted as an ordinary part of life. The boys' autism may make mothering them more difficult—more "hands-on" is how Moore describes it (267)—but there is no overt representation of autism as a disruption of the mother-child bond in the way that Maurice and LaSalle describe. In her typically understated way, Moore describes moments of both intimacy and distance from her sons. Near the end of the book, when she says, "Every day, the boys make me feel bored and irritated; equally, every day they provide me with delight, amusement, and joy" (273), these are responses that the reader is also likely to have experienced.

It is clear that Moore accepts the medical diagnosis of autism, accepts that her sons are both "autistic through and through," and attempts to minimise some of George and Sam's most socially unacceptable behaviours. However, in her representation of them she draws more from the socio-cultural paradigm of disability, acknowledging the part played by social and cultural norms in the construction of disability and viewing accommodation of difference as equally or more important than the attempt to change or rehabilitate the individual with a disability. *George and Sam*, then, is the more progressive of the three motherhood memoirs considered here because of the way in which the children are represented as specific individuals with personality and agency, the fact that the mother-child bond can accommodate difference, and the way in which wider social and cultural forces are shown to interact with individual bodies to create the experience of mothering autistic children.

There is a catch, however. At times, the tone of Moore's book introduces a discordant element which undermines its content. This tone, described by Mark Osteen as a "no-time-for-moaning attitude" (21), creates for the reader a kind of distance between the mother-author and the children she writes about. There are moments where Moore expresses empathy for her children, but in the main she simply describes what they are doing in a matter-of-fact tone mixed with dry humour. The effect of this narrative strategy is to distance the reader from the boys. The tone of detached, slightly deprecating humour becomes most problematic when it changes as Moore discusses Jake, her third and non-autistic child. Here the tone becomes much warmer and closer. Jake is often used as a comparison point, showing the eccentricity or abnormal development of George and Sam. Writing about her anxiety before Jake's birth about whether he would be autistic too, Moore says, "Five years later, the worry seems extraordinary. Jake is not only not autistic, he's the least disappointing child it's possible to imagine" (17). Comments like this suggest that the amused, distanced tone of most of the book (or of the 2004 version at any rate) may disguise other emotions that Moore doesn't wish to share or isn't aware of herself.

Whereas most motherhood memoirs about autistic children express grief and stress directly, Moore tends to avoid doing so. Compare Moore and Maurice, for example, on finding they have a second autistic child. Maurice says:

> I couldn't stand the thought of any of this. Dragging Michel back for those terrible, terrifying evaluations. Hearing those words.... Farewell to Michel. Farewell to the dream of who we

thought he was: the perfect child, the blessed baby. Good-bye to that self, so newly born and blossoming toward life. Now he too, blighted at the root. He too, slipping away. This was no bright morning he was traversing, but a somber twilight. (232)

Moore, however, says:

People have often asked me, why have you got two? And the only accurate reply is, I don't know. In a way, it doesn't really matter. I've never raged against fate, or cast about much for explanations. Nothing in my own childhood experience led me to expect that anything would be "wrong" with my children, but then there they were, and—well, you just get on with it. (16)

Even bearing in mind the very different prose styles, uses of metaphor and views about autism, it seems likely that Moore significantly understates her own maternal feelings about her sons.

The complexity introduced by Moore's tonal variations is also evident in her approach to the notion of normalcy. Like LaSalle, she dramatizes—partly through the use of Jake as a foil for George and Sam—an absolutist position on normalcy. George and Sam, and other autistic people, are abnormal whereas Jake, and other neurotypical people, are normal. While she clearly values George and Sam, the adoption of this strong division between normalcy and autism results in unspoken support for the medical view of typical development as "normal" and superior to non-typical development.

This view is further cemented by a chapter titled "Compensation." Here, Moore outlines what she considers are the compensations for having autistic children, including her sons' characteristic individuality, their "incorruptible innocence" (275), the low social demands they make on her, and their beauty. She ends by saying: "If you have to have a child with a disability, at least autism's an interesting one. On good days—on *very* good days—autism is its own compensation" (281, italics in original). A compensation noted in an earlier chapter is that autistic people "can be instruments for us to learn benevolence upon; unwittingly, they provide a yardstick for neurotypical moral behavior" (259). That disability has its own compensations and the disabled person provides a moral yardstick for the non-disabled (that is, they are objects of our experience rather than fellow subjects) are both paternalistic notions that the disability rights movement rejects and which contradict the socio-cultural paradigm of disability representation (Couser 22; Wendell 271). These aspects, read in conjunction with the rest of Moore's book, demonstrate the ambivalence that Mitzi Waltz and Mark Osteen note is so often found in parental memoirs about autistic children: the sense that autism is both gift and tragedy (for the parent, if not the child), both medical deficit and socially-constructed identity. This ambivalence is most evident in *George and Sam* through the way the 2004 edition of Moore's story is challenged by her distanced and distancing tone.

Interestingly, in the 2012 postscript entitled "What's wrong with being autistic?" this tone changes and the writing becomes more overtly warm and intimate. There is also some evidence of a shift in Moore's thinking around disability and normalcy. For example, she notes:

> Since I wrote the book, no new breakthroughs or theories have convinced me that a "cure" [for autism] is either possible or desirable. Some aspects of autism can cause great discomfort or distress. When one encounters an individual locked in a world of screaming and self-harming, it would be strange not to wish for some safe treatment that could alleviate the suffering. But a desire to control some symptoms is not the same as wishing autism undone. Gentle George, embarked on one of his huge, semi-abstract paintings, absorbed in his blues and pinks and greys; how should he be different? Sam, rollicking away at his keyboard in what feels like a one-man attempt to recreate Pink Floyd's recording studio at their most experimental phase, "singing" in an eldritch screech that gives him, at least, great satisfaction – this is what Sam is. (249-250)

Here, Moore not only directly adopts a socio-cultural paradigm of disability which values difference for its own sake, she also writes with great affection and intimacy about her sons, describing her boys in fully positive ways and using the phrase "Gentle George." She ends this postscript with a discussion of death, something that all parents of children with a disability are concerned about. She notes that George talks about his own death:

He says he wants to be "buried in the ground at Whatlington [our village]." I interpret this not so much as a death wish as a request for reassurance that the place with which he has been familiar all his life will always provide him with a haven. I think it's a variation on the desire—shared by many neurotypicals— that, when they come home, their bedroom should be just how they left it. I'm sympathetic to George's wish. I, too, want to be buried in the ground at Whatlington. And if I die in the knowledge that society will care for and respect my sons, I'll lie quietly in my grave. (253)

Once again, this moving end to the 2012 edition of her book focuses, in a way that neither Maurice nor LaSalle do, on the role of the wider community in valuing and caring for people with disabilities. This postscript also reads as though it is written by a woman now more comfortable with acknowledging her own emotions and expressing them in print.

My reading of these books suggests that all three memoirs demonstrate a central ambiguity in the representation of the mother-child connection, its shifting dimensions, and the play of distance and intimacy within the memoir. Maurice's memoir can be read as an advocacy book for behavioural therapy where the lost child is found by the heroic mother. Intimacy is broken by autism and then recovered through therapeutic intervention. By utilising the symbolic and medical paradigms without questioning them, Maurice has written a text that appears to confirm the stigmatisation of autism and autistic people.

LaSalle uses and then subverts both symbolic and medical paradigms in order to start to explore a socio-cultural approach which values difference and disability. LaSalle's memoir portrays a lost mother's journey of discovery to find and reconnect to her son. Distance becomes intimacy through the mother's re-education.

Moore takes this socio-cultural approach further, representing her autistic sons as individuals with value and influenced by and interacting with their environment. In her 2004 memoir, the mother-child bond is both intimate and distant and it is the full range of the mother's emotions—what could be described as the mother's intimacy with herself—that may appear to be lost. Distance and intimacy co-exist in an ambivalent relationship, becoming partly resolved only with the postscript of the 2012 edition.

This play of distance and intimacy, of lost and found relationships, animates all three motherhood memoirs and provides the primary metaphor for two of them. *Let Me Hear Your Voice* is powerfully written, but the narrative is neither complex nor ambiguous, disallowing anything beyond a straightforward reading. In contrast, the play of distance and intimacy in both *Finding Ben* and *George and Sam* result in complex and ambiguous texts that enable multiple readings. As a mother and writer, this is what I am interested in—the complexity and ambivalence of mothering represented in ways that open out the territory and allow us each to recognise aspects of our own experiences (our own distance and intimacy) in the memoirs of other mothers.

I am probably too close to the writing of my own memoir to unpack how intimacy and distance interact in the book. In our life, however, the dance of intimacy continues, sometimes becoming easier, sometimes more complex as my son Ben changes with age and I change from the experience of mothering him. And now, of course, my story of our relationship has become a part of this dance. On his last birthday, for example, Ben said: "Aren't you proud of me, mum, because I was once a two-year-old who muddled his pronouns, was afraid of noises and obsessed with numbers?" He will often quote slabs of the book to me—usually laughing, sometimes puzzled—an experience that is confronting for me but which seems to please him. If I wrote the memoir partly as a way to create intimacy between mother and son, equally it has the potential to create distance as Ben becomes older and may read it in a different light. This is not something I have any control over. Right now, he is mildly proud of his role in the book, but much more interested in his own life and his current hobby of making videos using cardboard cut-out characters and a range of wonderful accents for his large cast of characters. Like Moore says of George and his painting, of Sam and his shrieking, I am very happy to see Ben doing what he wants in the way he wants. I would like life to be easier for him, but I wouldn't change him one bit. As LaSalle's son says: "Here's the big secret: I never changed. I'm still the person I was when I was little. The world just caught up to me" (263). That's what we are doing, my son and I: waiting for the world to catch up.

I am grateful to Black Inc. for permission to reproduce an extract from my book Reaching One Thousand: A Story of Love, Motherhood and

Autism (2012) at the start of this article <http://www.blackincbooks.com/ books/reaching-one-thousand>.

[1]My son's name has been changed in order to protect his privacy. "Ben" is the name he has in my motherhood memoir, *Reaching One Thousand*.
[2]I use the term "autism" here to refer to the range of autistic spectrum disorders, including classic autism, high-functioning autism and Asperger's Syndrome. I have chosen to use the terms "autism" and "autistic person" (rather than person with autism) based on the views of autistic adults. (See for example "Why I Dislike Person First Language" by Jim Sinclair.)
[3]The term "neurotypicals" has been used by autistic people to speak of non-autistic or neurologically typical people.
[4]The paragraphs above are reproduced with permission (and very slight adaptation) from my memoir *Reaching One Thousand: A Story of Love, Motherhood and autism* (Black Inc., 2012).
[5]For a good discussion of maternal ambivalence see "The Production and Purposes of Maternal Ambivalence" by Rozskia Parker in *Mothering and Ambivalence* (Parker).
[6]In her article "Metaphors of Autism, and Autism as Metaphor: An Exploration of Representation," Mitzi Waltz traces—and critiques—the uses of the siege/fortress autism metaphor from Bruno Bettleheim's work to contemporary usages.
[7]Couser here makes a distinction commonly made in Disability Studies between impairment, the actual bodily or neurological anomaly, and disability, the resultant social response or cultural construction.

WORKS CITED

Couser, G. Thomas. "'Paradigms' Cost: Representing Vulnerable Subjects." *Literature and Medicine* 24.1 (Spring 2005): 19-30. Print.

Frank, Arthur W. *The Wounded Storyteller: Body, Illness and Ethics.* Chicago: University of Chicago Press, 1999. Print.

LaSalle, Barbara, with contributions by Benjamin Levinson. *Finding Ben: A Mother's Journey Through the Maze of Asperger's.* New York: McGraw-Hill, 2003. Print.

Maurice, Catherine. *Let Me Hear Your Voice: A Family's Triumph Over Autism.* New York: Fawcett Columbine, 1993. Print.

Moore, Charlotte. *George and Sam: Two Boys, One Family, and Autism.* London: Viking, 2004. Print.

Moore, Charlotte. *George and Sam: Two Boys, One Family, and Autism.* London: Viking, 2012. Kindle Edition.

Osteen, Mark. "Autism and Representation: A Comprehensive Introduction." *Autism and Representation.* Ed. Mark Osteen. New York, Routledge, 2008. 1-47. Print.

Parker, Rozskia. "The Production and Purposes of Maternal Ambivalence." *Mothering and Ambivalence.* Eds. Wendy Hollway and Brid Featherstone. London: Routledge, 1997. 17-36. Print.

Sinclair, Jim. "Why I Dislike Person First Language." *Jim Sinclair's Website.* np., nd. Web. 18 February 2010.

Waltz, Mitzi. "Metaphors of Autism, and Autism as Metaphor: An Exploration of Representation." 2000. *Interdisciplinary.net.* np, nd. Web. 18 February 2010.

Waltz, Mitzi. "Reading Case Studies of People with Autistic Spectrum Disorders: A Cultural Studies Approach to Issues of Disability Representation." *Disability and Society* 20.4 (June 2005): 421-435. Print.

Wendell, Susan. "Towards a Feminist Theory of Disability." *The Disability Studies Reader.* Ed. Lennard J. Davis. New York: Routledge, 1997. 260-278. Print.

8.
"Just Another Mother Who Has Lost Her Child"
Memoirs of Caregiving and Loss

KATHLEEN L. FOWLER

A voice was heard in Ramah, lamentation, and bitter weeping;
Rahel weeping for her children.
—Jeremiah 31:15, KJV

My plans for parenthood sat like scenery on an empty stage.
—Terra Trevor, *Pushing up the Sky* (216)

THE IMAGE of the bereaved mother has been a familiar archetype throughout history. We see her as Rahel (Rachel) Niobe, Hecuba, Demeter, Mary, or La Llorona. She is represented in sculptures and paintings, embedded in the imagery of many religions and equated with the wounded landscape and the torn nation. Her image is just as evocative now as in the past. Close-ups of grieving mothers dominate virtually any current news account of disaster or conflict. Still, her image is usually the object of an external gaze, and her story is usually told (if told at all) by others. Mothers' memoirs of caregiving and loss—including the three considered here, Barbara Peabody's *The Screaming Room* (1986), Maria Housden's *Hannah's Gift* (2002), and Terra Trevor's *Pushing up the Sky* (2006)—offer the story of caregiving and of loss directly from mothers themselves, each particular, unique, and personal. Through such works, Rachel's ancient lamentation takes on new forms of expression and a new urgency, pulling us into a community of love and pain and loss that includes other voices of pain just beyond our hearing. At the same time, as I will discuss later, these narratives interrogate and contest a powerful cultural gender script that defines the "caregiving mother."

Mothers' grief narratives unmake an assumptive world in which children do not suffer or die.[1] Mortality patterns in recent years—at least for the more privileged groups in the United States—have led us to consider a child's death as unnatural, untimely, and unacceptable, adding a further layer of discomfort, unfamiliarity, and anxiety to the contemplation of the grieving mother. As Terra Trevor records, "Jay's death meant that I was suddenly plunged into a role for which there was no name—a mother whose child had died" (208). Nancy Mairs asks: "Who can contemplate the death of a child ... dispassionately? It appalls in a way no other death could do because it violates the natural order. Never mind that the true nature of nature may be chaotic ... We don't readily tolerate any deviation from the script..." (104).

Caregiving memoirs blend the characteristics of illness narratives—what G. Thomas Couser has called the autopathography—and grief memoirs focused on sudden loss. In an earlier article from 2007, I looked at the nature of the relatively recent genre, women's grief memoir, with "its fusion of art and heart, of writing and reflection, of literary consciousness and personal and social analysis, of the story of the deceased and the story of the griever" (Fowler 525). As a subset of this genre, the mother's memoir of caregiving and loss attends more to the illness and caregiving journey itself than to the grief journey following the death. Their growing popularity reflects a current openness to sharing stories of illness, death, and grief as well as a recent tendency among grief theorists to focus on expressive forms of mourning, meaning reconstruction and storytelling (for example, Bosticco and Thompson). Anne Hunsaker Hawkins maintains that such caregiving narratives: "form a part of the process of grieving [interweaving] the witnessing author's feelings, thoughts, and organizing images and metaphors, as he or she goes about the work of mourning" (3).

Maria Housden[2] shares the story of her journey with her second child, Hannah, whose diagnosis at age three with an abdominal tumor leads Maria into the unfamiliar terrain of caregiving for a dying child and for her siblings. A chapter title, "Peeling the Onion of Grief," captures not only the multiple layers of grieving (before *and* after the death), but also the sense of a deliberate embracing of grief work as essential to healing and growth (Housden 81). Maria writes later, "My suffering wasn't something I was going to have to let go of; it had become part of what I had to offer, part of who I am" (Housden 187). Indeed, it is a new source of empowerment: "I was much more than a bereaved mother. My anger at the world had diffused into a determination to do something purposeful and real in my life" (Housden 187).

Housden's text is retrospective, written several years after the death of her child. So too is Terra Trevor's narrative. Trevor, a Native American mother of three children (two adopted from Korea), writes eloquently and movingly about caring for and losing Jay, her youngest child, who develops a brain tumor at age seven and dies at age 15.[3] Jay's story is richly interwoven with the stories of Terra's other two children and a host of other issues: family dynamics, multi-racial identity, transracial adoption, older child adoption, and cultural interchange. *Pushing up the Sky* is a narrative about living with complexity, ambiguity, and pain, and finding a way to "dance whole again, with a newfound rhythm" (Trevor 216). Comparing herself to the shattered Mt. St. Helen's after Jay's death, Terra says: "I began gathering the pieces that were left of me, and coaxing them into growth. I was starting out again but like the mountain, I'd lost all of my big trees" (Trevor 203).

An older narrative by Barbara Peabody (the mother of four adult children) shares the shock and anguish of the illness and loss of her son Peter, who dies at age 29 in the early days of AIDS. Unlike the Housden and Trevor narratives, Peabody's text is in the form of daily journals written as her son's illness progressed. There is none of the distancing found in the other two; instead, the power of the text inheres in its raw, urgent, almost overwhelming immediacy. Indeed, instead of being a typical grief memoir, its fusion of pathography with personal journaling and polemic gives it much of the didactic force of Audre Lorde's *The Cancer Journals*. Where Trevor's narrative of Jay's illness and death is part of a larger family story, Peabody's story, as Couser observes, "focuses narrowly and intensely on her son's last months of life, his suffering, and especially her emotions as his sole caregiver; ...The mother's book represents and enacts emotional catharsis, articulating and exorcising physical and emotional pain" (132). Couser, in fact, describes *The Screaming Room* as ... "probably the most agonized and agonizing illness narrative" among the many that he considers (133). Other family figures are momentary presences but, again and again, the text returns to the tightening focus on Barbara and Peter. When a friend accuses her of being obsessive, Barbara records plaintively: "I don't think I am. I just don't have time for my personal life now. Peter is my personal life.

How can I get anyone to understand this?" (Peabody 65).

For Barbara, at the end of the work, there is only the hint of healing achieved through giving back to others in the AIDS community and by speaking out about "this vicious disease" (Peabody 279). Peabody's book itself functions as testimony as the quote from the *San Francisco Chronicle* (included in the book's front material) makes clear: "The most compelling and poignant story of AIDS comes not from a doctor or professional writer but from Barbara Peabody." She is acutely aware of how a hostile society has intensified the horror of Peter's illness and left her feeling disenfranchised in her grief. Horror, pain, sorrow, and anger remain with her even as she accepts that "Peter lives on in each of us" (Peabody 279).

Trevor and Housden organize their stories around underlying metaphors and imagery. *Pushing Up the Sky* (as the title itself suggests) is deeply grounded in nature. Red-tail hawks, owls, ravens—and their feathers—signify wisdom and comfort throughout. The creek is a place of laughter, healing, natural transitions and transformations. The changing sky reflects and transforms emotional states. Blizzards and snow represent threats and loss and exhilaration. Her faith, she says at one point: "like a rope tied from the house to the barn in a blizzard, guided me" (Trevor 63).

Nature for Terra is home and healing and stability. It is echoed and answered by Trevor's other principal metaphor, culture. This second metaphor is also implicit in the book's title, taken "from a traditional American Indian story of the Snohomish tribe which testifies and speaks to the great power of what we can accomplish when people work together with a common goal" (Author's Note). Trevor's memoir is filled with the energizing but disorienting impact of cultural exchange and culture clash. These are located within the family itself and beyond it, as the family encounters others, at the Korean church, in visits to Korea itself, at the Indian family gatherings and at the powwows. Food, traditional clothing, rituals, language—all figure largely here. By drawing on both nature and culture, Trevor ensures that we recognize that Jay's illness and dying are both deeply natural and culturally contextualized. She pulls her two imageries together in the figure of the dance, a cultural construct—but one that connects the body with the earth and with its rhythms. Nature and culture merge as well in the image of the 1000 paper cranes folded for Jay by an invisible, international, and multicultural community of well-wishers: "Each paper crane was a loving tribute. We could feel the power, the precision and devotion in the folding, the unfolding of each wing, a prayer" (Trevor 180-81).

Housden's metaphors are primarily visual artifacts—the finger-paintings that she and Hannah construct (71), the magic wands at Hannah's birthday party (62), the waiting room where "There was no room ... for anything but two chairs and the truth" (41), an absurdly inappropriate and expensive ivory satin dress (89) that Maria impulsively buys for Hannah to wear at Christmas now that she has finally shed her hospital gown, and—most centrally—Hannah's impractical but deeply loved red shoes: "The image of them continues to live in my heart, a timeless reminder of Hannah's bright spirit" (222).

Peabody's text is the most prosaic of the three. It is almost completely free of figurative language beyond the central metaphor of the internal "screaming room" although Hawkins is surely right when she contends that, "the metaphor of 'fighting' disease is ... pervasive in *The Screaming Room*" (70). Hawkins sees the "battle myth" as essential to Barbara but problematic for Peter who is, perhaps "at some deep level not someone for whom combat, struggle, and fighting are desirable ways of coping with illness" (71). (It is interesting that Trevor's Jay also rejects the "battle myth," asking "So why do you suppose when a person dies from cancer they say he lost the battle?" and then quickly adding, "Don't worry, Mom, I know dying is not about losing" [182].) For Barbara, fighting a threat to her child is so fundamental to her conceptualization of the mother's role that it hardly functions on a metaphoric level any more than does her ongoing work as an artist, which could have readily served her as a metaphoric mine. Apparently, Peter's illness is simply too stark, too real, to allow her to reach for imagery for either comfort or meaning. Instead, Peabody piles up detail after detail of Peter's deterioration and the interventions he endures, focusing on his tormented body and the tortures of the medical system. As Couser comments, "This frank narrative is a salutary reminder of how sanitized most illness narratives are, how they minimize suffering and pain, how they insulate readers from contact with bodily fluids" (133).

The central imagery for each writer is closely linked to the spiritual/existential vision of the narrator. Terra draws spiritual healing from the natural world, from the Korean church that she belongs to, and from Native American rituals and ceremonies. She notes at one point the empowering blending of these different worships: "The Korean community was praying for Jay, there was the prayer line linking across the U.S., and now I knew Jay would be prayed for in the ancient way in the sweat lodge ceremony" (Trevor 112). Maria wrestles with her faith as Hannah sickens. Holding Hannah's sobbing brother, Maria anguishes: "Wasn't it enough for God that Hannah is going to die. Did he have to take Will's six-year-old innocence, too?" (Housden 115). She finds herself comforted by the support and understanding of her Methodist pastor, Laurajane, who resists offering conventional reassurance: "'I want more than anything to make sense of what is happening to you guys, but I can't even begin to pretend that this is something I understand.... it's hard to believe that the God I love would let a child suffer like this'" (Housden 44).

Hannah several times surprises Maria with an instinctive sense of ritual and prayer. When she can finally eat again after her transplant, Hannah is offered pizza, ice cream, cookies, "whatever you want" (Housden 93). She baffles the doctor with her selection. She explains in annoyance: "'I want a hard roll and grape juice,' she said holding her hands out palm side up in exasperation, 'like *Communion at church*' she added, as if it were so obvious that we were dolts for not seeing it" (Housden 93). Maria draws strength from Hannah's quiet assurance: "'Mommy,' she said quietly, 'do you know that even if I go to heaven, I'm going to come back?'" (Housden 146). A sudden vision of Hannah "dancing in the sparkly darkness, radiant, laughing and waving" (Housden 146) renews Maria's faith: "Faith is not about believing but about letting go of belief.... Faith is the still heart that refuses nothing, our willingness to trust things as they are" (Housden 147). She is further comforted by Will's dream that Hannah has visited him after her death: "'She says heaven is really cool, and she's not scared. They have baseball there, you know, and Hannah's on the green team'" (Housden 183).

For Barbara, in keeping with her spare and pained narrative, there is little discussion of faith or spirituality. God does enter the text, even appearing in the first line, but only in desperate apostrophes: "Oh, my God, no-o-o" (Peabody 1). "Oh God stop it stop it" (Peabody 125). "My God! Four weeks at least!" (Peabody 223). Barbara does at the end offer a vision of Peter's afterlife, but it is a firmly earthbound vision: "Now his spirit was free—free to watch the seasons change on the mountains above, free to see his sunsets, free to sing eternally through the groves of cedar and pinon and smell their pungent smoke rising from squat, adobe chimneys. Free at last" (Peabody 277).

Peabody's text is closest to what Arthur Frank calls the "chaos narrative." Frank writes:

> ...its plot imagines life never getting better. Stories are chaotic in their absence of narrative order. Events are told as the storyteller experiences life: without sequence or discernable causality.... The teller of chaos stories is, preeminently, the wounded storyteller, but those who are truly living the chaos cannot tell it in words. To turn the chaos into a verbal story is to have some reflective grasp of it. (97-98)

Yet Peabody's text evinces little such "reflective grasp." Instead we find acutely immediate journal entries transcribed apparently verbatim. Words stumble breathlessly into one another without regard for syntax or punctuation. Medical language, daily routines, and anguished outbursts mingle on the page as they do in the illness experience. Frank acknowledges that such stories are "anxiety provoking" (97) but insist that they must be attended to: "The need to honor chaos stories is both moral and clinical. Until the chaos narrative can be honored, the world in all its possibilities is being denied" (109). Suzanne Poirier and Lioness Ayres (2002) agree: "the best way to understand caregiving is as a story that is being written as it is lived" (170). This is precisely what Peabody offers us.

As they begin their unexpected caregiving journey, the three mothers find themselves lost in and struggling with a highly gendered cultural construct which will not safely house them in this new place. As Poirier and Ayres note: "caring has been too long devalued and understandably but misleadingly overdetermined by gender. As a result, caring remains vulnerable to the social and cultural conditions that devalued and gendered it" (167). While we have multiple names for the Grieving Mother, the caregiving mother has only *one* name: Mom. It is no accident that in a crowded setting when a panicked child's voice wails "MOMMY!" even mothers who have not had a small child around for decades swivel instantly toward the call. The caregiving mom is visualized in actions so familiar, so elemental, and so timeless that they have become anonymous snapshots: the mama bear defending her cubs, the sympathetic comforter kissing the scraped knee, the patient, silent figure soothing the child's "fevered brow," the bustling figure in the kitchen preparing chicken soup. Mom is conceptualized as body parts—enfolding arms, pillowy breasts, cool hands, busy fingers, tender lips, a welcoming lap, a ready ear. If she does have a voice, it is one that sings lullabies or chides lovingly or reads a children's story.

The power of the cultural script becomes most vividly apparent when the mother is absent or deceased. The absent mother looms in texts and images and psychiatrist accounts. But the living mother, if she observes the script faithfully, fades quietly into the background.[4] By tradition, Mom is not the central character of the narrative nor the consciousness through which the story is told. The focus of attention is on those for whom she cares. She sits lovingly but namelessly by the bedside in a painting by Edvard Munch; unsurprisingly, the title reads: "The Sick Child." Mom plays the essential supporting role. She is the launchpad; she must be outgrown and left behind. Even when the caregiving mom is appreciated in retrospect, that appreciation is for the value of that loving foundation for empowering the *child*.

This paradigm of the caregiving mother—supremely competent, defending her young from any threat, fierce, tender, courageous, inexhaustible, calm, warm, loving—holds its power in part because it is so deeply inscribed that it is almost beyond recognition or critique. Each of the mothers writing these memoirs finds herself consciously and unconsciously guided by, constrained by, and fiercely resistant to these cultural expectations. They themselves unpack and revise the paradigm in the course of their narratives. After all, the central premise of the script itself has failed them. The child they are caring for *is* dying and they cannot ultimately protect this child from that reality. In her examination of multiple narratives of parental loss, Ann Burack-Weiss concludes, "the severe disability or fatal illness of a child is an earthquake: the very ground on which their life has been constructed has shifted—and they struggle to find footing in an alternate universe" (48). Maria uses almost the same phrase "feeling as if I had passed through an invisible fold in the universe and landed in some altered state of reality" (Housden 25). For Terra it is a "deep dark hole" (Trevor 115), for Barbara a "void" (Peabody 96).

Grief itself is discohering, and what Therese Rando calls "anticipatory mourning" is a constant companion on the caregiving journey—but when does a caregiver have the time to "indulge" it? Terra writes: "I felt like I was on some kind of emotional layaway plan: experience life now and feel it later" (Trevor 181). Barbara has put her emotions "on automatic timer.... I cry for the five-minute trip to the grocery store, check my tears at the door, and cry again on the way home. Meanwhile, I carry my screaming room inside me. It has no doors" (Peabody 139). Maria tries to face the grief squarely: "I couldn't wall myself off from pain and fear. To turn away from them would be to turn away from Hannah" (Housden 44).

As caregiving mothers, the writers have tended to feel intensely alone, unique, and isolated. Terra writes: "We felt like we were the only two people in the world who knew this deep level of pain" (Trevor 111). Maria's words are almost identical: "We were like two people in a one-man life raft in the middle of a dark ocean" (Housden 33). Observing that "AIDS is such a terribly lonely disease, for the mother as well as the patient" (Peabody 279), Barbara finds brief respite in her sister's visit: "For a few days, I have someone to whom I can pour out my fears and anxieties. I have felt so alone, so weak, so helpless" (Peabody 96). Barbara, Maria, and Terra each seek support groups for themselves and for their children to try to ease the sense of isolation and to share stories and strategies. And all three feel the need to give back to these support groups after their own journeys.

The caregivers who write these memoirs feel that their strength (required by the cultural script, compelled by the illness situation, and perceived by everyone around them as a given) is really only an illusion. In fact, they are barely holding on. Barbara writes: "I don't like being thought of as some grand heroine. I'm just being a mother" (Peabody 109). Terra is irritated by friend's compliments: "'You look great and you're so strong.'" She retorts, "'Look beyond my freshly washed hair ... to where my mind aches'" (Trevor 114). Maria, by contrast, feels the need to maintain the façade: "It had been one of my guiltiest pleasures to tell people that I was 'fine' even when I wasn't. Although I knew it wasn't the truth, it kept me from feeling like a gigantic wound that wouldn't stop hemorrhaging" (Housden 131). Burack-Weiss finds a similar pattern in other parental caregiving narratives: "The authors want it known that they are not stoics, saints, or seers. They felt their children's physical and psychic suffering in their own bones" (50).

All along the caregiving journey, each mother finds that she has to write and enact her own script. Barbara records: "I have come to realize what it really means to be a mother, to fight for your child" (Peabody 32) and a little later: "I gave him life and now if he's to die, I'll be here for him. I have no choice" (Peabody 34). She acknowledges that Peter's illness has driven her back to the relationship of a mother and a very young child. As Peter writhes in a seizure, she reverts to talking to him as if he were a terrified toddler: "Peter, it's all right, Mom's here, Peter, Peter, Mom's here, it's all right, they're fixing it they're fixing it, it will be all right" (Peabody 80). Yet her inability to be that all-powerful mom batters her: "But I know it won't be all right, it'll never be the same" (Peabody 80).

Life, mothering, illness, dying, grieving are messy, without clarity, off-script, powerful, life-altering—and compelling. Recent studies of caregiving and caregivers offer a helpful context in which to view these memoirs. Such studies often emphasize "caregiver burden" and note the measurable impact on emotional, psychological, and physical health for the caregiver. Blood pressure, impaired immune system, injuries, and depression are all reported risks for caregivers (Caregivers of New Jersey). Poirier and Ayres, however, reviewing multiple recent studies that have questioned the primacy of this "burden," conclude: "burden is only one component of caregiving, and [caregivers] talk about the satisfactions of love, altruism, and other motives, meanings, or moral frameworks that sustain caregivers and buffer negative feelings of burden" (83). Burack-Weiss finds confirmation in caregiving narratives: "...caregiving was not an intrusion on family life but an intrinsic part of it, a crucible in which the crux of relationships was revealed, an occasion not only of stress and burden, but of growth, possibility and meaning" (xii).[5]

Many caregivers report feeling inadequately trained to meet needs and, in fact, only nineteen percent of caregivers currently report obtaining formal caregiving training (NAC/AARP). The urgency of learning medical information and nursing techniques is a major theme for all three memoirists. Barbara largely trains herself, seeking avidly for any possible information or technique: "we're going to need to know all we can. Where else are they doing research—New York Hospital, Mt. Sinai, Columbia, where?" (Peabody 23). She is not afraid to disagree with or even disregard the physician's instructions: "I've been rubbing acyclovir ointment into the four original lesions for three days now, even though the doctor said not to.... What can it hurt?" (Peabody 233). Later, she is trained by the nurse to use the "hyper—al": "Step by step we go over the procedure.... The whole procedure looks so complicated—so many joinings to be Betadine swabbed and taped—my mind reels. But I will learn it. I must" (Peabody 201).

Terra is given a crash course in handling the oxygen tank: "There were so many dials and valves and coils and hoses that at first it seemed too complicated. Frosty air escaped the overflow valve. Although I corrected the problem almost immediately, Jay's dark intelligent eyes regarded me with raw suspicion" (Trevor 185). Trevor too is determined to learn as much as she can about Jay's condition and possible treatments and manages to make herself an invisible witness in medical procedures and discussions:

> My act worked. I looked like an extra technician or a student observing and was allowed to stay in the room with Jay while the radiologist and a crew of others began to chart his treatment course.... Always I was mistaken for somebody else. "You are his mother? I had no idea; you seem so calm." ...The real me should have been reported as a missing person. (Trevor 135)

Maria's new assertiveness with medical professionals results from recognizing that her former compliance came from a sense of inadequacy and timidity. "Why hadn't I trusted myself more?" she asks; then, "The doctors knew symptoms of illness as they applied generally to children. I knew Hannah. We were authorities on different subjects ... I knew one thing: I was going to have to start speaking up" (Housden 20-21). She insists on staying with her daughter in the isolation room in the hospital for three weeks, recording scrupulously every dosage, every medication in a journal. She is triumphant that "Dr. Kamalaker had designated me the sole person responsible for handling and maintaining the Broviac and its site: even nurses and residents were given instructions not to touch it" (Housden 75). She comes to trust her own judgment enough to deviate from the rules: "Several times I quietly rebelled against the insanity of it all, lied to the nurses, and told them I had bathed her when I had actually let her sleep instead" (Housden 87). She supports Hannah's refusal to let the doctor examine her until he tells her his *"real* name" (Housden 27), and she insists that the hospital honor Hannah's request to have her red shoes with her during surgery (Housden 35). She refuses to accept restrictions on Hannah attending pre-school or going swimming: "I didn't want to expose Hannah to unnecessary risks, but I wasn't willing to postpone her joy, either" (Housden 75).

Each mother must face multiple difficult decisions. Dr. Markoff wisely advises Maria and her husband: "Make the best decision you can with the information you have at that time ... just keep telling yourselves, 'We did the best we could with what we knew'" (Housden 30). Barbara, alas, did not have Dr. Markoff to advise her. She is haunted by every decision that is to be or has been made: "Could I have done something, anything to prevent this?" (Peabody 17). She rages silently, "The anger, the pain, the hurt, every thing is boiling up and out of me—rage with everything, the whole world, AIDS, Peter, myself. I don't even know what it is" (Peabody 206). She is furious at insensitive physicians, opportunistic politicians, and those who are oblivious to the impact of the disease of AIDS. There is simple hatred for

> [Y]ou who think it's exactly what homosexuals deserve, that they're perverted and abnormal anyway....No one deserves this, no one. (Peabody 127)

The ground keeps trembling as the needs change. For Barbara the course is a straight plunge as Peter's condition hurtles swiftly downward: "Observing other patients, I see a pattern to the progress of AIDS. First the handicapped plaque for the car, next the cane, then the wheelchair and finally the hospital bed at home. I hate giving in to the signposts. I hate it" (Peabody 132). For Terra and Maria, it is the roller coaster between acute circumstances and treatments and the uneasy respite of a remission period that lasts almost long enough to feel normal again. Terra writes, "We held our breath. What if the brain tumor came back, dragging us away again? Each day when it didn't happen, I gained more confidence" (Trevor 119-120). Hannah's remission is shorter and Maria never fully feels secure: "I wanted to believe it was going to last, but I smelled the not-knowing in the air" (Housden 112). These narratives carry us with them, moment by moment, on an unsought journey, allowing us to appreciate the intricacies and the disorientation of a world that will not stop reshaping itself despite all efforts to control or slow it. It is this specificity and immediacy that gives the narrative account such power.

With the death, the caregiving mother can finally let her grief flood in, but as it does it also unexpectedly brings her into a sense of community with other grieving mothers both past and present. For Terra, identification is sudden, searing, but also healing as she recalls the multiple losses of her great-great-grandmother:

> It went on like that for years, grandma giving birth and grandpa making baby boards, digging holes and lowering those dead babies into the ground.... My mind glimpsed my great-great-grandma and I felt a distant memory pulling me back. I could hear her wailing like wind coming up, crying, swaying.... I wondered if [the nearby white settlers] knew the high, shrill sounds pressing against the night were from an Indian mother mourning her dead child. (Trevor 189)

For Barbara, the realization is so humbling that it almost invalidates the significance of her own personal anguish and threatens her identity: "I am just another mother who has lost her child, who holds his empty, wasted body in her arms and mourns, grieves, cries for the loss of part of her own body and soul" (Peabody 273). For Maria, the new understanding offers her a way to endure and forgive the obliviousness of those around her. Shocked at a woman who complains that her driver's license photo makes her "look like a *chemotherapy patient*, for God's sake!" (Housden 190), Maria muses: "I knew there had been a time in my life when I had been oblivious to suffering—my own and everyone else's" (Housden 190-1). She now reaches out to help other grieving mothers: "I had learned to have compassion for myself, and now recognizing suffering in others, I could have the same compassion for them" (Housden 193).

Many grief memoirists tell their stories in order to, like Housden, reach out to other parents facing such challenges and grief. Arthur Frank writes:

> People tell stories not just to work out their own changing identities, but also to guide others who will follow them. They

seek not to provide a map that can guide others—each must create his own—but rather to witness the experience of reconstructing one's own map.... Storytelling is *for* an other just as much as it is for oneself. (17)

The act itself of writing and publishing the narrative ultimately repudiates the cultural script's instruction that the caregiving mother should remain voiceless. The real mother—the flesh and bone mother caring for her dying child—must search for a new model that allows her a voice, a consciousness, a set of choices, a name. To tell the story of that caregiving, each memoirist struggles with multiple challenges. How to be other than "just another mother who has lost her child"? How to honor your own suffering without diminishing the importance of the child's experience? How to face again and retrace that journey as you write the story? How to admit others into the sanctity and intimacy of this place of pain and of memory? These are questions that demand great courage and extraordinary generosity.

In these memoirs, the dying child is indeed a central character, but so is the mother. More significantly, the mother is the consciousness through which the story is told. As Maria observes: "[I]t is my expectations, the story I weave around the truth, that make what is happening seem better or worse, good or bad, fair, or not fair" (Housden 38). Terra writes: "I shuffled out into the empty field of my mind to find enough words to make it through another winter of writing" (Trevor 203). Barbara says: "I gradually found my way out of my screaming room by sorting out and writing down all that happened to us. I have closed the door, but scars and bruises will always remain inside. Tears still come when least expected" (Peabody 279).

In choosing to share their stories with the world—to publish them— the memoirists compel us as readers to scrutinize the potent cultural script—to look beyond "Kleenex moment" tableaux into the emotional, physical, social, and existential reality of a real mother facing the life-altering illness and ultimately the death of her child. Emily Dickinson writes: "Essential Oils—are wrung—/The Attar from the Rose/Be not expressed by Suns—alone—/It is the gift of Screws."[6] Whether the "gift of screws" for these memoirists turns out to be beauty or wisdom or hope or faith or a passion for activism, they each generously share with us what their journey has yielded. In doing so, they contribute to our collective understanding of mothering, caring, grieving, and supporting one another in the face of the fragility of life and the vulnerability of the heart. We are privileged to be their witnesses.

ENDNOTES

[1]For a discussion of the assumptive world and bereaved parents see Laura Matthews and Samuel J. Marwit's "Examining the Assumptive World Views of Parents Bereaved by Accident, Murder, and Illness."

[2]To distinguish between the mother as author and the mother as narrator/character within the text, I will follow Hawkins' lead in referring by last name to the author and by first name to the narrator/character. Distinctions between author, narrator, and character are among many issues that have interested scholars of the memoir. Theorists have debated questions of authenticity, the nature of memory, narrative ethics, heteroglossia, positionality, embodiment, performativity and more. See Sidonie Smith and Julia Watson's *Reading Autobiography* for an excellent survey of such topics.

[3]The story of Jay's illness (my focus here) does not actually begin until page 105, when Jay's first symptom appears. Jay's illness story is paired with—and simultaneous to—the complicated and fraught journey of love, hope, and grief around Terra's oldest child, Kyeong Sook, who comes to the family at age ten as "a child so neglected and shuffled between so many homes that she contained the rage and sadness that defined her childhood" (161). Terra's own caregiving and grief story are as much about her troubled relationship with Kyeong Sook as it is about Jay. In focusing just on Jay, I regret that I must distort the full richness of Trevor's experience and her narrative.

[4]If Mom betrays the script, of course, she is unmaternal, even unwomanly. She is depicted as dominating, possessive, selfish, whiny, "stage mother," "helicopter mom," "Mommie dearest."

[5]The frequency of this theme in caregivers' narratives may, of course, be profoundly misleading in that those who have been overwhelmed or crushed or embittered by the burdens of caregiving may not be drawn to record their experience in writing or, if they do, editors and publishers may not choose to usher such works into publication.

[6] From poem 675 by Emily Dickinson, found in *The Complete Poems of Emily Dickinson*. Ed. Thomas H. Johnson. Boston: Little Brown, 1960.

WORKS CITED

Bosticco, C. and T. L. Thompson. "Narratives and Story Telling in Coping with Grief and Bereavement." *Omega* 51.1 (2005): 1-16. Print.

Burack-Weiss, Ann. *The Caregiver's Tale: Loss and Renewal in Memoirs of Family Life*. New York: Columbia University Press, 2006. Print.

Caregivers of New Jersey. Homepage. The Family Resource Network, n.d. Web. 18 Dec. 2012.

Couser, G. Thomas. *Recovering Bodies: Illness, Disability, and Life Writing*. Madison: University of Wisconsin Press, 1997. Print.

Fowler, Karen. "'So New, So New:' Art and Heart in Women's Grief Memoirs." *Women's Studies International* 36 (2007): 1-25. Print.

Frank, Arthur. *The Wounded Storyteller: Body, Illness, and Ethics*. Chicago: University of Chicago Press, 1995. Print.

Hawkins, Ann H. *Reconstructing Illness: Studies in Pathography*. 2nd ed. West Lafayette, IN: Purdue University Press, 1999. Print.

Housden, Maria. *Hannah's Gift: Lessons from a Life Fully Lived*. New York: Bantam: 2002. Print.

Lorde, Audre. *The Cancer Journals*. San Francisco: Aunt Lute Books, 1980. Print.

Mairs, Nancy. "Lost children." *A Troubled Guest: Life and Death Stories*. Boston: Beacon Press, 2001. 94-114. Print.

Matthews, Laura and Samuel J. Marwit. "Examining the Assumptive World Views of Parents Bereaved by Accident, Murder, and Illness." *Omega* 48.2 (2003/4): 115-136. Print.

National Alliance for Caregiving (NAC) and AARP. *Caregiving in the U.S.* Bethesda: National Alliance for Caregiving, and Washington, DC: AARP, 2009.

"Caregiving Statistics." *Caregivers of New Jersey*. The Family Resource Network, n.d. Web. 21 Jan. 2013.

Peabody, Barbara. *Screaming Room: A Mother's Journal of her Son's Struggle with AIDS—A True Story of Love, Dedication and Courage*. New York: HarperCollins, 1987. Print.

Poirier, Suzanne and Lioness Ayres. *Stories of Family Caregiving: Reconsiderations of Theory, Literature, and Life*. Madison: University Wisconsin Press, 2002. Print.

Rando, Therese A., ed. *Clinical Dimensions of Anticipatory Mourning: Theory and Practice in Working with the Dying, their Loved Ones, and*

Their Caregivers. Champaign, IL: Research Press, 2000. Print.

Smith, Sidonie and Julia Watson. *Reading Autobiography: A Guide for Interpreting Life Narratives*. Minneapolis: University of Minnesota Press, 2001. Print.

Trevor, Terra. *Pushing up the Sky: A Mother's Story*. El Dorado Hills, CA: Korean Adoptee Adoptive Family Network, 2006. Print.

SECTION THREE
MOTHERS WITHOUT BORDERS

9.
Transcending the Mind/Body Dichotomy to Save My Own Life

TARA MCDONALD JOHNSON

MOST PEOPLE take their ambulance ride after they almost drop dead in a shopping center, but I took mine before. While I was seven months pregnant with my first child, I innocently plopped down on the couch—for a much-deserved rest after some house cleaning—and a huge clot of blood fell out of me. Understandably alarmed, my husband called for an ambulance to rush me to the hospital. I spent a week hospitalized, undergoing many tests and seeing many specialists, but nothing about my condition changed. I was experiencing steady, painless vaginal bleeding, but otherwise, I felt fine physically, and my son was active in utero and not in distress.

The question—what was happening to me and my baby?—remained at the center of my existence for the next four weeks. After my weeklong hospital stay, the doctors had no answers. They sent me home on strict bed rest, and for four weeks, I lay on my left side. The only exception was my scheduled prenatal appointments, which always ended with an additional brief stay in the hospital where they ran more tests, hoping to arrive at some diagnosis. Meanwhile, I missed my own baby shower, and I missed putting the finishing touches on my son's nursery. In effect, I was simply missing—separated from all the excitement and anticipation that surrounds a baby's arrival. I became a body—my son's incubator—and it was this body that had taken over the primary responsibility for carrying and delivering my son safely. There wasn't anything else that anybody could do. The best medical minds at my disposal had all attempted to help me but to no result.

While the medical minds tried their best, my friends and family also hypothesized some optimistic amateur diagnoses. I heard in excruciating detail all about how a cousin's friend's sister-in-law had vaginal bleeding throughout her entire pregnancy, and her baby "came out fine." Or about how a neighbor's co-worker lost her mucous plug in the office during her sixth month only to give birth three weeks after her due date. I thought, Great! I've been lumped in with the world's weirdest, freakiest pregnancies.

Even though the doctors, my family, and my friends were thinking, thinking, thinking and trying to make some sense of the chaos I was experiencing, they actively encouraged me not to think. My stress and anxiety levels were so high that their advice, which was to basically shut down my brain and let my body do its job, made some sense. They told me:

"You're reading too many baby books and spoiling the surprise!"

"This is the perfect example of why women should give birth at home with no medical intervention."

"It can't be anything that serious. Women have been giving birth for thousands of years with no problem. How else would we be here?"

Knowing full well that these comments were completely idiotic at the time, my nascent mother's brain—the one with the Ph.D. in Victorian literature and the academic job—stopped thinking for a while, stopped asking questions for a while, stopped being engaged for a while and tried to relax. My brain let my unconscious, involuntary bodily functions be in charge of the well-being of my baby and myself.

Dividing myself into body and brain made sense at the time because it seemed that I had exhausted all of the mental and intellectual resources at my disposal: it appeared to be outside of my control and my doctors' control. Even though my bodily condition seemed unique, in that my doctors could not diagnose my condition, dividing the self into body and brain is not a unique condition and seems quite common for new mothers. Immediately after my son was born, a dear friend sent me a copy of *Mama, PhD*, a collection of short motherhood memoirs written by academics, sharing their experiences and challenges reconciling academic work and motherhood.[1] I found the essay format to be accessible because the shorter length was practical for me as a new mother: I could read one or two memoirs in their entirety during one breastfeeding session. As a brand new mother of a premature baby and as an academic on maternity leave, I found a community of mothers struggling with the same challenges I was facing. The details of our motherhood experiences were different, but the themes were the same: reconciling motherhood with career goals and an intellectual life with the physicality of motherhood. These ideas became even more powerful because they were discussed by different mothers from different perspectives, which was possible because the collection included various voices instead of one. Elrena Evans in her memoir "Fitting In" and Elisabeth Rose Gruner in her memoir "I Am Not a Head on a Stick" chronicle their struggles with the fragmentation that results from separating body from brain, and both memoirs focus on the challenges to and the rewards of a whole life. Elizabeth Grosz argues in *Volatile Bodies* that separating body from brain is detrimental because the mind/body dichotomy not only defines the two as opposites but also privileges mind over body. When I succumbed to the mind/body dichotomy, I showed a preference for one part of myself over the other, putting my life at risk.

In part, I can blame Descartes for this. Grosz explains that Descartes's "dualism is the assumption that there are two distinct, mutually exclusive and mutually exhaustive substances, mind and body, each of which inhabits its own self-contained sphere. Taken together the two have incompatible characteristics" (6). Grosz shows through her analysis that for about 400 years, not only philosophers but feminists as well, have subjected themselves to the mind/body dichotomy. The fact that a person has a mind and a body is simply assumed. We've grown quite comfortable with the idea. It's more than an understatement to say that overcoming it myself might be difficult. Nevertheless, it's worth the attempt (as Evans, Gruner, and I discover), because Grosz argues that subjecting oneself to the dichotomy is detrimental, especially for women who are associated with body. Philosophically, the body has been associated with woman while the mind has been associated with man, and therefore, the mind has been privileged, making the mind/body dichotomy especially pertinent to motherhood. One commonality between the memoirs in *Mama, PhD* is this struggle to reconcile motherhood (which is associated primarily with the body) and academic careers (which are associated with the mind).[2] The *Mama, PhD* memoirs written by academics are especially effective in regard to describing and analyzing this struggle because these academic mothers are under extreme pressure to divide themselves into the mind of an intellectual while at work and a physical body undergoing uncontrollable biological processes while mothering. Shorter motherhood memoirs in collections like *Mama, PhD* can mitigate this pressure and challenge the dichotomy by enabling readers to examine the different experiences of mothers from a variety of backgrounds who challenge the dichotomy, using a variety of strategies, some more effective than others.

Unfortunately, I was an academic mother who initially chose an ineffective strategy to cope with the mind/body dichotomy. During my last month of pregnancy, I privileged my body because for seven months my body had been doing a satisfactory job. My son was growing and developing right on schedule. Other than being tired and hungry all the time, like so many other pregnant women, I felt great. I was teaching, writing, researching, choosing the perfectly-patterned crib set, buying the latest and greatest cloth diapers and organic baby clothes, reading all the baby books, and all the while, my body was steadily doing its work. I was trying to keep things in perspective: My grandmother gave birth to my mother only to go pick cotton on the family farm the next day. My mom gave birth to me after working a twelve-hour day as a nurse. Perhaps during the dull, endless hours of bed rest, I had been guilty of over-thinking the situation. Obviously, I had genes on my side, coming from a line of strong women.

After four hospital stays, four weeks of bed rest, and too many injections and pills, I began labor that the doctors would not be able to stop. My first instinct was to go to the hospital immediately, but my obstetrician determined that my contractions weren't regular enough. He wanted me to labor at home until my contractions were closer together or until my water broke, whichever occurred first. After all the time I had already spent in the hospital, laboring at home a little longer was an attractive option. Meanwhile, the contractions intensified, only to go away again. I began to doubt that I was in labor at all. At that point, I began to doubt my own sanity. Then I had what turned out to be a terrible idea. Walking alleviated some of my pain, so my husband and I went shopping.

I waddled right through the store's sliding glass doors and down the aisle to the child safety section. Here I browsed through the array of childproofing equipment: outlet plugs, toilet and drawer guards, corner covers. I started filling up my shopping basket. I reached for a third package of outlet covers (can you ever have too many?), and my hand just froze in mid air. Suddenly, the irony of my situation occurred to me. Here I was shopping for safety equipment while putting my baby in danger by not going straight to the hospital. I panned around, still holding the package of outlet covers, and my gaze met my husband's. He was standing just behind me, frozen, his thumb poised over a stopwatch to time my contractions. We determined in that moment, without even speaking a word, that we were going to the hospital and would not be leaving without our baby in our arms. With both my brain and body now at work, I knew the doctors had been wrong all along.

Once I was at the hospital a new obstetrician—one I had never met before—arrived, only to impart the news that I would have to be stronger and more powerful than I had anticipated. He told us that he couldn't feel the baby's head. After a lengthy ultrasound, my new doctor determined that it wasn't the baby's head pushing against my cervix. It was the placenta. The placenta was completely blocking the birth canal. I was to have an emergency C-section. He then gave orders to the nurse to prepare the operating room but not to waste time mopping the floor. I thought he was joking. But, after being shaved, sterilized, partially restrained, pumped full of antibiotics, and given a spinal block, I knew that my birth plan—my romanticized dream of how my baby would be born—was dead. It was dead, so that my baby and I could live.

I met my son about 45 minutes later. He was the most beautiful, the most wriggly, the absolute reddest thing I had ever seen. Around that same time, my doctor introduced me to my diagnosis. After four agonizing weeks, I would finally know what was wrong. I would know what had caused all the bleeding, all the bed rest, all of the consequential abdominal stapling. He said, "Vasa Previa. Google it if you dare. I'll be back to talk to you about it if you decide you want to know."

Here I was, forced into making the same decision again. Should I turn off my brain and live in blissful ignorance? Should I just thank my body for doing a decent job with the assistance of a competent doctor? Should I just enjoy gazing into my beautiful baby's eyes and live happily ever after?

No, I made that mistake once.

According to the International Vasa Previa Foundation (IVPF), Vasa Previa is an extremely rare condition that involves the placenta separating into two parts, leaving the major blood vessels in the placenta exposed. My placenta was providing blood and oxygen for my son, but because it had split, the blood was traveling between the two halves in blood vessels strung out like power lines along a residential street. The vessels had no protection from the elements. This caused the painless bleeding that my doctors could not explain. Any baby kicks or contractions damaged the blood vessels, and blood leaked out. The IVPF claims that Vasa Previa is easily diagnosed but often is not. Consequently, it's most often diagnosed post-mortem because as the cervix dilates in preparation for birth the unprotected vessels come under stress and quickly rupture, leaving baby and mother to expire from exsanguination. Basically, the baby bleeds to death in a matter of minutes followed slightly more slowly by the mother. Mortality is as high as 95 percent. To make my situation worse, one of the placenta's parts had blocked my cervix, trapping my son inside.

It just so happened that my placenta's vessels were under the most stress while, at eight months pregnant, I was shopping, attempting to distract myself from the contractions my doctors said were too irregular to necessitate a trip to the hospital. After my emergency C-section and the subsequent biopsy of my placenta, I learned that if my water had broken while I had been shopping, my son and I would have died on the floor of the store most probably before an ambulance could have even gotten there.

My pregnancy and birth experience enabled me to realize that I need to live as a whole person—a life-changing realization. The *Mama, PhD* collection of motherhood memoirs suggests that life-changing self-realizations are the norm for new mothers. When teaching and researching, I am not just a brain on a stick; I am a body, too. While being a mother, I am not just a body, a breast-feeding, diaper-changing, food-preparing machine; I am a powerful brain, too. Even though I studied Cartesian philosophy for many years, I never internalized the consequences for myself as an individual: I did not consider the personal ramifications of these ideas until I became a mother. I don't think this lack of personal application is due to ignorance or lack of self-awareness. By comparison, many feminist writers also left the existence of the mind/body dichotomy unquestioned.[3] Perhaps my lack of personal application is due to the complexity of my personal experience. Even now, after years considering what happened during my pregnancy and labor, I don't know exactly what went wrong.

It's true that I entrusted my body primarily to care for my son during the last month of my pregnancy, but did I really privilege my body over brain? I often ask myself this question because my body was bleeding, in effect communicating to me that something was wrong, but when no diagnosis materialized, I distrusted my body's communication, allowing my brain to rationalize it away. This view indicates that I was not privileging my body, but my brain. And was it my brain that I was privileging or someone else's? The brains of my doctors, extended family, and friends were quite persuasive in that they helped to convince me that I was fine. Did I, in effect, negate my own body and mind by privileging other minds? It would be overly simplistic to say that during my pregnancy I privileged my body over my brain, and that as long as I avoid that mistake in the future, I will avoid similar negative consequences. However, these alternate views make my memoir of motherhood more ambiguous and problematic, and they also show how easily the mind/body dichotomy can shift. It's not that any one of these views more accurately describes my pregnancy than the others. All of the views accurately describe my pregnancy, but according to Grosz, my initial belief that my mind and body were separate was my life-threatening mistake. Overcoming fragmentation in order to live a whole life is a constant, ongoing struggle.

Grosz offers up an alternative view for our consideration to help us view the body not as separate but as all-encompassing: "New terms and different conceptual frameworks must also be devised to be able to talk of the body outside of or in excess of binary pairs" (24). We need a new vocabulary. We need a new word so that I can refer to myself as a whole without fragmenting myself into various parts and without intentionally and unintentionally referring to body negatively. Grosz permits the use of the words *mind* and *body* because she claims that only by engaging these terms can they be overcome (24). However, when the term body is used, it should be used with a more broad definition. Grosz suggests that:

> ...instead of participating in—i.e., adhering to one side or the other of—a binary pair, these pairs can be more readily problematized by regarding the body as the threshold or bor-derline concept that hovers perilously and undecidably at the pivotal point of binary pairs. The body is neither—while also being both—the private or the public, self or other, natural or cultural, psychical or social, instinctive or learned, genetically or environmentally determined. (23)

To achieve wholeness, I must transcend the mind/body dichotomy and adopt a more broad, unconventional concept of body. Perhaps I could start with the realization that the mind and body are not mutually exclusive and self-contained. My body can learn, teach, and rationalize: These are not capabilities exclusive to my mind as dualism argues. In this way, my body would exemplify Grosz's "borderline concept," one that does not adhere to the traditional role that dualism dictates.

This realization that the body and mind should not be separated is chronicled in *Mama, PhD* motherhood memoir, Elrena Evans's "Fitting In." Similar to my experience in my memoir, Evans chooses a failing and practically deadly strategy to cope with the mind/body dichotomy. She struggles to reconcile her mind (completing graduate coursework) with her body (managing a complicated pregnancy) and in the meantime almost dies from an embolism. In one particularly vivid image in her memoir, she is confined to a hospital bed surrounded by monitors, IVs, books from her graduate courses, and her laptop (51). This image is particularly important because it captures her struggle to meet external expectations to privilege her mind over her body. She specifically cites the academy's "floating head" syndrome: "People are expected to function as disembodied brains, not connected to bodies or families or any sort of life outside of academic pursuits" (52). This syndrome creates a work "environment that treats people like glorified computers" (53). Her efforts during her pregnancy imply that even though she criticizes academia and the workplace it creates, she eventually conforms to academia's expectations and privileges her mind over her body. The irony is that Evans begins her memoir by discussing how early in her graduate work she views herself as an academic outsider, exemplified by her love of dance, her wearing of ballet shoes and tights to class, and her dislike of alcohol and coffee. The mind/body dichotomy's power is reinforced: Even though Evans begins her academic career as somewhat of an outlier, she succumbs to pressure to conform to the mind/body dichotomy.

Evans's approach is consistent with Grosz's theory, which helps to explain why academics feel pressure to make this same choice. Grosz explains more specifically in *Volatile Bodies* that body "is the subordinated counterpart of mind" and is defined in "nonhistorical, naturalistic, organicist, passive, inert terms, seeing it as an intrusion on or interference with the operation of mind" (3-4). It's not just that the mind is preferred over the body or that the body is viewed less positively than the mind, but Grosz argues that the body is actually viewed negatively. The body is believed to affect the mind in a negative way by intruding or interfering in intellectual pursuits. For an academic like Evans who is devoted to intellectual pursuits, it is tempting to deny the body and live exclusively as a mind, especially if one believes that the body cannot contribute to those pursuits in a meaningful or positive way.

My academic specialty is in theories of aestheticism, so spending my days pondering questions like what is beauty and how is beauty defined[4] caused me to focus on my mind, but while pregnant, I was reminded that I had a body and that I needed it, too. Evans discovers that just because a person can live with the mind and body separated doesn't mean that a person should:

> So it's not about the fact that everyone knew I would somehow rise to the challenge and continue my graduate work without interruption, while trying to recover, trying to mother, trying to nurse with bleeding nipples that couldn't heal because my blood had been thinned to the consistency of water. It's about the fact that I shouldn't have had to. I should have been afforded the dignity of being treated as a whole person, not just a floating, disembodied head. (52)

For Evans and myself, a separated life is not a life at all. A separated life for us leads quite close to physical death. Her realization that a unification between the body and mind is necessary as well as possible seems to occur when her daughter reaches the toddler stage: "She is a whole person, a whole woman, and she fits in to herself just fine. Watching her I realize that, regardless of where I eventually end up with relation to the academy, that is what I want to do: I want to fit in to myself. Nothing more, and nothing less" (54). It is her daughter who models wholeness for her. Evans's experience reveals the life-and-death necessity of wholeness and her daughter illustrates that wholeness is possible, but her toddler daughter has yet to encounter the extreme external pressures that can quickly fracture this wholeness—pressures that adults encounter frequently. I wonder how long her daughter's wholeness will last, and if it does fracture, what then will serve as Evans's model for wholeness?

While Evans's daughter models wholeness for her, Elisabeth Rose Gruner is the model for her children in her motherhood memoir "I Am Not a Head on a Stick," and in this memoir Gruner explores how women can manage the external pressures that endanger wholeness. Gruner's experience shows that wholeness is quite fragile actually. Early in her memoir, Gruner recounts how she brings her two-year-old daughter with her to collect the final signature for her doctoral dissertation, and she was self-conscious because "by bringing my daughter with me that day, I made my own body visible, my own life a (tenuously) unified whole. There she was, unignorable evidence that I'd had other things than my dissertation on my mind for the past three years" (125). As a brand new academic, Gruner seems to be a unified whole, maintaining some balance between motherhood (the body) and doctoral research (the mind). However, this emotionally-rich image of Gruner with child on one hip and doctoral paperwork in hand becomes somewhat distorted after Gruner begins her first academic job. Similar to Evans, Gruner succumbs to academic pressure to privilege the mind over the body.

Gruner attempts to be "a head on a stick" or "that bodiless intellectual the academy seemed to want" because the academy privileges the mind at the expense of the body (126, 125). Evans's memoir, as well as mine, focuses on the physical consequences of privileging the mind over the body, but Gruner's memoir suggests that it can also affect one's self-perception. She explains that, to some degree, privileging the mind is inherent in the work because "we [academics] are, after all, valued for our particular expertise, our particular knowledge—our own particular minds. This makes it hard for us to imagine that anyone else could fill in for us, that we could share a job, that we are, in fact, not uniquely indispensable" (125-6). When a woman believes that she is indispensable for her mind only, she not only lives a fragmented life instead of a whole one, but she also privileges her mind over her body. The result is not simply separation of the mind and body, but a hierarchy forms.

This hierarchy can be quite destructive to maintaining balance between the mind and the body, which Gruner claims enables wholeness. She issues this challenge: "I want us to refuse to 'perform childlessness,' to make visible the strains and the costs of our striving for balance as we also insist on the centrality of our families to our work" (128). "Performing childlessness" is to suggest that the body—as well as sex, pregnancy, childbirth, and the resulting new body (the child)—does not exist. Grosz argues that philosophy has essentially done just that: "Philosophy has always considered itself a discipline concerned primarily or exclusively with ideas, concepts, reason, judgment—that is, with terms clearly framed by the concept of mind, terms which marginalize or exclude considerations of the body" (4). The body is discussed as "the hindrance of the production of knowledge" because the body "is implicitly defined as unruly, disruptive, in need of direction and judgment" (Grosz 3-4). If academics refuse to "perform childlessness" and intentionally credit the body's contribution to their intellectual pursuits, the body will be seen as an asset not as a liability, challenging the idea that the body interferes with intellectual pursuits. When academics view the body as Grosz's "borderline concept," the body does not interfere or contribute to the intellectual life: The body is the intellectual life. This assertion is especially important for academic women because historically the body has been associated with woman and the mind associated with man. If the mind/body dichotomy is not undermined, it will serve as an erroneous philosophical justification for man to be privileged over woman and for those who are "childless" to be privileged over those who are parents.

When academics make gains in regard to this ideological shift, these gains will benefit their own children and the next generation of academics. Gruner acknowledges that her challenge to live a whole life, to maintain balance, and to make this life visible is a formidable but beneficial one:

> My children ... can't remember a time when I wasn't 'a teacher and a doctor and a mommy,' and though they at times resent all three roles, this is the life they know. It's the life I know, too, and while I want to change it almost daily, I don't want to give it up. I want to fight, though, to have it acknowledged for what it is: a whole life, a life of both the mind and the body. So that no one expects them, or anyone else, to be a head on a stick. (128)

Young children like Evans's daughter in the memoir "Fitting In" may exhibit wholeness while they are young and may exhibit it so perfectly that they can serve as models for their parents, but as they age, external pressures and expectations will challenge and erode that wholeness. Gruner's memoir serves to remind parents that they will need to serve as a model for wholeness for their own children when this fragmentation inevitably takes place. Like Gruner and Evans, I suffered from the same "floating head" or "head on a stick" syndrome while working in academia, and I responded to my troubled pregnancy by choosing an even more extreme fragmentation. My success as a mother partly depends upon me combining my body and brain as thoroughly and seamlessly as I can. My life and my son's life may depend on it again one day.

In regard to achieving wholeness, Gruner and Evans use three verbs: to balance (mind and body), to reattach (head to body), and to fit (brain into body and into oneself). However, Grosz theorizes in *Volatile Bodies* that it is the very existence of the mind/body dichotomy that is the problem. Gruner, Evans, and I are, in effect, struggling to combine the mind and the body when they should not be viewed as separate in the first place. Grosz explains that "dichotomous thinking necessarily hierarchizes and ranks the two polarized terms so that one becomes the privileged term and the other its suppressed, subordinated, negative counterpart" (3). Grosz claims that a dichotomy is always accompanied by a hierarchy, and in the mind/body dichotomy, the mind and the body are not only separate and opposite but also ranked. Viewing myself as a mind and a body, according to Grosz, is at the very center of my struggle because two parts cannot exist in a dichotomy and be equals. If I want to live a unified, whole life, I have to get rid of the dichotomy. It's not a matter of balancing, reattaching, or fitting together the parts of myself to make a whole life. It's realizing that there are no parts.

Because I had assumed for much of my life that the mind/body dichotomy was real and applied to me, I left it unexamined, and it became, for me, an ideology—and apparently a quite powerful one because it escorted me close to death. My transcending it means not just wholeness or freedom from fragmentation. My transcendence means life. It is actually quite empowering to think of oneself as greater than the philosophy one studies, as being too complex to be contained within a set of ideas.

***

Eighteen months later, I'm surrounded by doctors and nurses again and in labor for fifteen hours with my second son. The doctor has agreed to a VBAC—vaginal delivery after Cesarean section. I'm fully dilated, fully effaced, but the doctors tell me that I've been in labor too long. They begin preparing me for surgery.

I muster all the knowledge gained from my experience and combine it with the intense passion, the courage, the clenched fists and teeth of a woman in labor, and I scream out in between breaths. Knowing that it's going to take all of my body's power—knowing that it's going to take my whole, unified self—I start to push.

ENDNOTES

[1]Other collections that include short motherhood memoirs featuring a variety of contributors are *Between Mothers and Sons*, *Mothers Who Think* (Stevens), *Literary Mama* (Buchanan and Hudock), and *It's a Boy* (Buchanan).

[2]See Alyson Bardsley's insightful review of *Mama, PhD* in *Feminist Teacher*.

[3]Grosz's introduction to *Volatile Bodies* argues that, historically, feminist thinkers have generally assumed that the mind/body dichotomy existed and, therefore, framed their arguments in such a way as to ameliorate the concept of the body while maintaining it as separate from the concept of the mind.

[4]Many of the theories of aestheticism in the eighteenth and nineteenth centuries debate where beauty exists: Does it exist in the artistic object itself? Does it exist in the perceiver of that object? Does the artistic object possess the capabilities of producing beauty but needs the perceiver's mind to act upon it in order for beauty to exist? In all three cases, the perceiver's mind is privileged over the perceiver's body. Many theorists of aestheticism agree that the body gathers sensory data from the external world, but that sensory data tends only to be useful and important in that it is manipulated by the mind. The mind uses the body's sensory data to form a perception of the artistic object in the mind or to form a new creation by the perceiver's imagination. Sometimes the body is even discussed as being an obstacle to the mind perceiving objects as they really are. For example, the body's five senses may be distorted, uneducated, or not sufficiently acute, and in this case, the body's sensory data would be unreliable. In some extreme theories of aestheticism, the

imagination is said to create the world, free of the body's sensory data all together.

WORKS CITED

Bardsley, Alyson. "Women Write about Motherhood and Academic Life." *Feminist Teacher* 20.1 (2009): 83-84. Web. 28 April 2013.

Buchanan, Andrea J., ed. *It's a Boy: Women Writers on Raising Sons.* Emeryville, CA: Seal, 2005. Print.

Buchanan, Andrea J. and Amy Hudock, Eds. *Literary Mama: Reading for the Maternally Inclined.* Emeryville, CA: Seal, 2006. Print.

Evans, Elrena. "Fitting In." *Mama, PhD.* Eds. Elrena Evans and Caroline Grant. New Brunswick, NJ: Rutgers University Press, 2008. Print.

Grosz, Elizabeth. *Volatile Bodies: Toward a Corporeal Feminism.* Bloomington: Indiana University Press, 1994. Print.

Gruner, Elisabeth Rose. "I Am Not a Head on a Stick." *Mama, PhD.* Eds. Elrena Evans and Caroline Grant. New Brunswick, NJ: Rutgers University Press, 2008. Print.

International Vasa Previa Foundation, 15 July 2004. Web. 13 November 2012.

Peri, Camille and Kate Moses, Eds. *Mothers Who Think: Tales of Real-Life Parenthood.* New York: Washington Square, 2000. Print.

Stevens, Patricia, ed. *Between Mothers and Sons: Women Writers Talk About Having Sons and Raising Men.* New York: Scribner, 2001. Print.

10.
We Are Family

Creating Lesbian Co-Motherhood Through Online Community

LISA FEDERER

One morning over coffee, I'm catching up on the blogs I follow when, out of the blue, I find myself looking at a photo of a new mother's placenta. It's enormous, fibrous, and bloody. In fact, it looks quite a bit like a lung that has just been ripped out of someone's chest. You'll forgive me for the graphic recounting, but I assure you, my powers of description cannot equal the vivid image of the midwife holding up this piece of tissue. So what has possessed someone to post a picture of a placenta on her blog? The writer is Lesbian Dad, a blogger whose partner was in her third trimester of carrying their second child at the time of the posting. Lesbian Dad posted the image of their first child's placenta as a "small gesture of humility and gratitude" for the work that has been required of her partner during her two pregnancies—the physically challenging and emotionally grueling work of creating a new life ("Hey pregnant ladies"). Lesbian Dad's placenta picture is not the only example of such illustrative glimpses into lesbian mothering. All over the Internet, non-biological lesbian mothers (or co-mothers) have hopped on the "mommy blogging" bandwagon, regaling their readers with harrowing tales of potty training, breastfeeding, sick babies, and the many travails of parenting.

For many, the blog is the confessional of the digital age, a place where they can vent their frustrations, tout their successes, and come clean about their most embarrassing transgressions in relative anonymity. Parents from a variety of sociocultural backgrounds have made their private lives quite public online, sometimes to criticism. The mommy blog has been dismissed as "an online shrine to parental self-absorption," and in the online world, a backlash against parental disclosure and self-congratulation has led to the rise of a rhetoric against mommy blogging (Hochman). For example, established in March 2009, the blog *STFU, Parents* posts user-submitted examples of parental TMI (too much information) from around the Internet, with frank and humorous commentary from the blog's creator, known only as B. (Incidentally, placenta pictures are a recurring complaint on *STFU, Parents*, with readers from around the world bemoaning the same sort of uninvited placenta viewing to which I was privy.)

The blogs of lesbian co-mothers are, on the surface, quite similar to those of their heterosexual counterparts. For co-mothers, though, the "blogosphere" also serves as an important space in which women do the cultural work of creating a concept of co-mothering identity and in which co-mothers, who often do not find acceptance in either the straight parenting or the general gay community, can turn to each other to find a support network that transcends geographical boundaries. Moreover, these bloggers share their often highly personal explorations of their new motherhood identities in the open and public setting of the Internet, where other women can learn from their experiences. Particularly for young women who have not previously envisioned themselves in traditional motherhood roles, the writing of these co-mothers can be inspiring.

In this chapter, I examine how the blogs of lesbian co-mothers act as more than just a place to recount stories, but also a site of individual and cultural identity negotiation. This chapter considers the blogs of several lesbian mothers and co-mothers primarily in the early 21st century. Of course, it should be acknowledged that forming a critique and analysis of any group based on their blogs alone presents certain limitations. First, one can only base analysis on what the blogger has chosen to present in their online presence, which may or may not represent the complete and accurate truth. Secondly, the group of individuals who blog about a certain topic represents a potentially small subset of any given community as a whole. During the time period in which this analysis was conducted, the lesbian "mommy bloggers" were primarily white, middle to upper class, well-educated women with the resources and know-how to create a blog, as well as the time to devote to updating it regularly. The blog as a medium is not necessarily inclusive, comprehensive, or completely representative, but blogs still provide a jumping-off point for considering communities, particularly those that are often "silenced" in mass and popular media.

CREATING A CO-MOTHER IDENTITY

The concept of lesbian motherhood is often considered an oxymoron, as Amy Hequembourg and Michael Farrell discuss in their article, "Lesbian Motherhood: Negotiating Marginal-Mainstream Identities." Cultural critics have posited several reasons for which the identities of lesbian and mother seem to be conflicting. First, societal expectations regarding gender and sexuality create a seeming incompatibility between homosexuality and motherhood. The American ideology of motherhood casts "mothering [as] a function of women's essentially female nature," while stereotypes portray the lesbian as androgynous or masculine, the "demonised 'dungaree wearing lesbian'" of popular convention (DiQuinzio xiii; Bell and Binnie 31). Lesbian mothers also trouble the notion of the traditional, patriarchal familial order by creating families without men.[1]

Even within the lesbian community, notions of lesbian identity do not typically include child-rearing. Many lesbians internalize society's assumptions that they will not become mothers, requiring a "re-exploration or restructuring of gay identity" that is also experienced by gay men becoming new fathers (Brinamen and Mitchell 525). The concept of the lesbian mother is thus often considered non-existent in both the heterosexual and the queer communities.

The co-mother faces even more significant challenges to the validity of her maternal status. Society's rejection of the co-mother as a parent with legitimate familial claims to her partner's child is often reflected in the legal system's refusal to grant her the protection that traditional families receive. As of March 2010, second-parent adoption, which gives the co-parent essentially the same rights as the biological parent, is recognized in 27 states ("Second Parent Adoption"). However, even where co-parents are afforded some rights, their legal status is tenuous, and many co-parents end up losing parental rights if the couple breaks up, in spite of second-parent adoptions and other legal measures. In the other 23 states, co-parents have almost no legal protection, even if they have actively participated in the child's life from conception.

In light of the contested validity of lesbian mothers' identities, blogging plays an important role in identity formation. Many schools of thought in sociology and psychology view language and narrative as means of production for both individual and communal identities. According to deconstructive narratology, "the author of a self-story must be seen as a person with many selves, constantly trying to reorganize him- or herself into a provisional unity" (Kraus 106). In other words, narrative serves as a way for multi-faceted individuals to negotiate identity and affiliation with different communities. Symbolic interactionism suggests that individual identity is not inherent, but is constructed through interaction with other people, groups, and symbols. Symbolic interactionists assert that "generalized others serve as reference groups with whom we negotiate our identities" (Bergen, Suter, and Daas 204). Co-mothers' blogs often reflect their attempts at figuring out what their own version of motherhood looks like, as well as negotiating a cohesive cultural identity for the co-mother.

A major aspect of identity formation and a topic of ongoing debate in the co-mother blogging world is the appropriate name or title for the co-mother. In this chapter, I use the term co-mother, often used in academic literature, but a multitude of other names exist for the partner of the lesbian mother: non-bio mom, lesbian dad, the "other" mother, and more. While such debate may seem trivial, defining a name for the co-mother plays an integral role in encouraging society's acceptance of the co-mother as a valid parent with legitimate rights. After all, "it is difficult to claim an identity without a linguistic term for that identity" (Bergen, Suter, and Daas 203).

Selecting a title also helps co-mothers define their role within the family, in part for practical reasons. Both parents and children may find it confusing if family members don't have clear names by which they can be addressed, as one co-mother humorously demonstrates: "I've seen other lesbians each use a variante [sic] of 'Mom', like 'Mama' and 'Mommy', but we're in the process of trying that and I just get confused... 'Let's go to the front door! Mama, I mean Mommy, I mean Mom is coming home!'" (Giddings, "On Becoming a SAHM"). Some co-moms have chosen the term Baba, a diminutive for "father" in many languages and for "grandmother" in others that poignantly captures the often ambiguous nature of the co-mother's role. Beyond simply making it easier for everyone to keep names straight, calling the co-mother by a term that is different from, but equal to, the biological mother helps to create a sense of equality between the mothers, both within the family and to outside observers (Bergen, Suter, and Daas 207).

The decision of what to call the co-mother is also significant in creating an outward image of family in a society that does not typically recognize lesbian and gay families. The general emphasis on the biological and genetic in the language of maternity obscures other important connections between non-biological parents and children through social bonding and needs fulfillment.[2] Having a recognized term by which the co-mother is called could help to communicate the legitimacy of her tie with her child. One co-mother observes that even lesbians without children are extremely interested in what her children call her, "as if they have some sort of stake in what the kids call me. As if, somehow, our movement depends on it" (Giddings, "More Name Games"). Although the blogger dismisses the name issue as unimportant, many would argue that defining a name for co-mothers *does* in fact play an important role in the move toward acceptance of GLBT families and the legitimacy of non-biological parents.

Deciding on a last name for the children can also be an important choice, as creating a tie between co-mother and child through a name can help in "identifying her as a legitimate parent both to external others and to those within their family of creation" (Bergen 209). While some couples stick to tradition and give their children the last name of the biological mother, many others decide to use both of their names, hyphenated, for their child's last name. Some couples use the co-mother's last name, reinforcing the notion that motherhood is about more than biology. Others get more creative, such as by each giving their last name to one child—for example, the first child has the co-mother's last name while the second child has the mother's last name.

Although most co-mothers consider themselves equally important as the biological mothers, they may question their role when challenged by outside observers. For example, when a stranger noted that a co-mother and her son looked so much alike, the co-mother felt like an "imposter," passing for a mother when no biological tie existed (Team Serrins; The Other Mother). Many co-mothers fail to receive recognition as a legitimate parent even from their own extended families, as Adital Ben-Ari and Tali Livni discuss in "Motherhood Is Not a Given Thing: Experiences and Constructed Meanings of Biological and Nonbiological Lesbian Mothers." One blogger confesses that she was "a little tiny bit disappointed how [my mom] kept looking at [my partner] and smiling and asking all these questions about what SHE was going to do…Like I have nothing to do with any of it. Now, I admit I might be a little tough on my mom but it's OUR baby" (othermother2b). The creation of a cohesive and widely-recognized term for co-mothers would go a long way in helping them to feel more secure and legitimate in their relationship to their children.

Some co-mothers struggle with the gender expectations that come along with the term "mother," feeling more of an affinity with masculinity than the femininity that often seems to be synonymous with motherhood. Many co-mothers use language in their blogs that reflect this masculinity. Recounting her partner's struggles with becoming pregnant via insemination, one blogger longs for a penis "so that I can just knock her up all by myself" (KK). Several bloggers describe looking to their fathers, rather than their mothers, as role models for parenting (Giddings, "Father Knows Best"; KK; The Other Mother). When one co-mother caught up with an old friend and announced that her partner had had a baby, her friend exclaimed "You're a DAD!?!" (Giddings, "Father Knows Best"). The term "lesbian dad" has been popularized by a well-known co-mother blogger who uses the title (Lesbian Dad).

Many names exist for co-mothers, and no two co-mothers will be the same type of parent, but what most do agree on is that motherhood is not based in biology, but is, as one co-mother poignantly puts it, "the sum total of dozens of skinned knees tended, hundreds of runny noses wiped, thousands of hurt feelings loved away" (Lesbian Dad, "Where the Diaper Meets the Road"). With so many people, from family to legal authorities, questioning the legitimacy of the co-mother's role in the family, blogs serve as a forum for the co-mother to reestablish the validity of her claims to parental status. Many blogging co-mothers, whether intentionally or not, use language that reasserts their equal importance in the family unit. In fact, some blogs require extensive exploration before the reader can determine whether the writer is the mother or the co-mother. Using first-person pronouns to refer to the children (my son, our daughter), telling stories about bonding experiences with the children, and discussing parenting techniques are all linguistic strategies of reclaiming the parental identity that many people would rather deny the co-mother.

THE ONLINE FAMILY

Parenting is not an easy task, even in the best of circumstances. As the saying goes, it takes a village to raise a child. For lesbian families, though, it may be difficult to muster a village. While heterosexual couples' extended families often step in to help, many lesbian parents do not find the same support from their families. One blogging co-mother described her frustration with an aunt who refused to acknowledge the blogger's child as a legitimate member of the family (Chicory, "I'm Sick of Being the Bigger Person"). Even when extended families are encouraging, co-mothers may not receive the same support as the biological mother, since many people still equate maternity with biology.

Since the 1970s, the larger GLBT community and its allies have come to be known as a rallying force, quickly mobilizing when GLBT rights are challenged or crimes are committed against a member of the community. As many GLBT individuals face discrimination and hatred, sometimes even from their own families, the GLBT community can become one's family of choice. Indeed, a great deal of the socialization in GLBT communities centers on communal activities, such as lesbian softball teams or the bar scene.

Most of the blogging co-mothers in this study had at least some connections within the GLBT community prior to becoming a parent, but in many cases, that connection ended or changed significantly after the birth of a child. Given the often-accepted stereotype that gays and lesbians do not have children, and the centrality of the bar scene and other adults-only activities in the GLBT community, new parents often find themselves excluded from the community they once called family. While the GLBT community generally emphasizes acceptance and openness, many new parents feel as though they are "outsiders in a gay community that they had once experienced as inclusive" (Brinamen and Mitchell 533). In some cases, parents step back from the community as the demands of raising a family begin to take up more of their time. One co-mother describes herself and her partner as "not very gay as gay people go," since they no longer spent time in the gay nightlife scene nor had many gay friends (Team Serrins Springfield). On the other hand, some lesbian parents find that they—or at least their children—are no longer welcome at GLBT events. One blogging co-mother expressed her surprise and disappointment that children were not welcome at a Sunday afternoon potluck held by a local GLBT group. After talking with other lesbian mothers in her area, she found that they, too, felt excluded by the GLBT community on the whole, and she regretted that "[parents] are not welcome at their homes, at their picnics, at their parties unless we set part of us aside" (Chicory, "Goddamn").

Many co-mother bloggers reflect on their experiences in public spaces with mostly heterosexual parents, but here again, they often fail to feel a sense of connection. Some lesbian couples face outright discrimination, especially in more conservative states. In other places, even when straight parents are welcoming, co-mothers may find it difficult to relate to either mothers or fathers. One blogger describes co-motherhood as "the nether-world of in-between parenting" and feels that she doesn't fit in to the straight parenting world, noting that, "unless I join a GLBT parenting group I will always be not-quite-mom and not-quite-dad" (Giddings, "Would You").

Since the advent of online communication, the Internet has served as a way of connecting people with similar interests regardless of geographical distance. New and expecting parents have taken advantage of bulletin board systems, blogs, and discussion groups to help each other answer questions about parenthood, share ideas and successes, and sometimes provide a place to commiserate with an understanding group of peers. The Internet abounds with such places for parental connection: a Google search for "expecting mom blogs" returns almost 8 million hits, and searches for "mom discussion board" and "dad discussion board" return 17 million and a surprising 33 million, respectively. Search for the term "lesbian mom discussion board," however, and you'll receive barely half a million hits.

With little advice or support in their own communities, some lesbian parents have taken advantage of the discussion boards for heterosexual mothers. Such forums can be useful for the expecting lesbian mother, as they can answer questions and calm fears about the experience of pregnancy and childbirth. For the co-mother though, straight moms' discussion boards may not answer the questions they have, while straight dads' discussion boards don't fit the bill either. One co-mother described an experience with her expecting partner at a bookstore: while her partner found stacks of useful books on pregnancy, the co-mother found that books on fatherhood emphasized the manliness of the role and offered little help to her (Klempnauer Miller 6). Co-mothers face a similar dilemma when finding online spaces for support, but many have found that blogging provides a useful outlet for their joys and frustrations. Several online communities exist to connect lesbian parents, including Mombian (touting the tagline "Sustenance for Lesbian Moms") and LesbianFamily.org, which provides links to lesbian moms' blogs (Rudolph; LesbianFamily.org).

With so many different bloggers from diverse backgrounds, living all around the world, no two co-mothering blogs are exactly alike, but many share some of the same qualities. Like straight mothers' blogs, most discuss the day-to-day business of being a mother and chronicle the children's milestones. Many co-mothers state that their original goal in keeping a blog was to keep far-flung family members up-to-date on the children. In so doing though, they join a community of blogging co-mothers, many of whom consider each other close friends in spite of having never met in person.

Although it is they who voluntarily post their family's information, many of the blogging co-mothers seem concerned about their family's Internet privacy. Some use pet names for their children and partners, like one co-mother who refers to her sons as "Cake" and "Trucker "and her partner as "my honey" on her blog, while others identify their loved ones only by the first initials of their names (oneofhismoms). However, in spite of these precautions, most of the blogging co-mothers frequently post pictures of their children (and of course, occasionally of their partners' placentas) and enough information for any reader to figure out the city, and even roughly the specific neighborhood, where a blogger lives. In some cases, blogging co-mothers have had to relocate their blogs or apologize for unflattering comments when friends or family members discovered their supposedly anonymous blog. Lesbian bloggers in general also face the very real possibility of anonymous strangers making rude or even threatening homophobic comments.

If, as new parents rightly should, blogging co-mothers worry about protecting their families from the masses of unknown people on the Internet, then why are so many extremely forthright in their blogs? One blogger, when asked by her partner why she didn't just keep a paper journal, responded that "the feedback from other people and the connections I've made with other people have been at least as valuable as the opportunity to record pieces of my life" (roundisfunny). Such is the case for many of the blogging co-mothers; beyond simply serving as a place to write down their thoughts, the blog itself becomes a source of community for co-mothers, many of whom lack the opportunities for such friendship in their everyday lives. Viewing the blog in this way—as a community of supportive friends—could go a long way in explaining why blogging co-mothers are willing to post intimate details about their lives. Rather than viewing the blog as simply another anonymous page in a vast network of web sites, blogging co-mothers see the blog as a means of communicating with people who have become close friends. Sharing the personal and sometimes graphic details of parenting allows blogging co-mothers to build camaraderie by providing the basis for sympathetic comments from parents who have experienced similar situations. Co-mothers' self-disclosure may also be viewed as a way of lowering barriers and extending boundaries to create friendship, given that the Internet does not permit the type of social and nonverbal cues of friendship that people recognize in their offline lives.

MODELING NEW FORMS OF MOTHERHOOD

Given the public nature of the blog as a medium of personal expression, co-mother bloggers also serve as models for other women who are exploring alternative ways of experiencing motherhood. I began researching co-mother blogs in my mid-twenties, as many of my heterosexual friends were having children and starting mommy blogs of their own. I found reading their blogs interesting, as they provided a snapshot of a life entirely different from mine. I have never felt a desire to have children, and as a bisexual woman who primarily dated women at the time, the idea of marriage, children, and the typical family life seemed very foreign to me. Throughout my life, women have knowingly assured me that I would want children eventually; the passing of the years has not changed the fact that I steadfastly do not want children of my own.

However, the role of co-mother fascinates me because of that intersection between mother and not-mother that so many co-mothers struggle with. The blogs of co-mothers reveal that there are many different ways of enacting motherhood that do not necessarily involve bearing one's own child, and that these different types of motherhood can be just as rewarding and meaningful as the traditional biological motherhood role. When I read the blogs of biological mothers' experiences of their pregnancy and motherhood, I am interested, but I cannot relate. On the other hand, when I hear about the experiences of co-mothers, I can imagine myself in this role. I suspect that most of the bloggers whose blogs I have studied would not view themselves as models or transgressors, but the act of recording their novel experiences with a sometimes controversial form of motherhood creates the space for other women to explore other ways of enacting motherhood.

While critics may continue to dismiss blogging as so much navel-gazing, blogs have played an important role in creating a concept of lesbian co-motherhood. As more and more lesbian couples start families of their own, co-mothers will increasingly need support and advice on how enact this unique type of motherhood, and undoubtedly, many will look to these blogs for that support.

ENDNOTES

[1]For a fulsome discussion of this idea, see Elena Marie DiLapi's article "Lesbian Mothers and the Motherhood Hierarchy."
[2]For a full discussion of this concept, see Sarah-Vaughan Brakman and Sally J. Scholz. "Adoption, ART, and a Re-Conception of the Maternal Body: Toward Embodied Maternity."

WORKS CITED

B. *STFU, Parents*. Web. 4 Mar. 2010.

Bell, David and John Binnie. "All Hyped Up and No Place to Go." *Gender, Place and Culture: A Journal of Feminist Geography* 1.1. (1994): 31-47. Print.

Ben-Ari, Adital and Tali Livni. "Motherhood Is Not a Given Thing: Experiences and Constructed Meanings of Biological and Nonbiological Lesbian Mothers." *Sex Roles* 54 (2006): 521-531. Print.

Bergen, Karla Mason, Elizabeth A. Suter, and Karen L. Daas. "'About as Solid as a Fish Net': Symbolic Construction of a Legitimate Parental Identity for Nonbiological Lesbian Mothers." *Journal of Family Communication* 6.3 (2009): 201-220. Print.

Brakman, Sarah-Vaughan and Sally J. Scholz. "Adoption, ART, and a Re-Conception of the Maternal Body: Toward Embodied Maternity." *Hypatia* 21.1 (Winter 2006): 54-73. Print.

Brinamen, Charles F. and Valory Mitchell. "Gay Men Becoming Fathers: A Model of Identity Expansion." *Journal of GLBT Family Studies* 4.4 (2008): 521-541. Print.

Chicory. "Goddamn, but I am bitchy." *An Accident of Hope*. 9 Feb. 2006.

Web. 1 Dec. 2008.

Chicory. "I'm Sick of Being the Bigger Person." *An Accident of Hope.* 27 Feb.2006. Web. 1 Dec. 2008.

DiLapi, Elena Marie."Lesbian Mothers and the Motherhood Hierarchy." *Journal of Homosexuality* 18.1/2 (1989): 101-121. Print.

DiQuinzio, Patrice. *The Impossibility of Motherhood: Feminism, Individualism and the Problem of Mothering.* New York: Routledge, 1999. Print.

Giddings, Lisa. "Father Knows Best." *Confessions from a Stay at Homo (SAHM).* 9 Oct. 2006. Web. 5 Jan. 2009.

Giddings, Lisa. "More Name Games." *Confessions from a Stay at Homo (SAHM).* 25 Sept. 2006. Web. 21 Jan. 2012.

Giddings, Lisa. "On Becoming a SAHM." *Confessions from a Stay at Homo (SAHM).* 8 May 2006. Web. 4 Jan. 2009.

Hequembourg, Amy L. and Michael P. Farrell. "Lesbian Motherhood: Negotiating Marginal-Mainstream Identities." *Gender and Society* 13.4 (1999): 540-557. Print.

Hochman, David. "Mommy (and Me)." *The New York Times.* 30 Jan. 2005: Sec 9:1. Print.

KK. "A 2 L of Semen—And Some Musings on the Injector's Inability to Properly Contribute to the Creation of this Sugar Patch." *Injection Reflections.* 2 Aug. 2007. Web. 27 Feb. 2010.

Klempnauer Miller, Annie. "Watching." *Confessions of the Other Mother: Non-Biological Lesbian Moms Tell All.* Ed. Harlyn Aizley. Boston: Beacon P, 2006. Print.

Kraus, Wolfgang. "The Narrative Negotiation of Identity and Belonging." *Narrative Inquiry* 16.1 (2006): 103-111. Print.

Lesbian Dad. "Hey pregnant ladies! No wonder you're exhausted!" *Lesbian Dad: Notes from the Crossroads of Mother & Father.* 29 Sept. 2006. Web. 3 Mar. 2010.

Lesbian Dad. "Where the Diaper Meets the Road." *Lesbian Dad: Notes from the Crossroads of Mother & Father.* 31 Jan. 2008. Web. 20 Jan. 2009.

LesbianFamily.org. n.d. Web. 21 Mar. 2010.

Lisa. "Would You, Could You, in the Suburbs?" *Confessions from a Stay at Homo (SAHM).* 24 Oct. 2006. Web. 4 Jan. 2009.

oneofhismoms. "Momming." *oneofhismoms.* 16 Oct. 2009. Web. 10 Mar. 2010.

The Other Mother. "I'm an Imposter…" *The OTHER Mother: Letters from the Outposts of Lesbian Parenting.* 16 May 2008. Web. 4 Mar. 2010.

othermother2b. "El Nino … meet Granny …not uncle T." *Life of the Other Mother2b.* 5 Feb. 2008. Web. 23 Feb. 2009.

roundisfunny. "The Drain." *Round is Funny: Adventures in Queer Transracial Adoptive Parenting and Other Mundane Things.* 10 Jan. 2008. Web. 3 May 2010.

Rudolph, Dana. *Mombian: Sustenance for Lesbian Mothers.* n.d. Web. 21 Mar. 2010.

"Second-Parent Adoption." Human Rights Campaign. Nov. 2009. Web. 4 Mar. 2010.

Team Serrins Springfield. "Farm Trip—Day Two." *The Mama Too.* 20 Jun. 2008. Web. 26 Sept. 2009.

A Partial List of Other Lesbian Parenting Blogs

Joy. *Another Other Mother.* 2 Nov. 2006. Web. <http://anotherothermother.blogspot.com>.

Rudolph, Dana. "Blogging for LGBT Families Day: Contributed Posts." *Mombian: Sustenance for Lesbian Moms.* 2 Jun. 2008. Web. <http://www.mombian.com/2008/06/02/blogging-for-lgbt-families-day-contributed-posts-2>.

h and l.babypants. *babypants.* 19 Feb. 2008. Web. <http://babypants.wordpress.com>.

Keri. Pieces of Gray: *My journey through losing a daughter and trying to conceive.* 13 Dec. 2006. Web. <http://piecesofgray.wordpress.com/>.

The Injector. *Injection Reflections.* 31 May 2007. Web. <http://injectionreflections.blogspot.com>.

Gail and Lyn. *First Time Second Time: Perspectives on Relationships, Roles, and Taking Turns from a Two Mom Family.* 26 Aug. 2008. Web. <http://firsttimesecondtime.blogspot.com>.

ohchicken. *We Are Fambly.* 29 M ar. 2007. Web. <http://wearefambly.wordpress.com>.

11.
Letter to a Young Black Mama on Writing Motherhood Memoir

DEESHA PHILYAW

JUNE 4, 2010

Hello, my name is Alexandra. I am taking a Race & Ethnicity class at XX University, and it was recommended that we visit the Addicted to Race blog. At the site, I listened to a podcast in which you are featured, about why there aren't more Black mommy memoirs. Since hearing the podcast, I've been plagued with the same question: Why aren't there more Black mommy memoirs? Are our mommy experiences not valued? Will the public not take our voices seriously? Do publishers not want to consider our stories?

I'm a full-time student pursuing a Bachelor's degree, employed full-time, and I'm a single mom to a beautiful little girl who is four. My daughter is my sunshine; she is how I breathe ... even though I had her at 19. I find it extremely challenging to relate to these mommy books because their experiences aren't like my own, so I feel somewhat secluded and a bit like an outsider.

I am interested in writing a mommy memoir.... But I have to admit, I am really nervous and worry that people won't want to hear what I have to say. A 24-year-old Black mother who has section 8, doesn't even have a degree yet, no professional writing experience, who used to be on welfare....."Why should I listen to her?" How do I silence these voices? Because they are very loud....

Dear Alexandra,

Thank you for reaching out. Like you, I didn't find myself in the pages of the mommy memoirs at the bookstore after my first child was born either. In the nearly twelve years since, I have perused memoirs by college-educated, stay-at-home moms who, like me, simultaneously wrestled with and delighted in parenthood, but none of these books made it to the check-out counter and none of their authors were Black.

These titles have paled in comparison (no pun intended) to Anne Lamott's *Operating Instructions: A Journal of My Son's First Year*, in terms of complexity and resonance. When I read this book about a year before becoming a mother, Lamott and I appeared to have little in common besides a love of words and confessed neuroses. Yet her wit, the authenticity of her voice, and the urgency of her story kept me turning pages. We can't all be Anne Lamott, but at the very least I needed a mommy memoir to yield some "Amen!" moments, something besides the usual fare of play-dates; Learning What's *Really* Important; lazy and/or clueless and/or inept husbands; ignoring the parenting experts; maintaining one's sanity; struggling to balance career and family demands; leaving the workforce; the loss of sexual or social identity; giving in to the minivan; the importance of martinis.

Black mama-writer Lori L. Tharps, author of *Kinky Gazpacho: Love, Life and Spain*, once approached her agent with the idea of writing a mommy memoir. The agent's response? "Please don't do that." In the 20 years since the publication of *Operating Instructions*, the mommy memoir market has indeed been oversaturated. I understand market forces are at play, but why weren't Black women authors included in this oversaturation? Where were the twenty-first century black mommy memoirs? Was it a problem of supply, or strictly one of demand?

I explored this question in a 2008 *Bitch* magazine article, "Ain't I a Mommy?" (paying homage to the "Ain't I a Woman?" speech attributed to abolitionist and former slave Sojourner Truth). I found that the answer was: *both*. Generally speaking, publishers don't believe there's a ready-made market for Black mommy memoirs, but Black women aren't breaking down their doors with these kinds of manuscripts either.

I asked my agent to give me her insider's assessment of Black women and mommy memoirs. She said: "Publishing is so 'me too', so cyclical. One person does it, and then suddenly everyone wants to do it. It's less about content than the face that you're putting on the book, and the face that's writing the book. As a result, issues that should not be considered fringe topics are treated as fringe topics in traditional publishing. So routinely, efforts to get books into a 'new' market get shut down, and this goes even beyond race and mommy memoirs. And because independent booksellers are dying, the market for taking chances is getting smaller and smaller."

I find it particularly problematic that the typical mommy memoirs were accepted by publishers on the strength of their supposed "universal" appeal: *This* is what American motherhood looks like. Except for many American mothers, it isn't. Many of us are not married White suburbanites. Seventy-five percent of working mothers earn $25,000 or less annually, which strongly suggests they must work in order to provide for their families and aren't wrangling with the question of whether or not to stay at home with their kids (Sweeney). When you add up all the women whose lives aren't reflected in *Dispatches from a Not-So-Perfect Life: Or How I Learned to Love the House, the Man, the Child* or *Sippy Cups Are Not for Chardonnay*, you'll find that these books are hardly representative.

Neither are these books bestsellers. And yet, hypocritically, publishers perpetuate the mythology that your face and my face are not the marketable faces of American motherhood, that Black women's motherhood journeys are "fringe," lacking in broad appeal, and therefore, not worth the investment. But a multiplicity of our stories, our voices—and those of other mothers of color, non-hetero mothers, and economically marginalized mothers—must be included on par with these other texts in the canon of motherhood writing for that canon to be truly legitimate.

Yvonne Bynoe, founder of soulfulaffluence.com and mom of an eight-year-old son, says "When I was shopping around the proposal for *Who's Your Mama?* [an anthology of women writing about motherhood], I had an agent who was a woman of color (but not Black) tell me, 'This book is not necessary. There are enough motherhood memoirs.' I decided that she didn't know what she was talking about. Sure, in a commercial environment, they publish what's tried and true. But I ultimately went with an independent press that was a good fit—and run by a White man, ironically. They were enthusiastic about the project."

Josie Pickens, a single mother, writer, and professor theorizes, "[Black mama-writing] is underrepresented because—and it pains me to say this—as much as Black women have mothered everyone ... we are not respected as women first. What is 'Mammy' if not the all-encompassing mother? There is not a space for Black women outside of stereotypes, outside of fabled constructs, therefore many believe that we only have one story, that we are monolithic, and so there is no need to tell our stories."

Josie's observation may explain in part why our stories aren't in high demand in the publishing industry, but what about the supply side of the equation? The response from the mama-writers I talked to varies.

Some, like Josie, have or had some ambivalence about writing about mothering. Josie shares, "In most parts of Africa, when you have children, your name changes. I would go from being 'Jo' to "Nailah's mother.' I used to have a big problem with that. I felt that it was stifling and an attempt to put me in a box. But I've settled into that thought now that I am growing in motherhood. I often mention Nailah in my writing because she is almost my entire life and reason for writing in the first place. I write in an effort to try and figure it out. I want to be able to guide her properly, and I want her to be courageous and unafraid to tell her story, however she chooses to tell it."

Lori Tharps told me that ultimately she dropped the idea of writing a mommy memoir, not because of her agent's reaction, but because once her post-baby hormonal haze wore off, she found that the moment and the desire had passed.

"'Why don't more Black women write motherhood memoir?' I don't know that a lot of Black women have the time to do it," says Tameka Allen-Mercado, a mixed media artist, award-winning essayist, and married un/homeschooling mother of two. "Plus, many of us aren't reading for the sake of reading, enjoying art for the sake of art, or interested in knowing for the sake of knowing. The storytelling isn't valued. I hear, 'Girl, please … what do *we* need to know about parenting?' Because it's what we do, what we've always done."

Yvonne observes, "Another reason some Black women don't care to write or read about motherhood: it isn't necessarily a good time for them. They love their kids, but the experience has been stressful, financially and other ways. Women are condemned for saying, 'I wish someone had told me…. Had I known this, I might not have had kids.' Women are pilloried for saying such things, so we're not comfortable talking about motherhood in real ways.

"And many of us as mothers still don't place a high value on motherhood, so we don't reflect on it. I can find White women who will gladly have the conversation, but for Black women, writing and telling our stories is not a priority, and if it is, the writing is not about motherhood, or anything personal, or family-oriented. We would rather talk topics like family on a macro level, perhaps because too much has been made of the 'dysfunctional' Black family for us to be comfortable writing about it on a personal level."

So the widening of the motherhood memoir canon requires shifts in supply as well as demand. Yvonne cautions, "We do ourselves a disservice by not contributing our stories to the motherhood genre. We have to participate in the public debate on women and family issues. Those of us who are able have to nurture these stories; the writers may not have the self-worth to tell them. But we have to provide access without overseeing. We need to respect diversity in terms of aesthetics and ethos."

Josie agrees that it's not always easy to write about her mothering experiences, but says she pushes past the fear and writes anyway. "It's not easy to say, 'I was scared or am scared. I am depressed and hurting.' But when I wrote a recent blog entry entitled, 'Self-Definition and the Slaying of Superwoman,' I thought of how many people I could heal by my saying those things. It took the focus off of me. Gloria Naylor says, 'Not only is your story worth telling, but it can be told in words so painstakingly eloquent that it becomes a song.' This is the quote I consider whenever I write. And so we have to be fearless because someone needs to hear our story."

Prompted by your letter, I asked some fellow Black mama-writers I know to tell me the first thing that came to mind when I said, "mommy memoir." Their responses (with one exception): "boring...they all say the same thing about how to balance work and family"; "either the über-mom who sacrifices all for her children, or the slacker mom, the 'bad' mommy"; "same stuff over and over again ... sanctimonious"; "older, White women, especially celebrities.... Mommy Dearest stuff, not anyone I know"; and "I find the whole culture irksome." If this is indicative of our perception of the genre, it's no wonder we're not all that pressed to contribute to it via traditional publishing.

I posed the same query—the first thing that "mommy memoir" brings to mind—to my agent, who is White. Her response: "A White woman with long blonde hair talking about herself for 300+ pages...." She added: "I get a lot of proposals from women who want to write this, but it's been done before. As a woman and a mother, I'm not getting anything from these stories. At its best, the genre is one woman speaking to another woman in a supportive way, not just me, me, me."

It's not that I can't relate to some aspects of the typical mommy memoir, and it's not that Black motherhood experiences are monolithic or esoteric or superior. The late educator and civil rights activist Dr. Dorothy I. Height observed, "A Negro woman has the same kind of problems as other women, but she can't take the same things for granted" (qtd. in Lewis par. 7). In her book, *I'm Every Woman: Remixed Stories of Marriage, Motherhood, and Work,* Lonnae O'Neal Parker writes, "Understand, it's not that I think that Black women have all the answers—only that we have struggled with the questions longer and that sometimes our tool sets are more expansive" (*I'm Every Woman* 14). Parker chafes at the "total obliviousness to Black women's history, and that it [has] always included work" that characterizes much of the public discourse on motherhood and work, a common concern in mommy memoirs (Philyaw, "An Interview" par. 4).

Black women's history also includes American chattel slavery, an institution which by its very definition mocked, violated, and devalued us as mothers. In slavery, our children did not belong to us and could be sold or taken away at any time. We were wet nurses and mammies on demand; we were mamas only at the whim of others.

From slavery forward, Black women have worked *and* cared for children—ours and other people's. By some estimates, the very existence of the Black middle class is owed to Black women's historical workforce participation. Yet there's this relative historical and contemporary silence where our work is concerned and where our mothering experiences are concerned. And this silence is reflected in the virtual absence of our voices in the motherhood memoir genre. In fact, according to Yvonne Bynoe, more than 90 percent of American women aren't reflected in the genre as traditionally published.

But while Black women's writing about motherhood has not had a significant presence in the traditional memoir publishing market, such writing does exist. Yvonne was tired of the one-note mommy memoirs, but was "blown away" by biracial writer Rebecca Walker's book *Baby Love: Choosing Motherhood After a Lifetime of Ambivalence.* She recalls, "It spoke to my age, education, background, economic concerns, identity, and relationship experiences." Memoirs like Walker's enrich and expand the motherhood memoir canon by raising questions about mothering at the intersection of race and personal politics.

Motherhood memoir isn't the only genre Yvonne found lacking. "In feminist books, motherhood is seen as a shackle, and I didn't see myself in those books," she says. "I'm a mother, a career woman who had a full life before motherhood, with a background of advocacy, and political and cultural concerns." Wanting to give access to the voices of "the average Jane" and to frame a broader, more inclusive discourse around motherhood, Yvonne edited the anthology *Who's Your Mama? The Unsung Voices of Women and Mothers* in 2009.

A motherhood memoir canon that includes texts like *Who's Your Mama?* has the potential to be a catalyst for social and political change. "There's this *Leave It to Beaver* assumption of family as a 'personal' issue," Yvonne says. "If we keep holding to this notion, then we don't have to talk about things like flex time or other public policies. We have to do a better job of chipping away at this antiquated thinking."

Another anthology our fellow mama-writers recommend to you: *Rise Up Singing: Black Women Writers on Motherhood*, a collection of short fiction, poems, and essays by established and emerging writers, including journalists, a doctor, and a minister, edited in 2005 by Cecelie Berry, at the time a freelance writer and stay-at-home mom. A motherhood writing canon that includes books like *Rise Up Singing* challenges the notion that any one demographic of women can be considered the "face" of American motherhood. Such a canon forces us to ask hard questions: *Why do we tolerate media and advertising that marginalizes and ignores us? What can we do as mothers and as consumers to change mainstream media and advertising messages that marginalize and ignore us? What alternative media spaces can we inhabit and create to reflect the diversity of who we are as mothers?*

Josie Pickens associates "mommy memoir" with her great-grandmother, who was a mid-wife. "I think of the delicate process of bringing forth life," she says, "and of course, my own birthing story." For Josie, "mommy memoir" also brings to mind an essay by Audre Lorde called "Man Child: A Black Lesbian Feminist's Response," where she discusses raising her son; Toni Morrison's *Beloved;* and slave narratives such as Harriet Jacobs' *Incidents in the Life of a Slave Girl.* "It struck me because what she wrote was so similar, yet dissimilar to my own experience. She went through the unimaginable in an attempt to free herself and her children."

Black women are writing about motherhood in virtual spaces as well. When I shared your questions about traditional publishing and silencing critical voices with other Black mama-writers and asked them to give you some sisterly advice, the predominant response was, "Tell her to blog. Write for online markets." Oprah's Book Club aside, traditional publishing doesn't treat our stories as having universal appeal as *women's* or *mothers'* stories. So the prevailing assumption is that we represent a niche market with a limited audience, a separate category from the existing motherhood writing canon. And without a proven, sizeable audience, black women's motherhood writing isn't generally seen as marketable. By contrast, the online writing market doesn't suffer from the same financial constraints and flawed assumptions. In cyberspace, *we* define and find our audience—and they find us. Thanks to social media platforms such as Twitter and Facebook, we can share our stories with a potential audience of thousands, instantly.

My agent confirms that the publishing industry "others" our writing about motherhood. She sees the Internet as an alternative space: "conversations about diverse mothering experiences are not happening in publishing because the industry doesn't see it as a valid 'category'." She believes that blogging and social media "allow writers to find a truer audience. You avoid layer upon layer of marketing considerations—typically via a White, male lens—before your story sees the light of day. You avoid criticism like, 'It's not sensational enough. It's not *juicy*. It's too much of a downer.'"

And online publishing can lead to traditional publishing opportunities. "Know that agents (and to some extent editors) scour the Internet, searching blogs for talent and how their body of work might translate into a book," my agent says. "A big part of their job is to seek out people who are currently on the margins but who have the potential to become the hot author or topic of the minute. But sometimes, agents become actual fans and keep you in mind. You may be gaining the respect of silent readers that you aren't aware of."

Online is where I got started in 2003. As an aspiring but terrified writer, I wanted to write and publish a novel. That process was slow-going, but in the meantime, I looked for opportunities to write shorter form. I subscribed to an e-list that compiled writing opportunities, most of which were aimed at Black writers. The opportunity that caught my eye was that of an unpaid columnist position at LiteraryMama.com. Though they had posted on a Black writer e-list, their call for submissions wasn't for a "Black mama-writer"; it was for a mama-writer to pitch an idea for a column. I could have pitched a race-related column since, at the time, none of the columns were regularly about race. But instead, I pitched an adoption-related column because my then-husband and I had just adopted a baby girl, our second child. My pitch was accepted, and I wrote *The Girl is Mine* column for four years.

From the outset, race naturally found itself in the center of some of my columns, as it was, at times, in the center of my mama-hood. As my columnist tenure wound down, I got divorced, began dating again, and suffered the loss of my mother, my father, and my grandmother. I wrote a lot less about adoption and lot more about motherhood in general, and grief. On LiteraryMama, I worked with great editors and gained exposure that led to other online writing opportunities and to paying gigs, most notably, *The Washington Post* and *Wondertime*, a now-defunct Disney parenting magazine.

And look at how you found me: online, on a podcast, on a blog. I was invited to be on that podcast after my print article "Ain't I a Mommy?" garnered Internet attention through online posting and re-posting. I was also invited to speak at a university on the strength of that article.

Jennifer James is an influential mom blogger, founder of *Mommy Too!* magazine, and creator of the Mom Bloggers Club, one of the largest social networks for mom bloggers at over 6,000 members. She has this to say about how you can leverage a mom blog: "As a writer, who do you want to speak to? Be creative and intelligent about finding out who your audience is. I would encourage you to write really well, approaching motherhood from different angles, maybe a really funny, unique angle. Years ago, people didn't think Black fiction would sell. But, oh my goodness, it sells! So there's hope. But unless you have a really good agent, the smaller publishing houses or academic presses are going to be the most receptive. For a Black mom to write a book about motherhood, you've got to have a different angle and a really good agent."

Perhaps that sounds daunting. But maybe your goal isn't to get an agent and turn your blog into a book. Jennifer adds, "It all depends on what your main objectives are. Is it to crack that Top Ten of mom bloggers? You know, that upper echelon who are the go-to moms, the ones that get the book deals and sponsorships? Realistically, most moms, regardless of color, aren't going to get into that circle at all. So how do *you* define 'success'?"

Yvonne's definition of success doesn't rely on traditional publishing's stamp of approval. "You don't need publishers to co-sign," she says. "Put your story out there via new media and keep writing." But she frames the issue not just in terms of new vs. traditional media or large vs. small presses, but rather in terms of ownership and entrepreneurship. She points to the need for presses that embrace our motherhood stories as central, not marginal. "Black people and people of color in general need to go back to starting their own presses," she says. "Decades ago, [the Black-woman owned] Kitchen Table Press and others came to pass because our stories weren't being told, and once again our stories aren't being told.

"Writers, like filmmakers, need to be entrepreneurial, to create their own publishing collectives instead of relying on narrow, traditional channels. You've got to fund your own freedom."

Regardless of the medium, there are some must-haves in your mama-writer survival kit. One is a mentor. You may feel awkward asking someone to mentor you, but both times I've asked someone to mentor me, they not only accepted, they were honored to be asked. Likewise, both times I've been asked formally to mentor, I've eagerly agreed. As someone who has been supported tremendously as an emerging writer by generous, thoughtful, established writers, I'm happy to pay it forward. So think about writers you admire, writers who write about the kinds of things you write about, writers with whom you've built a rapport, in person or through social media. Seek out and cultivate mentoring relationships, formally and informally, with writers to whom you have or can get access.

Other must-haves for your mama-writer survival kit: patience and perseverance. Tameka shares, "For me, writing is an art and it's so subjective. If you have a voice, use it. It really isn't about how big audience your audience is. You won't know that they're there until you start to shout. I blogged for a year without a single comment."

Like Tameka's, there's a very good chance that your path as a mama-writer will be a slow, windy, quirky one. My process certainly wasn't linear. The key factors for me were timing, effort, skill, connections, kind and capable editors, and being in the right place at the right time. My how-to advice would be this: Keep writing.

There's no shortage of advice and how-to books on how to get published, but I would encourage you not to focus primarily on getting published, but rather to focus on becoming a strong, confident writer. Read good writing. Ask questions. Seek out mentors and good editors. Ask them how your writing can improve, not if it's "good." Welcome constructive critique. Accept rejection without taking it personally.

Writing is an art, and sometimes a cathartic undertaking as well. But if you decide to write professionally, you'll need to think of it as a business too: Write for free, but only strategically. Write for free if it "pays" in exposure and opportunities to grow as a writer.

Despite the hard market realities and the myopia of the publishing industry, I still believe that good writing counts for something. My agent believes it too. Her advice to you: "Don't listen to those critical voices. There are so many people who care about what you have to say if you do it in a way that's true to your viewpoint without worrying about selling books. Think about who you are writing to and for, and stay true to what you want them to take away. Let that be your motivation. There are not a lot of writers writing the stories they really want to tell; they aren't writing the stories that will change people's lives. This isn't the way make a quick buck or get on *The Today Show*, but it is how you will sleep at night and feel good about what you're doing. I couldn't do my job if I didn't believe that there are great writers who are telling great stories that people will believe in, and be transformed and inspired by."

Even with your mama-writer survival kit fully stocked and with a commitment to writing well, the long journey to becoming a better writer can be a lonely endeavor. Some writers say, "I write for myself," and to a degree this is true. But to the extent that you're not limiting your writing to a private journal, you are writing to connect with an audience. You're looking to make this writing life a little less lonely, and other mamas are looking for voices like yours. So use your writing as a means of connecting with other mothers.

Carolyn Edgar, a single mama, lawyer, and writer says, "At each level of my writing, I've discovered that there is an audience for it, and it grows. I embrace that and take it as far as I can. Like Alexandra, I had doubts when I first began writing about motherhood. It took a while for me to realize that people weren't interested in hearing from 'someone like me' ... people want to hear from *me*. There's nothing special about my story except that I have an ability to tell it. My story doesn't have to be unique or extraordinary to be worth telling. When we write, we represent all those who don't have the ability to tell their stories.

"We so much want to write about 'our' [Black mama] experiences, that we forget about the universality of our experiences. Balance writing from your perspective as a Black woman, with projecting a voice relatable to mothers in general."

Alexandra, I know that you are specifically concerned about writing as a young, Black, working class, single mother, so Carolyn's comments may not feel applicable. But Carolyn clarifies: "We need to put a human voice and face to what motherhood means. Those of us who grew up more middle-class have class-based and race-based assumptions about your experiences: We think, 'This is the result of making bad choices.' We don't think about outside forces at play, or how people struggle to make different choices. Writing your story gives voice and humanity, and allows people to move beyond stereotyping. Write about your challenges—99 percent of them are the same as every other mom (health, safety, education)."

Yvonne agrees that we shouldn't worry about judgment or that no one wants to hear our stories. She says, "We need to borrow a page from other women's books. They aren't paranoid or worried about how they will be perceived. They value their stories, however mundane. They assume there will be broad interest in their stories. We too have to believe that women of all backgrounds will be interested in our stories, if we reach out to them."

Tameka adds, "Because I became a mom at 18 and have been a mom for my whole [adult] life, motherhood kind of found its way into the writing as part of my holistic approach to living. I am a Black mother: I know what my children may experience when they leave the house. Because my blog has an older, White audience, I want it to be educational [for them], and I want to get a discussion going. So, as angry as I am, I have to find my neutral voice when I write about race, racism, and prejudice where my family is concerned. If feelings and perceptions are evoked—that's the goal, you want that connection—then I've done my job. I feel a social responsibility as a Black writer because of how Blacks are perceived in the mainstream, but ultimately, I'm just telling my story.

"And Alexandra, your story is the *real* for more than a little bit of us—talk about 'keeping it real'! It's a story of triumph, but it's not *The Blind Side* kind of triumph because *you're* doing it and *you're* telling it."

Another reason it is imperative for us to tell our stories is that the oral tradition in our community is, sadly, a dying one. Josie reminds us, "We are a people of stories, all kinds, and we gain our worth and moral values from our narratives. This is where and how we have survived." But Carolyn notes, "We no longer have that continuity of stories passed from grandmother to mother to daughter in our families, so we have to seek them out."

And while we respect the mothering experiences and traditions of our foremothers, in many ways they can be different from ours. "Even when we have access to our grandmothers and mothers stories," Carolyn says, "we still seek other voices because what if, for example, we want to discipline but don't want to spank? Or, how can you instill the same drive and hunger in kids who are more privileged than we were growing up? How do we combat their sense of entitlement? Our foremothers didn't struggle with these questions."

Alexandra, our generation struggles with a whole new set of questions, owing in part to a whole new set of privileges, opportunities, and yes, challenges. But we owe it to our foremothers to claim our stake in motherhood memoir writing, even and perhaps especially when it means stretching the boundaries and creating literary spaces for our lived experiences. We can't wait for anyone to do it for us.

Alexandra, the process of writing this letter to you illustrates just how powerful and necessary diverse stories and conversations about our mothering experiences are. I felt that sharing my own mothering and mother-writing experiences, while possibly instructive and useful to you, was not enough. Just as there's no singular or universal *mothering* experience, there's not a monolithic *black mothering* experience. I knew that reaching out to some fellow mama-writers would yield a spectrum of ideas and perspectives. And when we seek out a multiplicity of mothering experiences, we gain context for our own. When we are aware and respectful of the context in which we and others mother—the personal, the economics, the politics, the social, the holistic—we become impervious to media and politicians' attempts to pit us against each other in fake "mommy wars." And we refuse to accept a "face" of American motherhood created by Madison Avenue and the publishing industry.

Instead, we take Lonnae O'Neal Parker's advice and "skim some of the best parts off the top" of a range of mothering experiences. We rally in support of each other and of social, cultural, and political change that not only improves the quality of life for mothers, but of *families*, including women who are not mothers. When we recognize that we aren't mothering in a vacuum, we make alliances across differences, acknowledge our privilege and use it to benefit others.

But despite all the sisterly conversations and connections, and all your hard work, sometimes those doubting, devaluing voices you mentioned may refuse to be silenced. In this case, we have to write our stories in spite of them. Precisely *because* these voices are telling us that we can't, we shouldn't—we must. Surely you aren't the only young mama hungering for stories that affirm, challenge, encourage, and change you. So you must write your story for all the Alexandras who are waiting for it.

In sisterhood,

Deesha

P.S. No mama's reading list would be complete without these:

WORKS CITED

Alexandra-Elizabeth.. *Alexandra-Elizabeth: Motivated. Inspired. Progress Desired.* Social Influenz, 24 March 2010. Web.

Allen-Mercado, Tameka. *Tea & Honey Bread.* 1 January 2007. Web.

Allen-Mercado, Tameka. *We of Hue: Intelligent Discussions for Raising Children of Color.* WordPress, 5 May 2009. Web. ‹http://weofhue. com/author/tameka›.

bandele, asha. *Something Like Beautiful.* New York: Harper Perennial, 2010. Print.

Berry, Cecelie S., ed. *Rise Up Singing: Black Women Writers on Motherhood.* New York: Doubleday, 2004. Print.

Bynoe, Yvonne, ed. *Who's Your Mama?: The Unsung Voices of Women and Mothers.* Brooklyn, NY: Soft Skull Preaa, 2009. Print.

Dwyer, Liz. *Los Angelista.* 19 August 2004. Web. ‹http://losangelista.com›.

Edgar, Carolyn. *Carolyn Edgar: Notes of a Lawyer, Writer and Single Mom.* 8 March 2009. Web.

James, Jennifer. *Mom Bloggers Club: Exclusive Community of 19,000 Mom Bloggers.* 2013. Web.

Lamott, Anne. *Bird by Bird: Some Instructions on Writing and Life.* Garden City, NY: Anchor Books, 1995. Print.

Lamott, Anne. *Operating Instructions: A Journal of My Son's First Year.* Garden City, NY: Anchor Books, 2005. Print.

Lewis, Jone Johnson. "Dorothy Height Quotes: Dorothy Height (1912-2010)." About.com Guide. Web.

Millner, Denene. *My Brown Baby: Smart. Confident. Fresh.* Shatterbox, 2011. Web.

Parker, Lonnae O'Neal. *I'm Every Women: Remixed Tales of Marriage, Motherhood, and Work.* New York: Amistad, 2006. Print.

Pickens, Josie. *Jo Nubian.* Word Press, 2 June 2009. Web.

Philyaw, Deesha. "Ain't I a Mommy?" *Bitch Magazine* June 18, 2008. Print.

Philyaw, Deesha. "An Interview with Lonnae O'Neal Parker | Literary Mama." *Literary Mama Home* 25 Novemnber 2007. Web. 3 July 2013.

Richards, Akilah. *Execumama: The Life Design Agency.* Web.

Richards, Akilah. *Execumama Online.* Web.

Stewart-Bouley, Shay. *Black Girl in Maine: Musings of a Black Woman Living in the Nation's Whitest State.* 22 January 2008. Web.

Sweeney, Jennifer Foote. "Banish the Boogeymom." *Salon.com.* 5 June 2001 Web. 9 Jan. 2013.

Tharps, Lori. *My American Melting Pot: A Multiculti Mix of Identity Politics, Parenting and Pop Culture.* 16 July 2012. Web.

Tharps, Lori. *The Original My American Melting Pot.* 2012. Web.

Walker, Rebecca. *Baby Love: Choosing Motherhood After a Lifetime of Ambivalence.* New York: Riverhead Trade, 2008. Print.

12.

In Search of Our Mothers' Memoirs

Redefining Mothering Through
African Feminist Principles[1]

NICOLE WILLEY

JUST AS AFRICAN AMERICAN WOMEN were kept out of membership to the Cult of True Womanhood in the Nineteenth century,[2] and felt marginalized in the feminist movement of the second wave,[3] "motherhood," as it is currently being practiced, preached, packaged, and sold, at least in the mainstream of the United States at this historical moment, is a place where African American women, particularly, working-class African American women, are once again marginalized, if not flat out rejected, from the Institution of Motherhood.[4] The injustice of this elision is made even more clear when we realize that "the intersections of maternal experience with class, race, and sexuality have created a divide between some White middle-class feminists who have historically seen the family as the locus of female oppression and some working-class women and/or women of color who have found refuge and resistance in their maternal praxis" (Stitt and Powell 3). And this marginalization is, unfortunately, felt in the world of motherhood memoir.

Memoir is a space for both writers and readers to collect and share a collective and cultural memory. Nancy K. Miller reflects the importance of memoirs to me personally, and to our knowledge generally, when she writes, "…what memoirs do is support you in the act of remembering. The memoir boom, then, should be understood, not as a proliferation of self-serving representations of individualistic memory, but as an aid or a spur to keep cultural memory alive" (432). If memoir becomes part of our cultural memory, then the presence of African American motherhood memoirs is a necessity in a collection such as this. So the question for me becomes, where are African American motherhood memoirs in this "boom"? Sure there are a few authors who come immediately to mind,

Rebecca Walker and ashe bandele to name two, but it is clear that the vast majority of women writers who are enjoying wider sales and name recognition in the motherhood memoir genre are white, middle-class women. *Literary Mama, Hip Mama, Brain, Child,* and other magazines and online journals aim to be representative, but there seems to be a much smaller number of African American women writing motherhood memoir. And perhaps those words, "motherhood" and "memoir," are an insight into part of the problem.

This article will first discuss some of the possible reasons for the relative dearth of African American writers in motherhood memoir due to the problematic definitions of the words "motherhood" and "memoir," while making a case for expanding our lens to include other genres within our search for these voices. Then, I will move into a discussion of transformative practices in empowered mothering created in two texts, Harriet Jacobs' *Incidents in the Life of a Slave Girl* (1861) and Richelene Mitchell's *Dear Self: A Year in the Life of a Welfare Mother* (1973; 2007). Their transformations occur specifically through the utilization of the African Feminist principles of adaptation and networking. Both Jacobs and Mitchell are able to show that mothering practice becomes possible for them only through the redefinition of "motherhood" that reflects their lived experiences, and through the necessary help of othermothers and other types of collectivism.

First, we must discuss the meaning of "Motherhood." If many (particularly white and/or middle class) women feel oppressed by their role within the family, it is often due to the "Institution's" demands on the mother. The time and attention required to mother by societal standards, Sharon Hays argues, changed dramatically after World War II (21). In an effort to get women back home (and satisfied with no longer being in the work force), the commercialized and patriarchal notion of the Institution of Motherhood began to require three things: "First, the mother is the central caregiver"; "mothering is regulated as more important than paid employment"; and mothering demands "lavishing copious amounts of time, energy, and material resources on the child" (Hays 8). Andrea O'Reilly revises Hays by noting that the post-war period brought about this notion of "custodial" mothering, but that the true period of "intensive" mothering didn't happen until the 1970s ("Introduction" 7).[5] O'Reilly differentiates the two roles, noting that custodial mothering is the precursor to, but not the same as, intensive mothering ("Introduction" 7). Custodial mothering required proximity, but intensive mothering requires "quality time" that puts the children's needs—physically and materially—before the mother's, or indeed, before the entire household's needs (7). Many African American mothers, for a slew of cultural and economic reasons, by choice or necessity, have not fit into this patriarchal construct of what mothering should be. If African American women are not permitted (or choose not) to join this construct of Motherhood, their stories will be by definition subversive, not a part of the Institution of Motherhood, and therefore, a harder sell all the way around.

I do not wish to impugn all white motherhood memoirs by suggesting that they are readily buying into Motherhood as an Institution and therefore their stories are easier published and sold. However, it is often the case that white motherhood memoirs are written by people who at least seem (on the surface—their subversion is often there) to be part of the comfortable confines of Motherhood. Many of the popular motherhood memoirists, such as Ayun Halliday, Michelle Herman, and Adrienne Martini, are the central caregiver for their children, many do not (aside from their writing) work outside of the home, or outside of their motherhood labor, and many do, indeed, spend large amounts of time and materials on their children. What makes these conditions possible? Usually, a partner who makes enough money to allow the writer to stay at home with her children, the invisibility of writing as work, and a story line that allows for the central importance of the children in the story—indeed, without the children, there would be no story. There is critique of Motherhood as an Institution in many of these stories,[6] and they don't always easily fit into the neat little boxes I'm suggesting here. However, at least at first glance, the mothers who are the writers and protagonists of these stories fit the notion of a mother in the Institution's definitions.

African American mothering is then, almost by definition, subversive. As Njoki Wane discusses in "Reflections on the Mutuality of Mothering: Women, Children, and Othermothering," "motherhood has been ideologically constructed as compulsory only for those women considered 'fit,' and not for women who have been judged 'unfit' on the bases of their social location" (235). She goes on to discuss that "unfit" mothers include "disabled women, Black women, First Nations women, immigrant women, Jewish women, lesbian women, women who are the sole-support of parents, poor women, unmarried women, young women, and others" (Wane 235). Since "mothering remains a site of struggle," indicating who in our society is able to live up to its demands and be considered worthy, African American women are once again placed outside of the Institution (Wane 235). And, as Alice Walker notes,[7] being placed outside of the mainstream is not always a bad thing and can lead to greater strength.

To counter the stereotypes of "two conflicting views of Black women's role in the family: 1) Black women are domineering, castrating females under whose hand the Black family and the Black community are falling apart, and 2) Black women are romanticized, strong, self-sufficient females who are responsible for the survival of the Black family and the Black Community" (Jenkins 204), we need more voices to show us what the realities for African American mothering can be. As Nina Lyon Jenkins suggests in "Black Women and the Meaning of Motherhood," uncovering writing by African American women about mothering will "fill the voids in our existing knowledge about the diversity of Black women's experiences" (Jenkins 208). Rather than being seen (solely) as a site of oppression, mothering within the African American community is often seen as empowering. As bell hooks writes, "Historically, black women have identified work in the context of family as humanizing labor, work that affirms their identity as women, as human beings showing love and care, the very gestures of humanity white supremacist ideology claimed black people were incapable of expressing" (134). African American mothers' voices will not only counter racist lies, but they also have the potential to transform mothering practice for all women—as I argue below—particularly through the model of utilizing African Feminist principles, creating models of empowered experience. Indeed, we should be seeking out (publishing and buying too) African American women's stories of mothering as a model for how we can subvert the dominant motherhood ideology that is isolating and crushing so many women under its burden.

Another problematic term for any discussion of African American motherhood memoir is the genre itself, "motherhood memoir." Elizabeth Podnieks and Andrea O'Reilly point out in their Introduction to *Textual Mothers/Maternal Texts* that

Autobiography (including the diary and memoir) is an especially valuable arena in which we can register and understand the ways that women inscribe an "I" or series of "I's" in the authoring of their own maternal selves, accounting for and expressing awareness of factors such as the body, sexuality, gender, race, class, and nationhood. Autobiographers tell their own stories through matrifocal speech, seeking agency as they shape and control both their lived realities and the textual representations of those realities. (7)

Autobiography is one of the forms Podnieks and O'Reilly highlight in their discussion of Daughter-Centric, Matrilineal and Matrifocal texts, and it is indeed a rich arena for dissecting the realities of lived mothers' lives and their presentations of those lives. Within this collection, *Motherhood Memoirs: Mothers Creating/Writing Lives*, one that explicitly celebrates and investigates the memoir form, it is necessary to point to both the marginality of motherhood memoir and the slippery nature of genre classifications.

First, as noted in the Introduction to this collection, in their otherwise thorough and impressive second edition of *Reading Autobiography: A Guide for Interpreting Life Narratives*, Sidonie Smith and Julia Watson spend only one sentence discussing motherhood memoir as a genre (270). It is listed almost as an aside under "Filiation Narrative" and Sidonie Smith and Julia Watson cite one work as an example—Anne Roiphe's *Fruitful: A Real Mother in a Modern World*. Margo Culley further demonstrates the marginalization of motherhood memoirs, at least obliquely, when she notes that "although contemporary autobiography studies looks like a free-form competition, a counter-canon anarchy, it has in fact dealt with only a tiny, tiny fraction of what has been published as autobiography..." (5). Certainly many more works have been identified and analyzed since she edited her collection *American Women's Autobiography: Fea(s)ts of Memory* in 1992, but her basic assertion that critics prize "highly "literary" texts and/or texts of writers known for their public achievement" is largely still true (5). And even if we can isolate those examples of African American motherhood memoir, as Deesha Philyaw's chapter in this collection does, we are still left with far fewer voices than we would hope to see.

Not only is motherhood memoir a somewhat marginal discourse within the larger terrain of autobiography studies, but genre itself is (wonderfully) hard to define and isolate. Celeste Schenck makes the case for looking for autobiography in other genres, specifically, poetry, in her article "All of a Piece: Women's Poetry and Autobiography," noting that "Western genre theory ... remains for the most part prescriptive, legislative, even metaphysical: its traditional preoccupations have been the establishment of limits, the drawing of exclusionary lines, the fierce protection of idealized generic (and implicitly sexual and racial) purity" (285). Her answer to this masculinist practice of the "banishment of women writers (and other marginalized groups) from the canon" (282) is to note that autobiographical practice runs through other genres as well.

In fact, and of course, African American women have been telling and writing their mothering stories as long as they've been mothering, but those stories are not always made public; therefore, they are often not available, and even more often they are not celebrated, at least not in the same category as more traditional motherhood memoirs. It is important to uncover these stories where they are—whether that means, searching for "our mothers' gardens" as Walker does in a more general attempt to uncover women's stories—or through looking for stories of mothering in different genres. If the "motherline" is a type of oral literature that exists outside the master narrative, then it is both suspect by the status quo and a possible agent of change (O'Reilly "Across the Divide" 255). These motherlines exist, and it is our job as scholars and critics to recover these maternal narratives.[8] Life writing in the form of slave narratives and diaries are exceedingly rich places to find the motherline, and in particular, the mother's own voice (as opposed to her story narrated through the daughter).

Searching for African American mothering stories in literature that is unquestionably memoir provides us with only part of the story. Those works are out there, such as Rebecca Walker's *Baby Love: Choosing Motherhood after a Lifetime of Ambivalence* (2007) and asha bandele's *Something Like Beautiful: One Single Mother's Story* (2009). But if we broaden our lens, we find that mothering stories, told by mothers themselves, have been here all along under different guises. Harriet Jacobs' slave narrative *Incidents in the Life of a Slave Girl* is a largely autobiographical account of her life as a slave, with a particular accounting of the abuses she suffered under her master, her decision to give birth to children who were not her master's, her escape from slavery, and her eventual reuniting with her children. As was painstakingly proven by Jean Fagan Yellin, the outlines of her story largely follow the contours of her life, but with names changed.[9] For access to Jacobs' life as a mother, we should look directly at her autobiography, because Joanne Braxton notes that exploring African American women's autobiographical writing helps us understand the particularities of their lives:

> The autobiography of black American women is an attempt to define a life work retrospectively and is a form of symbolic memory that evokes the black woman's deepest consciousness. Black women's autobiography is also an occasion for viewing the individual in relation to those others with whom she shares emotional, philosophical, and spiritual affinities, as well as political realities. (9)

So, through *Incidents*, we will be able to locate Jacobs' particular story with an eye toward the relationships that made her life meaningful. And these mothering stories do not stop with slave narratives, but have continued in the rich tradition of African American women's fiction and poetry, and sometimes, in memoir too. Richelene Mitchell's diary, *Dear Self: A Year in the Life of a Welfare Mother,* published by her children in 2007, but written in 1973, is clearly autobiographical. Though the writer had desires for publication, this was a personal accounting, one that had she survived, she would have edited and culled for public consumption. Neither Jacobs' nor Mitchell's memoirs fit the current mold for the "boom" in memoir generally, or motherhood memoir particularly, but both are affecting, instructive, and ultimately, transformative. These works expand the readers' minds into their own personal experience, enlarging the universality of the experience of motherhood in the specifics of the authors' lives. As Smith and Watson write, "The authority of the autobiographical, then, neither confirms nor invalidates notions of objective truth; rather, it tracks the previously uncharted truths of particular lives" (16). And through these particular lives, we see the legacy of African Feminist strategies and their effectiveness for empowered mothering.

It is significant that each of these works brings African Feminist principles to the table. Rosalyn Terborg-Penn in "Slavery and Women in Africa and the Diaspora" identifies the "two consistent goals valued by women of African descent—developing survival strategies and encouraging self-reliance through female networks" (218-219). Survival through networking (othermothering and collectivism) and adaptation (read here as redefinition) are traits that are continuous within communities of enslaved and free women of African descent throughout the Diaspora and are the bedrocks of African feminist thought and action (Terborg-Penn 218). These two basic principles are readily found in both of these books and provide possible transformative options for any mother struggling with the Institution of Motherhood and the challenges of mothering.

Each of these works recognizes the importance of a collective, of othermothers who share the specific load for individual mothers, but more generally the idea that we can collectively work together to enact positive change for mothers, children, and families. Braxton recognizes the extent to which female slave narratives are celebrations of "[the author's] liberation and her children's as the fruit of a collective effort, not an individual one" (20). As is true of most motherhood memoirs (as a subset of women's autobiography, discussed here by Smith and Watson), they are "interdependent and identified with a community" (278). While these authors are definitely mining their experiences and psyches for their own edification and the readers' benefit, they are also always writing within and about relationships. Their audience and purpose seems always to be one that shows the importance of the African Feminist ideal of social networks, of finding common ground, of forming mothering collectives—either in their lives or in the sharing of their lives, or both. The reason we may not see more motherhood memoirs by African American women may be rooted in this very fact—traditional (male) autobiographies are about the individual, and African American women have received and celebrated collectivist ideals that have been passed to them through the generations.

In addition to sharing their stories and creating bonds through that sharing, Jacobs and Mitchell are also engaged in the work of redefining motherhood. If the Institution of Motherhood does not allow women of color, then these authors rewrite motherhood in a way that will allow them to claim their place. As O'Reilly notes in her Introduction to *Mother Outlaws*, "In patriarchal culture, women who mother in the institution of motherhood are regarded as 'good' mothers, while women who mother outside or against the institution of motherhood are viewed as 'bad' mothers" (2). The Institution of Motherhood mandates a situation in which mothers cannot possibly measure up (thereby serving the system that wants them to be quiet and buy more things to improve their mothering) (O'Reilly "Introduction" 10). But many women have experienced and consciously enacted positive change through mothering outside of the Institution—either by choice or necessity. O'Reilly defines empowered mothering as "affirming maternal agency, authority, autonomy, and authenticity," noting that it creates a situation in which mothering can be "more rewarding, fulfilling and satisfying for women" ("Introduction" 26). Mothering is hard no matter the circumstances, but Jacobs and Mitchell must overcome many obstacles, often making choices and sharing truths that fall well outside of the accepted mainstream logic for "good" mothering. In their honest portrayals, in their ambivalence, anger and fierce love, they create new models, relying upon African Feminist principles that could help every mother transform her own mothering practice.

Acting as a sort of foremother to Mitchell, Jacobs both redefines the role of mother and shows the importance of collectivism in Incidents. Her life story is well known, with a veritable industry surrounding the criticism of her text, so we will only focus on a few of the most salient instances for our discussion. One of the most important features of her story, to my mind, is her unwillingness to let northern white women, the audience she assumes and addresses throughout her book, define her womanhood for her. As a teenager, in an effort to escape her diabolical master's control and sexual advances, she takes a white lover and has a son and daughter by him, believing that her pregnancy will make her repugnant to Dr. Flint while simultaneously creating a situation in which the father of her children can buy them all and make them free. She is loathe to admit her extramarital relationship to her audience of white, northern women, the proof of which is the existence of her children. In her own defense she writes, "I know I did wrong.... Still, in looking back, calmly, on the events of my life, I feel that the slave woman ought not to be judged by the same standard as others" (Jacobs 502). Hazel V. Carby sees the narrative in its entirety as the "most sophisticated, sustained narrative dissection of the conventions of true womanhood by a black author before emancipation" (47). I would add that this moment of redefinition is of the utmost importance in her redefinition and instruction to her white audience. In being born a slave, her purity was immediately in question, and rather than let her master make her his concubine, she chose an affair with a man who did not own her, and *then*, tells her readers that she should not be judged by their standards.[10]

It is this affair that causes Lydia Maria Child[11] to write in her introduction to the book,

> I am well aware that many will accuse me of indecorum for presenting these pages to the public; for the experiences of this intelligent and much-injured woman belong to a class which some call a delicate subject, and others indelicate. This peculiar phase of Slavery has generally been kept veiled; but the public ought to be made acquainted with its monstrous features.... (442)

Jacobs and Child were both keenly aware that their admittance to the Cult of True Womanhood, on the basis of purity, would be challenged by this work. Child (though admittedly already a member of the Cult and therefore in an entirely different position), just for helping the story to be published, would be accused of encouraging impure thoughts. But Jacobs' children's very existence proved her unworthiness as a woman, and she, through her eloquent writing and decidedly moral behavior, turns the tables and shows the hypocrisy of any "true" woman who would look the other way when rape was known, legalized, and allowed.

The first time I wrote about Jacobs, before I was a mother, I focused on the importance of her own definition of womanhood, her unwillingness to go along with the patriarchal notions that discounted her as a true woman. But, as Peter Carlton notes in a study of his own reading practice, "Every rereading is like returning to a familiar room and finding it changed" (238). I was different when I came back to Jacobs as a mother, and therefore, my interpretation of her work is different too, and deeper. I realize now that it was not just the Cult of True Womanhood that she was railing against, but the Institution of Motherhood as well. Her firstborn, a son, was sickly at birth, "but God let it live" (Jacobs 508). She seems unwilling in this phrase to admit to her son's personhood, and she is clearly ambivalent about his survival. Later she writes:

> As the months passed on, my boy improved in health.... The little vine was taking deep root in my existence, though its clinging fondness excited a mixture of love and pain. When I

was most sorely oppressed I found a solace in his smiles. I loved to watch his infant slumbers; but always there was a dark cloud over my enjoyment. I could never forget that he was a slave. Sometimes I wished that he might die in infancy. God tried me.... I had prayed for his death, but never so earnestly as I now prayed for his life; and my prayer was heard. Alas, what mockery it is for a slave mother to try to pray back her dying child to life! Death is better than slavery. (Jacobs 510)

Of course she bonds with her child, and loves him fiercely, but she knows that because he is a slave his life is not hers to protect or his to keep. Slavery is the cause of her sorrows and her inability to see her son's life in a wholly positive way. The fact that she could mention this ambivalence[12] goes against unwritten codes for suitable expressions for mothers, then and now. All mothers, regardless of conditions, should unconditionally love and wish to bond with their babies, so the Institution tells us. But the complicated position of mothering for a slave woman is the reality, and she doesn't shy away from it.

When her daughter is born, she writes, "When they told me my new-born babe was a girl, my heart was heavier than it had ever been before. Slavery is terrible for men; but it is far more terrible for women ... they have wrongs, and sufferings, and mortifications peculiarly their own" (Jacobs 526). Again, not only is she unable to feel or describe joy at the birth of her child, but she is clear in her ambivalence about the new life and the sorrow this "link to life" will bring her and the child herself. In fact, when her master's abuses cause her to faint and become ill four days after the birth of her daughter, she "begged [her] friends to let [her] die rather than send for the doctor" (Jacobs 527). Granted, the only doctor they had to call was her master, but the plea to end her suffering, not just as a woman but as a mother, is clear.

The fact that Jacobs refuses to fall into line with the prescribed role for a mother of the time is understandable and unavoidable in her situation, but it is also a tool she uses to further her escape and her children's protection. Her master's family cannot believe that she would want to be separated from her children, so they believe that ruses like sending Linda/Jacobs and her daughter to a family plantation in the country will prevent her from escaping. As I have written elsewhere, it is precisely this emotional blackmail that spurns her to action, to escape, for herself and her children (Willey 277). When she does escape, they think that imprisoning her daughter will bring her out of hiding—it does not. She misses her children terribly, but she knows that they are in good hands with her grandmother and uncle, and she knows that her own escape is the best she can do to ensure her children's freedom. Relying on social networks, allowing for othermothering, and using every tool in her arsenal of survival strategies are African Feminist notions that allowed African families to continue under slavery. But more than ensuring survival, Jacobs' mothering playbook—which does not follow the same rules as her white master's—enables her to escape and arrange for her children to be free as well.

Writing is a central part of her escape plan. She writes letters from the attic garret, and has them shipped north, then sent with New York City postmarks, back home. Her master believes the letters to be authentic and wastes a tremendous amount of money, money he doesn't have, to go and recapture her. Once she is in the North, her letters home are her only real connection with her family that remains in the South. But her biggest triumph in the world of writing is her autobiography. At first, she thinks that maybe someone like Harriet Beecher Stowe should write her story, and she sends a letter to her outlining that idea. Stowe agrees that Jacobs' story would make a lovely paragraph in her Key to Uncle Tom's Cabin. Jacobs, rightly, removes her offer and decides that she should write the story herself (Yellin, "Introduction" xxi).

She feels underprepared as a writer, but perhaps even more importantly, she has the full-time care of her employer's child, as well as housework, to fill her days. Finding the time to write is a struggle, and she does it mostly at night, taking five years to finish at this pace (Martin 264). While she needed to have forewords and appendices to authenticate her work (though, as Couser notes, she subverts the tradition of the time by including her own words first and a free black man's words last "thereby subverting the hierarchy of race (and gender) characteristic of authentication" [136]), and while Child herself claims that her work is "more romantic than fiction" (441), disparaging her writing, the work itself is solid and admirable, and what's more, it is transformative—for mothering and for genre. It bridges several genres; at turns it is a sentimental novel, slave narrative, spiritual memoir, and pure autobiography;[13] it is Jacobs' own story, in her own words. As Smith and Watson note, "Any utterance in an autobiographical text, even if inaccurate or distorted, is a characterization of the writer" (15), and this writer is able to share her experience of mothering. Knocking down the walls that would keep her from the Institution of Motherhood, she prefers to mother on her own terms.

Her story is of course not an unmitigated success. She famously writes at the end, "Reader, my story ends with freedom; not in the usual way, with marriage. I and my children are now free!" (Jacobs 664). She has no home of her own, but she has provided the most important thing to her children that she could—their freedom. Of course, there are losses. She loses her son and brother in a trip to California, a trip they take to find success, something they are not able to find in Massachusetts (Willey 267); she never sees her Grandmother or Uncle Phil alive again. Her desire to have a home of her own with her family surrounding her is thwarted. It is important to note, as Couser does, that "the thrust of the whole narrative has been to establish a nonpatriarchal home on the memorable (and memorialized) model of her grandmother's. Jacobs wants not a husband but freedom from a life of service in a white home" (140). And eventually, this is what she gets, through her activism for her people, in working as a nurse during the Civil War, and running schools in the South for freed slaves with her daughter. And she continued to write—utilizing the press to "report back to the reformers on conditions in the South" (Yellin "Introduction" xxvii). As Braxton notes, "the early autobiographical writings of black Americans linked the quest for freedom with the quest for literacy. To be able to write, to develop a public voice, and to assert a literary self represented significant aspects of freedom" (15). Jacobs' writings *won* her freedom, but African American mothers still had much ground to cover.

Jacobs set the tone, allowing women to define and practice mothering in their own way, while proudly telling their own stories. Moving forward a century, there is no more legalized slavery in the United States, and the Civil Rights movement has gone a long way in correcting the inequality that states' rights following the Civil War legalized and enforced, though there is still a long way to go. Jenkins reminds us that "The Moynihan report ... officially labeled the African-American female-headed family inferior, nonproductive, pathological and dysfunctional" in 1965 (205). It is in this contested terrain that Richelene Mitchell has made a resolution to keep a diary for a year, to record her struggles and aspirations as a divorced mother of seven who is struggling to raise her family within the welfare system. Her book, *Dear Self: A Year in the Life of a Welfare Mother*, may have never been published had her son (Ricky in the book), Imam Zaid Shakir, not become a prominent Muslim scholar and activist who was able to advocate for its publication through the publisher New Islamic Directions. The book became public in 2007, but was written in 1973. Patricia Bell-Scott asserts in her book *Life Notes: Personal Writings by Contemporary Black Women* that "there is a verifiable tradition of Black women who have made contemporaneous notes of their lives, though these writings almost never reach a national audience" (17). We are fortunate that this example survived and was finally published. Sadly, many of the problems related to poverty and discrimination that Mitchell exposes and explores in her book are still with us, some even more potent than they were then. Mitchell, too, shares her own story of mothering, defining it for herself and in contrast to stereotypes. Her work is also interested in mothering as a collective action.

Mitchell is not a stranger to writing as she begins her diary. In fact, she says that she is afflicted with "letter-writis" and "itchy fingers," and has spent years writing letters to politicians, authors, and newspapers about any number of issues that concern her. She is in a somewhat unique position—though not college educated, she was a "pet" at her white high school, and was encouraged to read and write. Mitchell owns a typewriter, and has subscriptions to *Reader's Digest* and a Book of the Month club (though she cancels her subscription to this because they never feature African American authors). Though she is raising seven children on her own, when this book begins all of her children but one are in school all day, and the youngest is in Headstart for half days. She is on welfare and finds that working is an exercise in diminishing returns—she reports the income, and her welfare subsidies go down while her well-being suffers. Because she has no transportation, and because the jobs she can attain and keep do not pay well, staying strictly on welfare suits her finances (such as they are) and her health (which is compromised by severe bouts of seizures due to epilepsy, which she keeps secret). Therefore, Mitchell is an educated woman, widely read, with the ability and some time to devote to her craft. Her birth family is firmly middle class, and so was she, until she divorced her abusive husband. In refusing her any support, he forced her entry into the welfare system, just as he forced, through the destruction of any contraception she was able to procure, the many years of her life she spent pregnant, nursing, and caring for children. Mitchell has seen poverty from a variety of angles, and her intelligence, skill, and time allow her to write about class, race, gender, and mothering from the position of one who actually is a member of the so-called underclass.

For a woman like Mitchell, her diary project can be seen as a wonderfully "dangerous activity, because it allows [her] the freedom to define *everything* on [her] own terms. For those seeking to defy culturally imposed negative identities, personal writing has offered avenues for resistance and re-creation" (Bell-Scott 17). Mitchell's diary project for the year of 1973 has several purposes, which she outlines in the beginning. First, she has hope that this will be the year she turns her life on welfare around. With her children getting older, her opportunities for herself expand, and she feels a turning point is coming. She also sees the diary as a tool for personal enrichment, as well as a private outlet for her thoughts. Her diary, she says, is for herself. About her habit of writing letters, she explains:

> I am always striving to enlighten, and to make people a little more understanding and loving. Trying to save the world! Suddenly it dawned on me that the world would most definitely remain the same, and I, least of all, would never be the one to change it. After all, who am I but a poor miserable welfare recipient who can't even pay my own way through life? …So, self, in December of 1972…. I vowed that henceforth when my fingers began itching to write a letter, I would simply sit down and write a letter to myself, and this is it. (Mitchell 1)

Mitchell's sense of humor and irony is present here—the self-deprecating tone should not be taken at face value. She does feel powerless at many points in this book, but often, she feels that her writing *can* make a difference. Sometimes, particularly in the first quarter of the year (or the first half of the book—she is more prolific early on), she chooses to write about topics rather than daily events. She focuses on her readings, and how she can apply those readings (notably, Norman Vincent Peale's *The Power of Positive Thinking*) to her own life situation for improvement. She feels that examining her situation will allow her to understand it, fix patterns, and create change.

The voice is personal throughout, and each entry starts with "Dear Self." This "Self" that Mitchell postulates is another side of herself—the side who can listen without judgment and offer reason in answer to emotional duress.[14] Despite this personal focus that is a necessary part of the diary form, Mitchell continues to write public letters, and sends out her letters and some diary entries for perusal by editors. Though she is rejected, she decides toward the end of the book that she knows now that she needs to write a novel, and that becomes her new goal. Sadly, it is never carried out, as she ends her diary in despair on December 18, writing that she has no money for Christmas for her kids, and that events have kept her from writing. Like many diarists, and "despite a compelling need to write, a majority have put their writing on hold at least once" to deal with the busy-ness of life or a crisis (Bell-Scott 22). She seems to know that this will be the last entry, as she writes, "Suffice it to say events have continued to conspire in such a way as to make me despair of encountering that miracle that 1973 promised me in glowing terms at the beginning of this year. Faith is at an all-time low ebb as of December 18, 1973; hope is almost dead, and charity is seriously questioning its existence" (Mitchell 420). Mitchell's last line is, "And so, dear Self, in case I don't get back to you this year, Merry Christmas" (Mitchell 421).

The stark contrast of her first entry and her last is stunning, but exceedingly understandable to anyone who has read her book. Mitchell starts the year with ideas and hope. But, as work opportunities sour and health problems emerge, she focuses more, and repetitively, on the daily issues she must circumnavigate to keep her house warm and her children clothed and fed. Some might feel that this repetition (though clearly a product of the format—a daily and personal diary that was not edited for style or culled of painful material) is a weakness, but I would argue it is one of its great strengths. Diaristic writing is about the "dailiness" of the subject's life, and while this piling up of events "may seem incoherent or haphazard in their preoccupations" they build meaning through the piling on of experience (Smith and Watson 266). Getting a welfare check late, which happens several times, creates huge problems for her. If her check is not on time, she cannot get to the bank on time, and then she cannot get to the store in time to restock the nearly empty cupboards. Not having a car leads to indignities that are made worse by taxi drivers who charge more on "check day," knowing their clients have few choices. It is also made worse by ice, or rain, or the cost of eggs rising by 15 cents per dozen. Grocery shopping is certainly not a task I relish (and I'm happy to let my husband do most of it), but while it can occasionally make me grumpy—someone cuts me off in the parking lot, or disbelief at how few bags I've filled for how much money, or disgust with myself for once again forgetting my canvas bags—it does not decimate my bank account, or cause people to judge me for how much I'm buying on food stamps, or become impossible if no taxi is waiting and I have to simply leave my cart and walk home to enlist my children to come back and help me carry the many bags. As a reader, I would likely not be as impressed with the problems associated with check day for her, if I did not read about her going through it each month. The repetition of the book is the repetition of this mother's life, a repetition that is filled with small and large hurts, based on the limitations of her position.

And repetition, really, is one of the big issues for anyone who is mothering. Laundry, messy bedrooms, cooking, homework, money for shoes, floors that become dirty as soon as they're cleaned—these repetitions are a part of almost any mother's life. Kids need to eat everyday, and need clean clothes everyday, and mess up the floors and the walls and the furniture, everyday. Her pile of laundry, with seven children, of course, is bigger than mine. And anyone's washing machine can break. But when mine broke, I could use a credit card to purchase a new one. When it wouldn't be ready for delivery for a couple of weeks, I could use a friend's, or the laundromat. Mitchell had no coins for the laundromat, and buying something new, or even fixing the old one, was something she couldn't imagine how to do. A hiccup, a hiccup I complained about, was nonetheless a hiccup I could manage. This same problem for someone who is living on very little and barely making ends meet leads to all out despair. And here is the difference. Women in the kind of poverty that Mitchell is living do not usually write their stories. Many reasons, like the lack of time, access, and opportunity, conspire against mothers' stories being told, but particularly conspire against mothers who are in survival mode, and that is what this welfare mother describes—survival: "Money can do so much to make life more livable. If I were wealthy, released from the constant grind of just trying to survive, I could thoroughly enjoy raising my own children, every one of them. They're really pretty nice people, all things considered"

(Mitchell 45). Part of her hope and dream is simply to get to a place beyond scrimping and saving and piecing together an existence, so that she can enjoy her life and her children.

Of course, Mitchell's burdens would be less if she didn't have seven children. Added to these seven, her oldest daughter became a teenage mother and has two children as well. This daughter lives with her sons and her husband, but still expects Mitchell, a "premature" grandma, to watch her children at any time. And here is where Mitchell's redefinition of mothering comes into play. First, she admits, again in a humorous but painful moment, that she had too many children: "Admittedly, I may have caused the population explosion" (Mitchell 8). Podnieks and O'Reilly note that maternal "ambivalence is sanitized and domesticated through the device of humour, for it is only in this context that these taboo feelings and responses can be articulated 'safely'" (15-16). In this instance, humor is clearly used to diffuse the difficulty of her burden, but most of her maternal ambivalence is clearly spoken, with no filter of humor. She writes later, "If only God had given me the strength and courage to break away after the first one, all of these other mixed-up little souls wouldn't be here. Sometimes I say awful things to them because they have such unsettling and hurting personalities. I pray to God to hold my tongue because I know they're not responsible" (Mitchell 231). And still later, in referring to family size, "Anything over two is just too many" (Mitchell 254).

At first the reader knows she has seven children, but doesn't realize that she had no say in the number of her pregnancies. Her husband was controlling and abusive, and refused her the use of contraception. She is quite literally saddled with the complete burden of raising them on her own, since her own family was disgusted that she left her husband (and middle-class existence), and because her ex-husband refuses to pay any child support. (In fact, he moves frequently and will never tell her where he is so that he cannot be tracked.) The untenable situation that her ex-husband and birth family have left her in are part of the cause for her maternal ambivalence. Though "ambivalence and anger are typical and expected dimensions of motherhood" it clearly still "takes candour, courage, and community for mothers to 'out' them-selves in public, never mind in print" (Podnieks and O'Reilly 4). Of course, Mitchell doesn't know that this writing will reach a public stage without the chance of her ordering it first, and so her ambivalence may be more clearly spoken than most. Still, uncovering her anger—at herself, her ex-husband, her family, and importantly, her children—gives all of us mothering a mirror, one that lets us know it is okay to express these feelings.

So, she is clearly doing the best she can in an unideal situation. Like Jacobs, she is often ambivalent about her children—the fact that they exist, and their presence in her daily life. She shows that they can hurt her, "these kids can cut you to the quick, with no qualms" (Mitchell 222). She calls her youngest "wild," and writes, "Those preschoolers can really work on your mental processes, it's literally psychological warfare. Between alternating periods of howling for the sheer pleasure of seeing you disintegrate before their eyes and fighting because they like the way you referee, they look at you with wide-eyed innocence" (Mitchell 7). She recommends both spankings and tuning them out. She writes clearly and unapologetically about just how hard being a mother is, and offers this as a definition of her job:

> My work is trying to maintain a somewhat stable home for my children. That this is a thankless and even maligned job, especially in circumstances like mine. [sic] That there are those that count me as nothing, since I am a welfare recipient, I am well aware. And yet I feel that I am of as much worth, in the total scheme of things, as … the president who rules America and the Queen who rules England. For as long as I give my best to the job that is mine, and if, by God's grace, I can present these young lives to society as decent, stable, self-sustaining, contributing adults, have I not done as monumental and important a job as any human being? Even failing to accomplish this, if I do my best, have I not done all that is required? (Mitchell 65)

She has redefined mothering as her own, though she is black, poor, and on welfare, and is therefore considered "nothing." She dies young, of an aneurysm, about a year and three months after she finishes her diary, so she does not know how her charges presented to society. As the epilogue shows, all of her children turn out well, by her own and society's standards. Several get advanced degrees, all hold down jobs, none have been to prison or have addiction problems, and five of the seven have been married for 20 years or more at the time of publication.

In fact, several of them have spent their careers working with welfare recipients and others at risk in our society. Indeed, she did all that was required. She is proud and loving and shows tremendous self-sacrifice for her children, but can also show great anger and frustration at them, and even show regret that they were born. In other words, she is a real woman, a real mother, and she is not afraid (in this diary) to show it.

Jacobs railed against slavery, and the "peculiar" institution's particular problems for female slaves. Mitchell rails against the welfare state, and how "powerfully hard [it is] to be happy when you're black, poor, and walled in all around" (20). Like Jacobs, she relies on her community to help her through. She enjoys her bowling league (until racism forces her out), she relishes phone conversations and time spent with friends, and she relies on other women to help out with transportation and childcare—often providing whatever services she can for friends as well. Collective mothering in her apartment complex is a necessity, and she notes, "When I talk to other welfare mothers, both black and white, it is amazing how similar is the fabric of which our lives are woven" (Mitchell 38). Indeed, there is more to connect mothers than separate us, if we look closely.

Mitchell's writing here is a kind of *testimonio*, in which "the narrator intends to communicate the situation of a group's oppression, struggle, or imprisonment, to claim some agency in the act of narrating, and to call on readers to respond actively in judging the crisis" (Smith and Watson 282). Her connection to others, others whose lives are so entwined with her own, shows that these are not only her own particular truths, but truths for her collective. Ruth Behar in *The Vulnerable Observer* writes, "The genres of life history and life story are merging with the testimonio, which speaks to the role of witnessing in our time as a key form of approaching and transforming reality" (27). Mitchell's desire to connect with other mothers and share her struggles points to her desire to transform not only her own, but other mothers' realities as well.

Her diary seems to provide her with some personal fulfillment and consolation. She writes, "But at least I can express my innermost feelings and thoughts here, on paper, and it's a wonderful catharsis" (Mitchell 107). But this personal fulfillment belies her larger ambitions. She writes later,

Oh I'm so sick of being poor. But, I see no change in sight. Wouldn't it be great if I could sell this "year's journal" to a publisher and get rich? Dreams! Dreams! I really do think that some of the things that I've observed and experienced might be enlightening to people that want to be enlightened about the human side of poverty. (Mitchell 157)

She is writing for herself, but also for her dreams, for a public audience. Mitchell is like other women who have created diaries, and who, "In spite of isolation, multiple disadvantages, and attempts by others to stop them, they write defiantly of lives lived and dreamed in all their complexities" (Bell-Scott 25). Luckily, for us, her work became public. I can only say that while she never lived to see her work published, it has been appreciated. It won the Bronze medal for Foreword Reviews Book of the Year in Family and Relationships 2007, and it was the 2008 winner under the Parenting/Family category of the Next Generation Indie Book Awards. Upon uncovering this work, I myself have been unable to let it go—thinking through the ways in which she uncovers and redefines mothering for all of us.

Writing these books are singular acts of extreme courage on the part of Jacobs and Mitchell. For them, as for so many mothers, the "tension between the oppression experienced by mothers and our often simultaneous experience of resistance through our mothering has been difficult to mediate" (Podnieks and O'Reilly 3). Jacobs and Mitchell are ambivalent about their motherhood, *and* they embrace it as empowering work. They recognize that the Institution of Motherhood does not deem them worthy on one account or many, and they fight mightily against stereotypes thrown their way about their position as mothers. Further, they recognize that mothering is not done alone. The specifics of their lives speak to truths in other women's lives, about the effects of slavery, poverty, teenage mothering, single mothering, racism, and sexism. But with collective action, through social networks and othermothering, good friends, and shared responsibilities, mothering can become more manageable for every mother.

The experience of reading these books, through time and genre, gives me hope about the future of mothering, mothers, children, and families everywhere. As the founders of *Brain, Child* write, "…every time a mother's voice is heard—this is what my life is like, this is what I struggle with, this is what makes life worth living—it is a political statement, because we've been invisible, dismissed for so long" (Niesslein and Wilkinson

74). These stories, all of our stories, create a shared experience. Smith and Watson remind us why we all care about autobiographical writing, and specifically motherhood memoirs when they write, "…we read other people's narratives as spurs to self-understanding, self-improvement, and self-healing" (231).

Jacobs and Mitchell help us to understand mothering in new ways—redefining the role and providing models of collectivism. If we can all learn to rely more on the African feminist principles of social networking and adaptability—in this case, through adapting definitions that don't serve us and creating definitions that do—then we can all, I hope, come closer to valuing children—our own and all of them, everywhere—while being honest and true to our own needs and experiences.

ENDNOTES

[1]As I revise this piece, the massacre in Newtown, CT, happened less than a month ago. I am one of many millions of mothers whose hearts broke that day. Transforming ourselves and our world has never taken on such urgency for me personally, and yet I know that mothers' hearts break around the world minute by minute, for atrocities that are equally unspeakable. I dedicate this chapter to all mothers who need us to transform our practices, our very world, to protect our children.

[2]Barbara Welter's amalgamation of works from the time period and definition of "true womanhood" locates the four most important characteristics of the domestic ideology cult: "piety, purity, submissiveness, and domesticity" (152). Of course, women living during the time of the cult were well aware of its pervasiveness and boundaries, even though it was not studied and perhaps less clearly defined.

[3]bell hooks in *Feminist Theory: from margin to center* addresses head on the divide between white middle class feminists and feminism from black women and working class women; Alice Walker discusses the same divide in her book of essays *In Search of our Mothers' Gardens*. Indeed, many writers—Hazel V. Carby, Patricia Hill Collins, and Harryette Mullen, to name but a few, have all discussed this breach in detail.

[4]I will capitalize "Institution of Motherhood" throughout the essay to remind us of the artifice of this patriarchal notion. As discussed in the Introduction to this collection, we are assuming that Motherhood refers

to the patriarchal expectations put on mothering roles, while the word "mothering" refers to any number of practices that individual mothers enact (O'Reilly "Introduction" 2).

[5]I would suggest that "intensive" mothering was not on display in my own childhood (I was born in 1974) and that it really began with the materialism of the 1980s and has extended deeply into the present. Perhaps the growing popularity of Dr. Sears' "attachment parenting" in the 1990s is also part of the pressure for increased intensity in mothering. Certainly mothers do not have to be believers in, or even readers of, Dr. Sears to know some of the basic premises of attachment parenting (bonding, breastfeeding, babywearing, co-sleeping, etc.), and "Dr. Bill" has been advising parents through *Parents Magazine* and a variety of talk shows for years.

[6]O'Reilly argues in "The Motherhood Memoir and the 'New Momism': Biting the Hand That Feeds You" that motherhood memoir "ultimately reinscribes, or more accurately naturalizes and normalizes, the very patriarchal conditions of motherhood that feminists, including the motherhood memoir writers themselves, seek to dismantle" (205). I agree with her assertion for many motherhood memoirs, indeed for the ones I am characterizing here, but the works I will discuss in this chapter, as well as many discussed in this collection, actually show a desire to transform mothering practice rather than simply discuss it.

[7]Alice Walker opens her book *In Search of Our Mothers' Gardens: Womanist Prose*, with definitions for womanism that highlight the word's relationship to feminists of color, strong women, willful behavior, and the like. She ends with the analogy: "Womanist is to feminist as purple is to lavender" (xii). There is strength in being on the outside of the mainstream feminism, which Walker points out here.

[8]O'Reilly in her article "Across the Divide" uncovers motherlines in the genre of fiction.

[9]Jean Fagan Yellin corroborated (through the letters and papers of principle people in Jacobs' life) that Jacobs did, indeed, write her own story (Preface vii-viii). Furthermore, the question of Jacobs' authenticity as an author was probably less in question during her own life than it had been in the time up to Yellin's authoritative study (Yellin "Texts and Contexts" 262).

[10]William L. Andrews calls her redefinition of true womanhood an "ambivalent summation of her confession" (229), and believes that "the

extent to which she was able to escape the ambivalence and contradic-
toriness of her own moral position to articulate an alternative standard
of morality of black women in slavery remains a matter of debate"
(230). I disagree. Yes, she owns up to her part in this drama, but also
meticulously shows the reader how she would never have been able to
remain "pure" as a slave girl/woman, and so she chose the best option
among bad options. If there is ambivalence remaining, it is toward an
audience that would judge her without taking into account the miti-
gating circumstances of slavery.

[11]Though Child has sometimes been accused of being too invasive in
her editorial policies, G. Thomas Couser notes that "…Child proved
respectful of her manuscript. Although she reorganized what Jacobs had
supplied, asked for elaboration of some episodes, and suppressed a final
chapter on John Brown, her editing was not particularly aggressive—it
apparently involved no major changes of substance or style" (139).

[12]Mary McCartin Wearn finds Jacobs' ambivalence to be one of the
organizing principles of the narrative, and quite problematic. She
writes, "Jacobs's ambivalent maternity, however, reflects more than just
anguish over her children's slavehood or a sense of guilt about her own
role in their captivity. For her children not only failed to be the vehicle
of freedom that she had hoped for, but they actually served as new im-
pediments to her much-longed-for liberty" (148). I contend that this
ambivalence is both normal and "off script" for mothers then and now.

[13]For a full discussion of the many genres this narrative utilizes, see my
work in *Creating a New Ideal of Masculinity for American Men* (214).

[14]Katherine R. Goodman in "Elisabeth to Meta: Epistolary Autobiography and the Postulation of the Self" articulates a similar characterization
of the two characters in the autobiography she is studying—one is the
self (mediated through representation as always), and the other is a
reasoning friend (312).

WORKS CITED

Andrews, William L. "The Changing Moral Discourse of Nine-
teenth-Century African American Women's Autobiography: Harriet
Jacobs and Elizabeth Keckley." *De/Colonizing the Subject: The Politics of
Gender in Women's Autobiography*. Eds. Sidonie Smith and Julia Watson.
Minneapolis: University of Minnesota Press, 1992. 225-241. Print.

Behar, Ruth. *The Vulnerable Observer: Anthropology That Breaks Your Heart.* Boston: Beacon Press, 1996. Print.

Bell-Scott, Patricia. "Black Women Writing Lives: An Introduction." *Life Notes: Personal Writings by Contemporary Black Women.* Ed. Patricia Bell-Scott. New York: W.W. Norton, 1994. 17-28. Print.

Braxton, Joanne. *Black Women Writing Autobiography: A Tradition within a Tradition.* Philadelphia: Temple University Press, 1989. Print.

Carby, Hazel V. *Reconstructing Womanhood: The Emergence of the Afro-American Woman Novelist.* New York: Oxford University Press, 1987. Print.

Carlton, Peter. "Rereading Middlemarch, Rereading Myself." *The Intimate Critique: Autobiographical Literary Criticism.* Eds. Diane P. Freedman, Olivia Frey and Frances Murphy Zauhar. Durham: Duke University Press, 1993. 237-244. Print.

Child, Lydia Maria. "Introduction by the Editor." *Incidents in the Life of a Slave Girl.* By Harriet Jacobs. *The Classic Slave Narratives.* Ed. Henry Louis Gates, Jr. New York: Signet Classic, 2002. 441-442. Print.

Collins, Patricia Hill. "Black Feminist Thought." *Theories of Race and Racism: A Reader.* Eds. Les Back and John Solomos. London: Routledge, 2000. 404-420. Print.

Couser, G. Thomas. *Altered Egos: Authority in American Autobiography.* New York: Oxford University Press, 1989. Print.

Culley, Margo. "What a Piece of Work is 'Woman'! An Introduction." *American Women's Autobiography: Fea(s)ts of Memory.* Ed. Margo Culley. Madison: University of Wisconsin Press, 1992. 3-31. Print.

Goodman, Katherine R. "Elisabeth to Meta: Epistolary Autobiography and the Postulation of the Self." *Life/Lines: Theorizing Women's Autobiography.* Eds. Bella Brodzki and Celeste Schenck. Ithaca: Cornell University Press, 1988. 306-319. Print.

Hays, Sharon. *The Cultural Contradictions of Motherhood.* New Haven: Yale University Press, 1996. Print.

hooks, bell. *Feminist Theory: From Margin to Center.* Boston: South End Press, 1984. Print.

Jacobs, Harriet. *Incidents in the Life of a Slave Girl. The Classic Slave Narratives.* Ed. Henry Louis Gates, Jr. New York: Signet Classic, 2002. 437-668. Print.

Jenkins, Nina Lyon. "Black Women and the Meaning of Motherhood." *Redefining Motherhood: Changing Identities and Patterns.* Eds. Sharon

Abbey and Andrea O'Reilly. Toronto: Second Story Press, 1998. 201-213. Print.

Martin, Terry J. "Harriet A. Jacobs (Linda Brent)." *Nineteenth-Century American Women Writers: A Bio-Bibliographical Critical Sourcebook.* Ed. Denise D. Knight. Westport, CT: Greenwood Press, 1997. 262-269. Print.

Miller, Nancy K. "But Enough about Me, What Do You Think of My Memoir? Reading Spaces." *Yale Journal of Criticism* 13.2 (2000): 421-436.

Mitchell, Richelene. *Dear Self: A Year in the Life of a Welfare Mother.* Hayward, CA: NID Publishers, 2007. Print.

Mullen, Harryette. "Runaway Tongue: Resistant Orality in *Uncle Tom's Cabin, Our Nig, Incidents in the Life of a Slave Girl,* and *Beloved.*" *The Culture of Sentiment: Race, Gender, and Sentimentality in Nineteenth-Century America.* Ed. Shirley Samuels. New York: Oxford University Press, 1992. 244-264. Print.

Niesslein, Jennifer and Stephanie Wilkinson. "Well-Behaved Women." *The Maternal Is Political: Women Writers at the Intersection of Motherhood and Social Change.* Ed. Shari MacDonald Strong. Berkeley: Seal Press, 2008. 70-74. Print.

O'Reilly, Andrea. "Across the Divide: Contemporary Anglo-American Feminist Theory on the Mother-Daughter Relationship." *Mother Outlaws: Theories and Practices of Empowered Mothering.* Ed. Andrea O'Reilly. Toronto: Women's Press, 2004. 243-261. Print.

O'Reilly, Andrea. "Introduction." *Mother Outlaws: Theories and Practices of Empowered Mothering.* Ed. Andrea O'Reilly. Toronto: Women's Press, 2004. 1-28. Print.

O'Reilly, Andrea. "The Motherhood Memoir and the 'New Momism': Biting the Hand That Feeds You." *Textual Mothers/Maternal Texts: Motherhood in Contemporary Women's Literatures.* Eds. Elizabeth Podnieks and Andrea O'Reilly. Waterloo, Ontario: Wilfrid Laurier University Press, 2010. 203-213. Print.

Podnieks, Elizabeth and Andrea O'Reilly. "Introduction: Maternal Literatures in Text and Tradition: Daughter-Centric, Matrilineal, and Matrifocal Perspectives." *Textual Mothers/Maternal Texts: Motherhood in Contemporary Women's Literatures.* Eds. Elizabeth Podnieks and Andrea O'Reilly. Waterloo, ON: Wilfrid Laurier University Press, 2010. 1-27. Print.

Roiphe, Anne Richardson. *Fruitful: A Real Mother in the Modern World*. Boston: Houghton Mifflin, 1996. Print.

Schenck, Celeste. "All of a Piece: Women's Poetry and Autobiography." *Life/Lines: Theorizing Women's Autobiography*. Eds. Bella Brodzki and Celeste Schenck. Ithaca: Cornell University Press, 1988. 19-44. Print.

Smith, Sidonie and Julia Watson. *Reading Autobiography: A Guide for Interpreting Life Narratives*. 2nd ed. Minneapolis: University of Minnesota Press, 2010. Print.

Stitt, Jocelyn Fenton and Pegeen Reichert Powell. "Introduction: Delivering Mothering Studies." *Mothers Who Deliver: Feminist Interventions in Public and Interpersonal Discourse*. Albany: SUNY Press, 2010. 1-18. Print.

Terborg-Penn, Rosalyn. "Slavery and Women in Africa and the Diaspora." *Women in Africa and the African Diaspora: A Reader*. Ed. Rosalyn Terborg-Penn and Andrea Benton Rushing. 2nd ed. Washington: Howard University Press, 1996. 217-230. Print.

Walker, Alice. Epigraph. *In Search of Our Mothers' Gardens: Womanist Prose*. San Diego: Harcourt Brace & Company, 1983. xi-xii. Print.

Wane, Njoki Nathani. "Reflections on the Mutuality of Mothering: Women, Children, and Othermothering." *Mother Outlaws: Theories and Practices of Empowered Mothering*. Ed. Andrea O'Reilly. Toronto: Women's Press, 2004. 229-239. Print.

Wearn, Mary McCartin. "Maternal Fetters: Motherhood and Slavehood in Harriet Jacobs's *Incidents in the Life of a Slave Girl*." *From the Personal to the Political: Toward a New Theory of Maternal Narrative*. Eds. Andrea O'Reilly and Silvia Caporale Bizzini. Selinsgrove, PA: Susquehanna University Press, 2009. 143-155. Print.

Welter, Barbara. "The Cult of True Womanhood: 1820-1860." *American Quarterly* 2 (1966): 151-174. Print.

Willey, Nicole L. *Creating a New Ideal of Masculinity for American Men: The Achievement of Sentimental Women Writers in the Mid-Nineteenth Century*. Lewiston, NY: Edwin Mellen Press, 2007. Print.

Yellin, Jean Fagan. "Introduction." *Incidents in the Life of a Slave Girl: Written by Herself*. By Harriet Jacobs. Ed. Jean Fagan Yellin. Enlarged Edition. Cambridge: Harvard University Press, 2000. xv-xli. Print.

Yellin, Jean Fagan. "Preface." *Incidents in the Life of a Slave Girl: Written by Herself*. By Harriet Jacobs. Ed. Jean Fagan Yellin. Enlarged Edition. Cambridge: Harvard University Press, 2000. vii-viii.

Yellin, Jean Fagan. "Texts and Contexts of Harriet Jacobs' *Incidents in the Life of a Slave Girl: Written by Herself.*" *The Slave's Narrative.* Eds. Charles T. Davis and Henry Louis Gates, Jr. Oxford: Oxford University Press, 1985. 262-282. Print.

Contributor Notes

Rachel Epp Buller weaves together personal and professional interests in her art and scholarship on mothering, the maternal body, and mothering in academia. Her writing appears in many journals and books, including *Woman's Art Journal, Mothering in the Third Wave* (2008), and *Academic Motherhood in a Post–Second Wave Context* (2012). Her exhibitions and curatorial projects highlight diverse themes of mothering, as do her newest books, *Reconciling Art and Mothering* (2012) and a co-edited volume, *Mothering Mennonite* (2013). She holds a Ph.D. in art history and is assistant professor of art at Bethel College.

Pamela S. Douglas is an Australian general practitioner and adjunct senior lecturer at The University of Queensland. She is Director of The Possums Clinic for Mothers and Babies, and her Ph.D. is in Women's Studies. Her current writing project is a memoir concerning her medical research interest, the crying baby. Pam and her husband have five grown-up children between them, and four grandchildren.

Justine Dymond is an assistant professor of English at Springfield College, where she teaches writing and literature. She holds an MFA in Creative Writing and a Ph.D. in English from the University of Massachusetts at Amherst. Her publications include essays on Linda Hogan, Mourning Dove, Virginia Woolf and Gertrude Stein, and she is the editor of a special cluster in *Modern Language Studies* on 9/11 literature and culture. Her fiction and poetry have been published in numerous journals, including *The Massachusetts Review, Pleiades*, and *The Briar Cliff Review*. Her short story "Cherubs" was selected for an

O. Henry Prize and also appeared on the list of distinguished stories in the 2006 *Best American Short Stories*. She lives in western Massachusetts with her family.

Lisa Federer is a Health and Life Sciences Librarian at the UCLA Louise M. Darling Biomedical Library. Prior to completing her Masters of Library and Information Studies at UCLA, she received an MA in English and was an adjunct instructor of English at the University of North Texas, where her research interests included gender and sexuality, queer theory, and new media.

Kathleen L. Fowler, Ph.D., FT, was a professor of Gerontology and Women's Studies at Ramapo College of New Jersey, where she taught courses in women's studies and in thanatology (the study of death, dying, and bereavement). She was certified as a Fellow in Thanatology. Fowler published articles in thanatology, women's studies and literature, and was the Editor of *The Forum: The Quarterly Publication of the Association for Death Educators and Counselors*. We feel privileged to publish her work posthumously with the permission of her husband, Robert Dilly.

Lori Lyn Greenstone was a graduate student in Literature and Writing Cultural Studies at California State University, San Marcos when she wrote her thesis on motherhood memoir and ekphrasis, from which her chapter arose. She is an artist whose work has won several awards and been published in *Strokes of Genius: The Best of Drawing* by Northlight. She sold the blueberry farm and now lives and skis in Bend, Oregon with four of her six children and her husband. She teaches at Central Oregon Community College.

Melissa Shields Jenkins is an assistant professor of English at Wake Forest University, specializing in nineteenth-century British literature and culture. Her research interests include the history of the novel, gender and masculinity studies, and ethnic studies. Her first book, *Fatherhood, Authority, and British Literary Culture, 1840-1900*, is forthcoming. Her writing has appeared in *Victorian Literature and Culture*, the *Victorians Institute Journal*, the *Journal of British Studies*, *Modern Language Studies*, and in edited collections.

Tara McDonald Johnson teaches literature and composition at California State University, San Bernardino. She earned her Ph.D. from the University of Alabama and is a research specialist in nineteenth-century British literature as well as theories of aestheticism and the aesthetic personality. Her work has been published in various journals and books. She lives with her husband and two sons in Southern California.

Deesha Philyaw is the co-author of *Co-Parenting 101: Helping Your Children Thrive After Divorce.* She is a freelance writer whose work has appeared in *Essence* and *Bitch* magazines, and *The Washington Post.* Her writing has been anthologized in several collections including *Literary Mama: Reading for the Maternally Inclined; When We Were Free to Be: Looking Back at a Children's Classic and the Difference It Made;* and *The Cassoulet Saved Our Marriage: True Tales of Food, Family, and How We Learn to Eat.* She is a co-founder of CoParenting101.org.

Yelizaveta P. Renfro is the author of a collection of short stories, *A Catalogue of Everything in the World* (Black Lawrence Press, 2010), winner of the St. Lawrence Book Award. Her fiction and nonfiction have appeared in *Glimmer Train Stories, North American Review, Colorado Review, Alaska Quarterly Review, South Dakota Review, Witness, Reader's Digest, Blue Mesa Review, Parcel, Adanna, Fourth River, Bayou Magazine, Untamed Ink, So to Speak,* and elsewhere. Her writing on motherhood has appeared in the *Journal of the Association for Research on Mothering* and *Literary Mama.* She holds an MFA from George Mason University and a Ph.D. in English from the University of Nebraska. She currently lives in West Hartford, CT, and teaches English at Westfield State University in Westfield, MA. Her virtual home is at <http://chasingsamaras.blogspot.com>.

Rachel Robertson is a Lecturer in Professional Writing and Publishing at Curtin University in Western Australia. Her first book, *Reaching One Thousand: A Story of Love, Motherhood and Autism,* was published by Black Inc in 2012. She has also published short fiction, personal essays, academic articles and book chapters and was winner of the Australian Book Review Calibre Award for Outstanding Essay in 2008. Her academic interests include life writing, disability studies, mothering and writing creative non-fiction.

Nicole Willey is an associate professor of English at Kent State University Tuscarawas, where she teaches African American and other literatures, along with a variety of writing courses. Her research interests include mothering, memoir, nineteenth-century American literature, and slave narratives. She wrote *Creating a New Ideal of Masculinity for American Men: The Achievement of Sentimental Women Writers in the Mid-Nineteenth Century*. She lives in New Philadelphia, Ohio with her husband and two sons.